Motor City Champs

Motor City Champs

*Mickey Cochrane and
the 1934–1935 Detroit Tigers*

S<small>COTT</small> F<small>ERKOVICH</small>

McFarland & Company, Inc., Publishers
Jefferson, North Carolina

LIBRARY OF CONGRESS CATALOGUING-IN-PUBLICATION DATA

Names: Ferkovich, Scott, author.
Title: Motor City champs : Mickey Cochrane and the 1934–1935
  Detroit Tigers / Scott Ferkovich.
Description: Jefferson, North Carolina : McFarland & Company, Inc.,
  Publishers, 2018. | Includes bibliographical references and index.
Identifiers: LCCN 2017059942 | ISBN 9781476666594 (softcover :
  acid free paper) ∞
Subjects: LCSH: Detroit Tigers (Baseball team)—History. | Cochrane,
  Mickey, 1903–1962. | Baseball players—United States—Biography. |
  Baseball managers—United States—Biography.
Classification: LCC GV875.D6 F47 2018 | DDC
  796.357/64097743409043—dc23
LC record available at https://lccn.loc.gov/2017059942

BRITISH LIBRARY CATALOGUING DATA ARE AVAILABLE

ISBN (print) 978-1-4766-6659-4
ISBN (ebook) 978-1-4766-2950-6

Front cover: Detroit Tigers Catcher Mickey Cochrane running on
field, wearing catcher's protective gear (courtesy of the Ernie Harwell
Sports Collection, Detroit Public Library)

Printed in the United States of America

*McFarland & Company, Inc., Publishers
  Box 611, Jefferson, North Carolina 28640
  www.mcfarlandpub.com*

To my dad,
who loves baseball

For whatsoever from one place doth fall,
Is with the tide unto an other brought,
For there is nothing lost, that may be found, if sought.
—Spenser

Sing a song of seasons!
Something bright in all!
Flowers in the summer,
Fires in the fall!
—Robert Louis Stevenson

Table of Contents

Acknowledgments

The assistance and encouragement of so many individuals has been vital in guiding this book through it birth, maturation, and completion. I would be remiss if I did not give them my heartfelt thanks. Many of them are probably unaware of my gratitude, but that is even more reason to make mention of it here.

First, I consider myself blessed to have such a wonderful family. During the nearly two years it took to put this book together, they have been a precious anchor.

Gary Mitchem, my editor at McFarland, saw the potential in the book from the very beginning. His faith in its success helped get the project off the ground. His direction and expertise proved invaluable.

To fellow writers Dan Holmes and Bob Davis, who both took the time to read the manuscript and offer sound feedback and counsel, I am especially grateful.

Bill Nowlin, the vice-president at the Society for American Baseball Research (SABR), was an encouragement from the start.

Mickey Briggs, the grandson of former Tigers owner Walter O. Briggs, is a fine gent if ever there was one. He is also full of wonderful stories of the 1935 champions. My gratitude for his telling them to me knows no bounds.

To the professional staff at the Detroit Public Library, I owe a debt of gratitude. Whether I needed their help locating rolls of ancient microfilm, or loading them onto the temperamental readers, they were always eager to lend a hand. Mark Bowden, the Coordinator for Special Collections, and Carla J. Reczek, a special librarian in the digital lab, were both very giving of their time and energies in providing me with access to digital images.

Many thanks go out to the wonderful personnel at the Purdy-Kresge Library on the campus of Wayne State University. I spent countless hours scanning their fine collection of Detroit newspapers on microfilm, and the knowledgeable staff was always ready to give aid.

Kelli Bogan, Photo Archives Manager at the National Baseball Hall of

Fame's Giamatti Research Center, is especially deserving of mention. Her assistance with photos was vital. An additional shout-out goes to Connie Robinson, Finance Associate at the Hall.

This has been said before, but I'll say it again: Every baseball researcher is beholden to Sean Forman, the president and founding partner of Sports-Reference.com. His great work has made our jobs infinitely easier (and more enjoyable).

A bevy of benevolent souls freely offered thoughtful inspiration along the way. Among those worthy of thank you notes are Phil Archer, Larry Armstrong, Alexis Battenfeld, Bob "Bronco" Bellini, Maxwell Benz, Justin Bologna, Karen Bush, Darren Carlisle, Sebastian Clay, Maurice Cobb, Molly Crapps, Peter Dunne, Frank Foy, Tom Gage, Gary Gillette, Debbie Good, Donnie Grugliasco, Enrique Hernandez, Tommy Hudson, Kostya Kennedy, Elroy Lebenne, Charles Leerhsen, Jana McBurney-Lin, Bob McGee, Jerry Nechal, Bartlett W. Neusbaum, Malcolm Oglivie, Mary Louise O'Hara, Woody Phelps, Julie Reilly, Rusty Remmerswaal, Sam Kim, John Savoy, Bob Soo, Monte Swift, Kenji Takahashi, Bruce Thurmond, Barry Vetter, Fritz Von Boors, and Robyn Wilde.

Preface

The world of the early 1930s could be a bleak, chaotic, and threatening place. The Great Depression had thrust global economies into turmoil. Like dominos falling, dark events in Europe and Asia would lead to a cataclysmic clash of nations in just a few short years. Hope was a rare commodity, and the future looked cheerless and unwelcoming. The city of Detroit, in particular, endured hard times. Following the events of the stock market crash of 1929, automobile production had dropped, leading to layoffs and massive unemployment. Money was scarce. Food was even scarcer. Long lines at soup kitchens were a common sight. The Motor City, however, did have one thing to feel good about, and that was its baseball team.

As of this writing, the Detroit Tigers have won four World Series, and it is remarkable how every one of those championship teams has served as a kind of catharsis from calamity for the residents of the city. In 1984, for example, Kirk Gibson, Alan Trammell, and Lou Whitaker gave Detroit a reason to celebrate in the midst of a sour economy, a stagnant auto industry, a tanking housing market, and high interest rates. In 1968, Mickey Lolich and Al Kaline helped to heal the wounds from race riots that nearly burned the city to the ground the summer before. In 1945, it was Hal Newhouser and Dizzy Trout pitching the way to a new era of peace and prosperity following the horrors of World War II.

In 1934, still reeling from the Depression, Detroiters fell in love with Mickey Cochrane and his colorful cast of characters who went to the World Series. They lost in seven games to the St. Louis Cardinals, but came back even stronger in 1935, beating the Chicago Cubs to take the franchise's first World Series championship.

Cochrane, the erstwhile catching star on Connie Mack's pennant-winning Philadelphia Athletics teams, rode into town as the Tigers' new player-manager for the 1934 campaign. He may have single-handedly saved baseball in Detroit. His leadership and drive transformed a group that had resembled a country club rather than a baseball team. To borrow a modern phrase, he changed the culture. He also re-ignited the passions of a fan base that had been dormant for years.

The 1934–1935 Tigers had no less than four future Hall of Famers in their lineup. Cochrane was one. The other three, collectively known as the "G-Men" (a nickname borrowed from the special agents at the Federal Bureau of Investigation), were Hank Greenberg, Charlie Gehringer, and Goose Goslin.

Greenberg, the young Bronx native, had overcome ethnic slurs to become a slugger of the first magnitude. He had his breakout season in 1934, amassing 63 doubles and hitting .339. He also gained national notoriety when he made the tough decision to play on Rosh Hashanah, the Jewish New Year, banging out two home runs in the process. He followed it up with an MVP season in 1935, and hit Detroit's only home run in that year's World Series.

Gehringer, known as "The Mechanical Man" because he was as reliable as a fine wristwatch, had already established himself as the American League's premier second baseman. He finished second to Cochrane in the AL MVP vote in 1934, after hitting .356. By the time he retired following the 1942 season, he had amassed 2,839 lifetime hits in his 19-year career (all with Detroit), and a .320 average.

Leon Allen Goslin was a brilliant batsman, but an atrocious outfielder. Fly balls hit his way were an adventure; with his large proboscis pointed skyward, his arms flapping wildly like a bird, it was no surprise he earned the nickname "Goose." One of Cochrane's first moves was to acquire Goslin, a veteran leader whose Washington Senators had gone to the World Series three times, winning once.

In addition to the quartet of Hall of Famers, the 1934–1935 Tigers boasted a bevy of smart, aggressive position players who fought for every inch the opposition would allow.

Hardnosed shortstop Billy Rogell was known as "The Fire Chief." He was a fine clutch hitter, driving in 99 runs in 1934. He backed down to no one, a quality that served him well later in life when he became a longtime member of the Detroit City Council.

Third baseman Marv Owen had a mild-mannered, professorial look about him, but he never shied away from an oncoming baserunner. His famous dustup with the St. Louis Cardinals' Joe Medwick in the 1934 World Series led to one of the most ignominious on-field events in baseball history. Detroit's vaunted infield became known as the "Battalion of Death," mainly because it was the ruin of ground balls.

Right fielder Pete Fox hit over .300 five times in his career and was also a fine fly chaser. A fan favorite, he led Detroit with a .385 average in the 1935 World Series.

Outfielder Gerald Holmes "Gee" Walker is largely forgotten today, but he was one of the most popular players ever to don the Old English "D." A .294 lifetime hitter over 15 seasons, Walker had good speed on the basepaths, but his lapses in concentration often drove Cochrane crazy.

The 1934–1935 Tigers had an impressive collection of talented pitchers. The charismatic Lynwood Thomas "Schoolboy" Rowe was one of the most talked-about athletes in America. Only 24 years old in 1934, the right-hander won 16 consecutive decisions at one point, still tied for the American League record. He finished the year with 24 wins and won 19 each of the next two seasons before arm problems derailed his career.

Tommy Bridges won 20 games three consecutive years beginning in 1934. His slight frame (5'10" and only 155 pounds) belied his bulldog nature. His virtuoso performance in the ninth inning of Game Six of the 1935 World Series remains one of the gutsiest displays of pitching in the annals of the game.

Elden Auker, known as "Big Six," was a former college football player who sustained a shoulder injury on the gridiron. As a result, he could only throw underhand. Football's loss, however, was baseball's gain. His submarining pitching style carried him all the way to the major leagues, where he won 15 games in 1934 and 18 the following year.

The rise of these Detroit Tigers is a rousing tale of triumph. An underdog outfit at the onset of the 1934 season, they surprised the baseball world by hanging near first place in the early months. In midsummer, they took on Babe Ruth's New York Yankees in a series of titanic clashes, and prevailed. The Tigers could have wallowed in their own failure following a humiliating loss in Game Seven of the 1934 World Series. Instead, they came back the following year with a chip on their shoulders and some unfinished business. This book will chronicle their story, from the time in 1933 when Tigers owner Frank Navin contacted Yankees boss Jacob Ruppert about acquiring a certain home run king, until the denouement two years later, when Goose Goslin strode to the plate in the ninth inning at Navin Field with a world championship on the line.

Just how good were the 1934–1935 Detroit Tigers? Comparisons across eras make for fun conversation and debate, but ultimately do not accomplish much. The professional game that we follow today is profoundly different from the one that our grandfathers and great-grandfathers knew. There were a mere 16 teams in the major leagues in 1935, and only one of them was west of the Mississippi River. Players wore flannel uniforms, sweated out doubleheaders every Sunday, and did not know what to make of the arrival of night baseball. For the most part, they did not earn much more money than the fans who paid to watch them play. Indeed, the intimacies of the player-fan dynamic seem quaint to our modern perspective. Many players lived not far from the ballpark. They were just as likely to strike up a conversation about baseball with the fan they met on the streetcar, as they were to chat with the butcher or baker as they visited his shop on their way home from a game.

The relationship between players and the media (although in those days it was just "the press") was also startlingly different. They ate together, rode the train together, played cards together, and drank together. As a rule, newspapermen did not divulge the peccadillos of players in print.

On the field, there were no designated hitters, no batting helmets, and no ninth-inning closers throwing 100 miles per hour. Pitchers went the distance or suffered disgrace. Rare was the batter who struck out over 100 times in a single season. There were no free agents, no arbitration hearings, and no three-minute, between-inning breaks for television commercials. Players today are bigger, stronger, and faster (and a whole lot richer). To its shame, Major League Baseball in 1935 was an exclusive bastion of the white player. The integration (and indeed the gradual globalization) of the national pastime was far off in the future.

Nevertheless, the game on the field today remains virtually intact in its essence. It is still played, as it was in 1935, with a round ball and a round bat. Three strikes you're out, four balls take your base. Nine men on defense, and 27 outs in a regulation game. The beauty of baseball is in its continuity, its dependability, even as the rest of the world undergoes changes both seismic and unsettling. Humanity may careen toward catastrophe, but baseball is a reliable respite from reality. Bart Giamatti, the late baseball commissioner, once wrote that baseball was "our best invention to stay change."[1]

The Detroit Tigers of 1934–1935 were a talented club that gave hope to a city in trying times. For that, they are worth remembering, and that is why I have written this book.

A Note on Statistics and Quotations

Fans of baseball have had an enduring enchantment with its statistics. In our age of computers, perceptions of the game's numbers (and the "how" and "why" behind them) have undergone a revolution of sorts. Statistics such as batting average, runs batted in, and wins for pitchers carried much more weight 80 years ago than they do today. Primarily indicators of volume (25 home runs, 32 doubles, 15 wins, etc.), they were a limited gauge of a player's value to his team. Today, baseball analytics is an industry unto itself, with its passionate proponents and detractors. Esoteric formulas such as OPS+, Ba*bip*, FIP, and RA9*def* are transforming the way we view player performance. What I have attempted in this book is to employ a mix of traditional "baseball card" statistics, infused with a fair portion of modern sabermetrics (nothing too complex or off-putting for the average fan; just enough to provide something for everyone). I hope I have done that well. All statistics I use (yes, even WAR!) are taken from the great folks at BaseballReference.com.

While chronicling this team history, I often utilize quoted matter from newspapers of the day. I could have chosen to edit these quotes, as they sometimes do not conform to the rules of spelling or syntax. However, I feared that doing so would rob them of their authentic, evocative voice. Instead, I have recorded all quotations exactly as they originally appeared in the source material.

Chapter One

"Detroit is not my lucky town"

Our story of how a baseball team went from mediocrity to the World Series begins with a knock on a door. The date was September 23, 1933. The knocker was Bucky Harris, manager of the Detroit Tigers. The door he knocked on led into the office of Frank J. Navin, the team's owner. Harris had some weighty news for his boss.

Navin was not expecting the meeting, although he probably should have been. The 1933 Tigers were not a good team. Perhaps the greater sin, however, was that they played a dull, uninteresting brand of baseball lacking in discipline, which is often an indictment of the manager. Harris had hoped he could turn things around in the season's final month. Beginning a 16-game East Coast swing on September 6, the club was in fifth place, already 22 games behind the eventual-champion Washington Senators. Still, Harris figured that a solid road trip could increase Detroit's chances at third-place money. Instead, the Tigers went 5–11 before slouching back home, and the skipper knew he had seen enough. Less than an hour after a victory over the St. Louis Browns, Harris entered Navin's office to announce his resignation. It was agreed that coach Del Baker would handle the final two games of the season.

It was not as if Harris had arrived in the Motor City without a pedigree. He had, after all, won two pennants, including a World Series title as a young manager in Washington. However, in his five seasons in Detroit, his clubs had never finished higher than fifth, with a 76–75 high-water mark in 1932.

Navin seemed genuinely surprised at the turn of events. He had always liked Harris, whom he affectionately referred to by his given name Stanley. "I had no intention of changing managers," Navin admitted. "Stanley could have stayed. This year he had a young ball club and it made mistakes for which he could not be held responsible. In 40 years that I have been in baseball, I have never been associated with anyone, player, manager, or owner, whom I liked as well as Stanley. I tried to get him to change his mind, but he seems set on his decision."[1]

"Mr. Navin did not ask for my resignation," a stoic Harris told reporters. "He didn't even hint that he planned to ask it. I just felt that Detroit is not my lucky town and that it would be for the best interests of all concerned if I quit."[2]

To be sure, Detroit had not been any baseball manager's idea of a lucky town for a long time. Hughie Jennings, with a young Ty Cobb roaming his outfield, had skippered the Tigers to three straight World Series beginning in 1907, losing every time. Those days, however, were ancient history. Since then, Detroit was a perennial middle-of-the-pack club. Jennings hung on until 1920, when Cobb himself replaced him as player-manager. After six years, "The Georgia Peach" gave way to George Moriarty, and finally to Harris, none of whom had been able to lead Detroit to the land flowing with milk and honey.

Worse yet, attendance at Navin Field had dwindled. The Tigers drew only 320,972 fans to their ballpark at the corner of Michigan and Trumbull, good for fifth in the eight-team American League in 1933. It was the second-lowest turnout since the park had opened its gates in 1912. Frustrated denizens of Detroit were beginning to wonder if their Tigers were ever going to win a World Series, something the team had yet to do in its 33-year history. Indeed, the city's only major baseball championship had come back in 1887, when the National League's old Detroit Wolverines won a 15-game post-season tournament (a precursor to the modern World Series) over the St. Louis Browns of the American Association. By the end of the following season, the franchise was unable to meet expenses and unceremoniously folded.

On the heels of the Tigers' 75–79 finish in 1933, and desperate for a winner, Navin looked around and realized that he was not getting any younger. Born in 1871 in Adrian, Michigan, a village about 70 miles southwest of Detroit, he had aspired to the law and earned his degree from the Detroit College of Law (now Michigan State University Law School). As a young man striving to make his way in the world, he had been attracted to the political arena and ran unsuccessfully for justice of the peace. Having a head for arithmetic, he switched careers and found work in the Detroit office of one Samuel Angus, an insurance agent. Navin kept the books and sold policies, and generally ingratiated himself to Angus.

A bookish, introverted fellow lacking in charisma, Navin could well have spent the rest of his life crunching numbers in a dusty office, but his fortunes changed for the better in 1902. That was the year Angus led a syndicate to purchase the Detroit Tigers, bringing Navin along to be his business manager.

Just how much Navin initially knew about the game of baseball is debatable. He was no more or less likely to have played it growing up than any other typical American boy of his era. But Angus needed Navin's flair for business. It turned out, however, that Angus had greater aspirations; within a year, he sold the team to William C. Yawkey in order to focus on a mayoral run. Yawkey, who had garnered his millions by virtue of being the son of a Michigan lumber baron, retained Navin.

Soon after taking over the reins of the organization, Yawkey died, and ownership fell to his son, William H. Yawkey. No particular fan of the national pastime, the younger Yawkey was more than happy to let Navin run the team as he saw fit. Navin proved to be a shrewd judge of baseball talent; piece by piece, he put together the squad that would soon dominate the American League.

Among his assemblages were "Wahoo" Sam Crawford, the slugger who still holds the likely unbreakable record of 309 career triples, and Wild Bill Donovan, who won 25 games in 1907. His most brilliant acquisition, however, was Cobb, for whom Navin paid a pittance of $700 to the Augusta Tourists of the South Atlantic League. Cobb became the greatest batsman of his day and the sporting world's biggest star. By 1908, Navin had purchased a nearly 50 percent stake in the Tigers; ten years after that, he became the majority owner following the death of Yawkey from the Spanish Flu.

Those giddy days, and those talented Tigers clubs, were now a distant memory. Navin's beloved baseball team had gone without a pennant for 24 years. With the departure of Harris, the search for a new field boss became his top priority.

⚾ ⚾ ⚾

Navin's pursuit was not going to be easy. He needed a man with a tough, no-nonsense approach, able to instill a winning attitude into his Tigers. In recent years, Detroit had gained a reputation as a soft team with an easy-come, easy-go attitude. Soon after Harris's departure, a *Detroit Free Press* headline blared:

WE WANT TIGERS—NOT TAME KITTENS

Maybe it was a product of Harris's managerial style. Brought on five years earlier primarily to rid the club of the numerous cliques that were eating away at it like a cancer, he had accomplished that goal, but conversely was accused of letting the pendulum swing the other way. He had placed too much emphasis on team harmony, his detractors argued. If he had to choose between a player of marginal talent but sunny disposition, versus one of greater skills who had a tendency toward irritability, he would pick the former. When recruiting players, he valued character over natural ability. On the field and in the clubhouse, reprimands were rare. Harris never nagged. Account-ability was lacking. If he criticized a player in the fifth inning, he did it in such a mild, nonthreatening way that it was invariably forgotten by the sixth. Whoever the Tigers' new manager might be, that laid-back atmosphere could not be allowed to continue.

But Navin had an additional problem on his hands: The sparse crowds at Navin Field. The Depression had hit Detroit hard. People simply did not have the disposable income for a trip to the ballpark anymore. All throughout the major leagues, teams were playing in front of legions of empty seats, as atten-dance plummeted 40 percent from 1930 to 1933. (The numbers would not reach pre–Depression levels until after World War II, when soldiers numbering in the millions returned from overseas.) Not helping matters was the ten percent Federal Amusement Tax added to the price of a ticket beginning in 1932. That year, only the Chicago Cubs and New York Yankees, pennant winners both, turned a profit. In 1933, only the New York Giants and Philadelphia Phillies were in the black. The Tigers averaged a scant 4,115 fans per game at Navin Field, a venue that seated 30,000. "Economically, it was a very tough decade for baseball," notes Andrew Zimbalist, a sports economist at Smith College.[3]

In short, Navin had to put more people in the seats if he wanted his baseball team to remain solvent. He required a manager, but also a gate attrac-tion. He had a man in mind that he felt could fill both roles.

His name was George Herman "Babe" Ruth.

Frank Navin's pursuit of the Sultan of Swat is a tale retold by nearly every Ruth biographer and countless Tigers historians. It remains a classic case of missed opportunity, of what might have been. While the details differ depend-ing on the source, the gist is the same.

Ruth, 38 years old and nearing the end as a player, had long expressed a desire to manage a major league team, the Yankees especially. Team owner Jacob Ruppert, however, would have none of it. In his eyes, the Babe was still a carouser, a clown who could not be taken seriously as a leader of men. Rup-pert once told him, "You can't manage yourself, Ruth. How do you expect to manage others?" In truth, Ruppert would just as soon dump his aging star. The Sultan of Swat was coming off a season in which he had hit "only" .301 with 34 home runs and 104 RBI. Solid numbers, by any measure, unless you were the Babe.

To Navin, however, Ruth was an enticing option, not merely as a player, but as a player-manager. Ruth could still hit the ball a mile, just not as often. Navin figured the Babe could bash a few homers and give fans a reason to come down to the corner of Michigan and Trumbull. Who knows, he just might prove to be a capable manager. It was a calculated risk. If Navin was harboring the idea, however, he kept it mum (he wasn't known as Old Poker Face for nothing). As one writer put it, "Frank J. Navin, who accepted Harris' resignation with regret, is saying nothing, except that Ruth and a lot of other good men have been suggested to him."[4]

During the 1933 World Series between the Washington Senators and the New York Yankees, Navin contacted Ruppert about the possibility of acquiring Ruth. The two men agreed to a deal in principle, and it looked for a while as if Navin had his man. All he had to do was get Ruth to come to Detroit to work out the financial arrangements.

That was easier said than done. Navin phoned Ruth, who seemed excited by the news. He maintained, however, that he had plans to travel to San Francisco to board a Hawaiian-bound ship. Once on the islands, he would play a few pre-arranged exhibition games (and a round or two of golf on the side). Could Navin wait until he got back? Navin suggested that Ruth take a later boat. Not possible, Ruth countered, ending the call.

That did not get the negotiations off on the right foot, since Navin was not a man who liked to wait for anybody. When Ed Barrow, the Yankees' general manager, heard about the conversation, he phoned Ruth to tell him he was making a mistake, and that he should see Navin right away or risk losing his big chance.

Ruth did not listen. Indeed, he only made things worse. While in California, he rang up Navin at his home, apparently forgetting the time difference, as it was two o'clock in the morning in Detroit. While Navin wiped the sleep out of his eyes, Ruth, in a crackly long-distance voice, demanded a percentage of the gate receipts, on top of his high salary. Navin, who had a reputation as a skinflint, immediately saw visions of money flying out the window. He hung up the phone, ending his flirtation with the Sultan of Swat.

The idea of Babe Ruth playing (and managing) for the Detroit Tigers seems the stuff of fantasy, and yet it is not entirely implausible. Navin *did* need a new manager, he *did* need a drawing card, and Ruth *was* available. At the time, however, Ruth never made any mention of an offer from Navin. Upon his arrival in Honolulu, a brief paragraph appeared in the *New York Times* stating flatly, "Ruth was unwilling to discuss the game in which he is the home run 'king,' except to say he had not as yet received an offer of a managership from any major league club."[5]

To his dying day in 1948, Ruth insisted that nobody in Major League Baseball ever gave him the opportunity to manage a team. While Ruth admitted that Navin had indeed approached him, he could be vague as to what exactly they had discussed. Years later, Harry Grayson, the longtime sportswriter and editor, wrote, "Despite reports to the contrary, Ruth says he was never made any kind of an offer to manage a major league club. The late Frank J. Navin telephoned him in San Francisco as he was about to sail for Honolulu in the fall of 1933, said something about wanting to see the old home run king."[6] What exactly was that "something?" Surely, Navin did not want to get together with Ruth simply to have tea and crumpets. Big plans must have been in the works.

As for Barrow, he always believed Ruth blew it. According to one writer, "Barrow says that the Babe was offered the management of the Detroit Tigers and only his slowness in visiting the Motor City to sign his contract" caused the deal to fall through.[7]

So, if not Babe Ruth, who was going to be the new manager of the Detroit Tigers?

Among the potential names bantered about in the press and public were Del Baker, the Tigers' interim manager for the final two games in 1933, along with Bill Killefer, former St. Louis Browns skipper. Also believed to be in the running were Steve O'Neill, the catcher on the world champion Cleveland Indians of 1920 and currently the manager of the Toledo Mud Hens of the American Association, and Oscar Vitt, the former Tigers third baseman who had some experience managing in the Pacific Coast League. Marty McManus, recently removed as manager of the Boston Red Sox, and Billy Evans, the longtime umpire and erstwhile general manager of the Indians, rounded out the possibilities.

Perhaps the most intriguing candidates were former Tigers star Harry Heilmann, who had retired following the 1932 campaign with a lifetime batting average of .342, and Charlie Gehringer, Detroit's brilliant second baseman, who was still in his prime. Heilmann, however, quickly put an end to any discussion of becoming the Tigers' new manager when he entered the race for Detroit city treasurer on October 10.

As for Gehringer, a story circulated that Navin had offered him the managerial post only to change his mind soon after. When Gehringer appeared in Navin's office in late October to sign his new contract for 1934, both men shot the rumor down.

The man whom the Detroit Tigers eventually hired, however, was none of the aforementioned. Indeed, it was a selection seemingly out of left field. Navin did not get Ruth, but the fellow he landed instead was destined to change the course of baseball history in the Motor City. The great irony is that were it not for the Depression, it may never have happened.

Having passed on Ruth, Navin turned his direction to Mickey Cochrane, the Philadelphia Athletics' catching star. The Athletics were owned by Connie Mack, who was struggling just like every other team in the poor economy, and perhaps more so. His team had drawn only 297,138 fans to Shibe Park in 1933, an average of 3,910. Attendance had fallen every season since the stock market crash of 1929, when the team drew 839,176. That year the Athletics won their first of three consecutive American League pennants, including World Series championships in 1929 and 1930. It was a star-studded squad featuring future Hall of Famers Jimmie Foxx, Al Simmons, Lefty Grove, and Cochrane. Nevertheless, by the end of the 1933 season, Mack could no longer stay afloat financially. Just as he had done with his first Athletics dynasty nearly two decades earlier, he planned a fire sale of his players in order to pay the bills.

Tigers owner Frank Navin, known as "Old Poker Face," had a reputation as one of the game's great horse traders (courtesy National Baseball Hall of Fame, Cooperstown, New York).

His one untouchable was Cochrane, an excellent defensive receiver and strong batsman who captured the American League Most Valuable Player award in 1928. In his nine seasons in Philly, he compiled a batting average of .321, with extra-base power, including 23 home runs in 1932. He had four straight years of +5.0 Wins Above Replacement (WAR), including 6.3 in 1933.[8] Cochrane's value, however, could not be measured in statistics alone. An inspiring leader, he was the sparkplug of those great Athletics clubs, a man driven to excel, who demanded nothing less from his teammates. At 30 years old, he was still in his prime.

A native of Bridgewater, Massachusetts, he was born Gordon Stanley Cochrane on April 6, 1903. Although of Scottish heritage, he was assumed to be Irish when signed to his first pro contract by scout Tom Turner. Consequently, he was always referred to as Mickey, at least in public. His parent just called him Gordon, but to the rest of his family he was Mike.

Ironically, baseball was not Cochrane's first passion, football was. While at Boston University from 1921–1924, he starred on the gridiron as well as the basketball court, winning a total of ten sports letters (four of them in football). According to one story, "He was a halfback. He did the punting, drop-kicking, most of the ball-carrying, and was the best thrower of forward passes the eleven had."[9]

He played baseball, too, but mostly as a shortstop and outfielder. It was only later, while with Dover in the Class D Eastern Shore League, that he first donned the tools of ignorance. The team needed a catcher, and Cochrane, because of his overall athleticism and quickness, was deemed the best candidate. He maintained that it was not entirely his choice. "I didn't want to be a catcher, it was thrust upon me, as they say in the classics. In other words, I was shoved into it," he told baseball writer John Kieran in 1931.[10]

Cochrane dropped out of BU to focus on professional baseball. In two minor league seasons with Dover and Portland, he hit a combined .328 before making the Athletics out of spring training in 1925. Barely 22 years old, he became an instant star, hitting .331. He benefitted greatly when former Tiger Ty Cobb joined the Athletics for his final two seasons in 1927 and 1928. Perhaps the most intense competitor ever to wear spiked shoes, Cobb taught Cochrane how to play the game to the last out, to fight for every advantage and never give an inch. The likeable Cochrane was a bright, articulate man and a student of the game, and Mack viewed him as future managerial material. Before the conclusion of the 1933 season, Mack insisted that he would "never sell or trade Cochrane, no matter what tempting offers of cash and players" were made for him.[11] Cochrane was a student of human nature, a quality beneficial for any who would be a manager. "I guess I just took naturally to psychology at school," he once remarked, "because I like to study folks."[12]

Navin pitched Mack the idea of the Athletics sending Cochrane to Detroit to be player-manager. Mack initially asked for $125,000 and catcher Ray Hayworth.[13] A solid receiver with a strong, accurate arm, Hayworth broke into the big leagues with the Tigers back in 1926. In 134 games in 1933, he hit only .245 with one home run and 45 RBI. It was not the kind of offense expected from the catching position. Navin made a counter-offer of $100,000 and catcher John Pasek, an expendable player whose big-league career consisted of 28 games for the Tigers in 1933, when he hit .246. While Mack did not initially accept the counter-offer, he did not reject it outright, either.

Navin personally lacked the cash anyhow. Even though he was the owner of a baseball team, he was not a particularly rich man. Most of his fortune had been lost following the stock market crash in 1929. At this stage, Walter O. Briggs enters the narrative. The founder of the Briggs Manufacturing Company (a producer of auto bodies), he was also a co-owner of the Tigers. Briggs had held a stake in the team since 1919, with his percentage gradually increasing until by 1933 he was nearly a full partner with Navin. While the latter was the public face of Tigers ownership, with Briggs preferring to stay behind the scenes, it was Briggs who had the deeper pockets. When he asked Navin how much Mack wanted for Cochrane, Navin told him $100,000. Briggs declared that Cochrane was worth every penny. Navin agreed, but insisted he himself could not afford such a price. With Major League Baseball's winter meetings scheduled for Chicago in December, Briggs decided to loan Navin $100,000 in order to get their man. Additional phone conversations took place between Navin and Mack, during the course of which a verbal agreement was made to trade Cochrane to Detroit. They did not want it leaked to the press, however. Not yet, anyway.

Word got out nevertheless. On November 1, the *Associated Press* claimed that Cochrane was spotted in Detroit "some weeks ago."[14] Reporters buttonholed Cochrane wherever he went, asking him his opinion on the potential move. "I'll be happy to manage the Tigers for Mr. Navin," he told one writer. "[He] impresses me as a great fellow and a man who will help me build. I see no reason why I can't make the grade as manager."[15]

Pundits predicted that the cash-poor Mack would eventually agree to a deal. Cochrane's trade value was simply too high to ignore, and the Athletics looked to be a team on the decline. It was better for Mack to get something for Cochrane while he could. As for Detroit, they would be getting a catcher who, in the words of sportswriter James C. Isaminger, "overtowers all rivals like the Empire State Building."[16]

Even before the meeting in Chicago, Navin was talking as if Cochrane's acquisition were a foregone conclusion. "I'll see Connie Mack in Chicago," he said, "and the chances are, if there are no upsets and things go as planned, Cochrane will be our next manager."[17] Rumors circulated that banks were hounding Mack for repayment of loans of $250,000. He wanted to delay the official announcement of the Cochrane trade, as he was still embroiled in efforts to get relief from his creditors.[18] Until his financial options were exhausted, his desire was to hang on to Cochrane.

Navin made his way to the winter meetings in the Windy City. After his arrival at the Palmer House on December 12, he and Mack made official what had been the worst-kept secret in baseball: Mickey Cochrane was headed to the Detroit Tigers. Mack remained reluctant to part with Cochrane up to the very end, and probably would not have done so if he did not feel that it was a great career move for the catcher, who could finally get his chance to manage a team.[19] In addition to the money, the Tigers threw Johnny Pasek into the deal. The paperwork would not be officially signed until January 1934. Discussing Cochrane, Navin proclaimed, "I would much rather have him with us than against us. Cochrane has been baseball poison for Detroit ever since he's been in the league."[20]

It was the darkest day in Philadelphia Athletics history, as Mack also traded away future Hall of Fame pitcher Lefty Grove to the Boston Red Sox, along with star second baseman Max Bishop and former 20-game-winner Rube Walberg, receiving little in return. Wrote the *New York Times*, "[The deal] all but completes a break-up of the famous Athletics who won the world's championship in 1929 and '30."[21]

As for Mack, he tried his best to put a spin on the trades. "I am not breaking up my ball club," he emphasized. "In my opinion, anybody who thinks so is all wrong."[22] Mack's words ultimately were ignored, and the Athletics would plummet to fifth place in 1934.

Cochrane, who was also in Chicago, did not waste any time trying to improve his new club. He wanted Al Simmons of the White Sox to shore up his outfield, but could not work out a deal. He later asked Mack if Pinky Higgins, Philadelphia's third baseman, was available. Mack, the dynasty-destroyer, replied sheepishly, "Nothing doing. I'm not helping any more ball clubs and that's final. You've been helped enough already."[23] When Cochrane mentioned to Mack that his former boss had not sold *him* any players, Mack replied, "I sold you a pretty fair catcher, didn't I?"[24]

Navin, for his part, was more than pleased with the results of his Chicago sojourn. Before leaving town, the former insurance salesman promptly purchased two policies on Cochrane's life, totaling $100,000.[25] According to the *New York Times*, "Cochrane appeared in the pink of condition during the insurance physical examinations. He weighs 175 pounds and believes he will catch about 125 games next season."[26]

Before heading back home, however, Cochrane made a bold move. The 1933 Tigers were a young, inexperienced team, almost completely lacking in veterans who had battled it out in the post-season trenches. Only two current Tigers had played in a World Series: pitchers George Uhle with Cleveland in 1920, and Firpo Marberry with Washington in 1924 and 1925. Detroit's position players were the American League's youngest, with an average age of 26 years and seven months. Cochrane knew the Tigers desperately needed a skilled veteran bat if they were going to compete in 1934.

The man Cochrane set his sights on was Leon Allen "Goose" Goslin. A dynamite hitter for over 12 seasons with the Washington Senators and St. Louis Browns, Goslin had compiled a lifetime .325 batting average. Six times, he had had a WAR of more than 5.0. With his propensity for slashing line drives, he was able to take advantage of the vast expanse of Washington's Griffith Stadium, banging out 151 triples. The Senators won their first and only World Series championship in 1924, with Goslin slugging three home runs versus the New York Giants in a matchup that went the full seven games.[27] He hit three homers again in the Series the following year, but the Senators were denied by the Pittsburgh Pirates. After a brief three-year exile to the lowly Browns, Goslin returned to D.C. in 1933, leading the Senators to yet another World Series. He homered again, but Washington was no match for the Giants of Mel Ott and Carl Hubbell, losing out in five games. With seven home runs in World Series play, he was tied with Lou Gehrig for second place on the all-time list. Goslin's idol, Babe Ruth, held the mark for most Series homers, with 15.

Goslin was a proven winner and a gamer, a popular player who made it easy for managers and fans to forgive him his fielding follies. (On Goslin's glove work, Senators skipper Donie Bush once noted that he was "sincerely lacking in that department."[28]) Years after Goslin retired, Lawrence Ritter interviewed him for his classic oral history book, *The Glory of Their Times.* In it, Goslin recalled how much fun he had playing the game. "They didn't have to pay me. I'd have paid *them* to let me play. Listen, the truth is it was more than fun. It was heaven."[29]

From early on, Goslin emulated Ruth's all-or-nothing swing, contorting his body into a pretzel when he whiffed. Like Ruth, he was often accused of "breaking training" as a major leaguer, which was baseball code for carousing. Goslin developed his great strength from working on his father's New Jersey farm as a young boy. It was obvious that he possessed a fair fastball, and the game became his ticket out of a life of manual labor. He landed a gig with DuPont, ostensibly repairing elevators, but the company primarily wanted him to pitch for its industrial league team. He eventually signed a minor league contract with the Columbia (South Carolina) Comers of the South Atlantic League. It did not take long for the club to discover that he could hit the ball a country mile; very soon, the Comers converted him to the outfield. In Goslin's second year of pro ball, he hit .390, and by the following September, he was playing regularly for the Senators at the tender age of 20.

Now, over 2,100 hits and three World Series appearances later, he was going to be a Detroit Tiger. Like Mack, Senators owner Clark Griffith was struggling to keep his team financially afloat, and could no longer afford to keep Goslin. In a straight-up swap of outfielders, Griffith dealt Goose to Detroit for John Stone. The deal raised more than a few eyebrows; it looked like the shrewd and experienced Griffith had fleeced the novice Cochrane on his first day on the job. Goslin would be 33 by Opening Day, five years older than Stone, and by most indications was on the downside of his career. After all, he hit only .297 with 64 RBI for the Senators in 1933, far below his norms.

Stone, on the other hand, looked to be trending upward. He batted .306 in his six years in Detroit and put up good extra-base numbers. In the words of *Detroit News* sportswriter H. G. Salsinger, however, Stone was "lack-lustre. He is totally void of aggressiveness, and Detroit has too many players who are void of aggressiveness."[30] Another scribe accused Stone of "losing interest" in his work, and asserted that he was at times "downright lazy."[31] He was still considered a player with great potential, however, and Griffith appeared to be the winner in the deal.

Cochrane, however, was confident he had pulled off a coup. "Goslin is the winning type of player, if I ever saw one. He has been on championship and contending clubs. He thinks in terms of victory and will be a big help to our morale, in addition to being able to park the ball in the right field bleachers now and then."[32] It was also well known that Goslin and Senators manager Joe Cronin did not always see eye-to-eye, having gotten into a heated argument one afternoon in the dugout. Cochrane and Goslin, on the other hand, had been friends for years and occasionally went on hunting excursions. Cochrane figured that getting Goslin out of Cronin's doghouse might reinvigorate the slugger. Still, many fans were left wondering if the Tigers' new manager had paid too high a price for a player past his prime.

Chapter Two

City on the Strait

In 1701, Antoine de la Mothe Cadillac landed his canoe at a high bank on a narrow strait connecting Lake Erie to Lake St. Clair. Viewing the uninhabited land with favor, he plunged a stake bearing the flag of France into the soil, claiming the territory in the name of King Louis XIV. Cadillac's mission was to establish the Fort Pontchartrain du Detroit, named after his benefactor, the Comte de Pontchartrain. Ostensibly, the fort was intended as a haven for displaced Native Americans. The grasping Cadillac's real motive, however, was to establish a monopoly on the local fur trade. In little over 200 years, the terrain he traversed would be utterly transformed as far as the eye could see.

The fort that Cadillac built took the latter half of its name from the waterway that it overlooked. *Le detroit du Lac Erie* (meaning "the strait of Lake Erie") is today known as the Detroit River. French settlers both hardy and industrious were attracted by the free, tillable virgin land that surrounded the fort for miles. In 1760, following the capitulation of Montreal near the conclusion of the French and Indian War, Fort Detroit was handed over to the British. Three years later, an Ottawa chief named Pontiac, having failed to capture it by surprise, laid siege to the fort with a contingent of nearly 900 warriors, leading to the Battle of Bloody Run. Pontiac lived to see another day, but after nearly six months, he lifted the futile siege and went in search of easier conquests.

A British post during the Revolutionary War, Fort Detroit was used primarily as an armory for allied Native American tribes, who led raiding parties on settlers to the south. In 1796, the fort and the village surrounding it were handed over to the United States as part of the Jay Treaty.

A fire in 1805 rapidly reduced nearly the entire settlement of wooden structures to ashes. Its people persevered, building Detroit up from the rubble, officially incorporating the erstwhile village as a city just a year later. Augustus B. Woodward, in his role as Chief Justice of the Michigan Territory, put his stamp on Detroit's topographical destiny, laying forth a sweeping vision of streets radiating out like spokes on a wheel, with a central axis known as Grand Circus Park. Detroit's wide avenues would be reminiscent of the beautiful streets of Paris.

Like any city, it had its growing pains. Today, Detroit-bashing is a veritable cottage industry. Here is an early antebellum example, courtesy of a traveler from New York City in 1854:

> As we reached the dock in Detroit, we were saluted by a grand peal of Heaven's artillery, while the clouds poured down their welcome in overwhelming torrents. Detroit as mapped out, and Detroit as we saw it, appear two very different places: the Detroit on paper being, as we doubt not it will be some day, a very large, beautiful and regular city; the Detroit we looked at from our cab appeared one interminably long and wide street, across which it was neither easy nor pleasant for neighbors to communicate. This main artery is, however, healthy, and new veins are fast shooting out on either side. It compares favorably with what it was, and hence those who have grown with the place feel very proud of it. Their Common Council, judging from the condition of the streets, are as derelict as was ever ARCULARIUS, of mud and dirt celebrity in New York. The channels are very unclean, and send up a most unhealthy effluvia in the noonday heat. We were not surprised to hear of a few cases of cholera.[1]

During the Civil War, Detroit's relatively easy access into Canada made it a key stop on the Underground Railroad. A disgruntled segment of the city's white population blamed blacks as the cause of the war. Resentment simmered between the two groups, which boiled over into violent unrest in March 1863. The Michigan Infantry had to be called in to restore a fragile harmony. Before the disturbance was over, fires had destroyed over 30 buildings, an estimated 200 blacks were left homeless, and two people had been killed. It would not be the last time that Detroit would experience deadly race riots.

By the late 1800s, Woodward's grand plan was taking shape, and Detroit had come to be known affectionately as "The Paris of the West." With its stately Gilded Age mansions, its grand tree-lined avenues, its green spaces, fountains, and culture, it was certainly an appropriate appellation. Its citizens gloried in their majestic opera house, excellent library, and beautiful art museum. Moneyed lumber barons and their fashionably dressed wives strolled together along the Woodward Avenue shopping district. They might partake of the pleasures of Campus Martius Park, or sample the sweet delights at Fred Sanders' confectionary, before heading back to their stately brick homes in the Brush Park neighborhood. On weekends, crowds packed Belle Isle, the 982-acre oasis in the middle of the Detroit River.

As the twentieth century approached, the city grew to a population of nearly 300,000. Among them was a young engineer named Henry Ford, who, on a damp, misty morning in 1896, took his quadricycle out for its first test run along Washington Boulevard—only to have the fancy contraption break down.[2] In less than ten years, he formed the Ford Motor Company with $28,000 in capital.[3] Already an important transportation hub due to its proximity to the Great Lakes, Detroit's destiny was to become the automobile capital of the world. During the Roaring Twenties, the burgeoning metropolis sprouted skyscrapers rivaling those of New York: The Book-Cadillac Hotel, the Guardian Building, the David Stott, the Fisher Building, the Penobscot, the General Motors Building, and the beaux-arts Michigan Central Depot. All of them bespoke prosperity, high finance, and industrial might. That prosperity did not reach to all, however. As one observer of the city wrote in 1934, "Big skyscrapers [were] next to wooden shacks. No symmetry in anything. Like a fat boy too big for his pants."[4]

The Motor City was built on the backs of men like Ford, the Dodge Brothers, the Fisher Brothers, Alfred Sloan, and Walter Chrysler, automotive giants who transformed the sleepy town of the late 1800s into an ever increasing, ever expanding, frenetic, fast-paced urban jungle. Immigrants streamed into its streets, lured by the prospect of steady factory work. The Packard Automotive Plant, completed in 1911 and encompassing 3,500,000 square feet, was considered the most state-of-the-art facility in the world. The Ambassador Bridge, connecting the city to Windsor, Ontario, was the longest suspension bridge in the world when it opened in 1929. Detroit's population, just below 1,000,000 in 1920, was set to explode by almost 60 percent before the decade was over.

The Big Three automakers were on top of the world, as motor vehicle production ratcheted up to more than 5,300,000 in 1929. Car factories hummed around the clock. Men eager for work descended on the city now known as Detroit the Dynamic. Occupancy rates reached 100 percent, and once-elegant mansions were converted into crammed rooming houses to meet the tight demand. Landlords employed a systematic rotation, renting beds to multiple workers in eight-hour segments, just long enough for one man to get some shuteye while another put in his shift at the plant. The bed-sheets barely had time to cool.

The stock market crash of 1929 tapped the brakes on Detroit's roaring economy. In February 1933, two of Michigan's largest banks, Union Guardian Trust and First National, failed to meet their obligations. In an effort to stave off a run on other financial institutions, Governor William Comstock instituted an eight-day bank holiday, effectively freezing the assets of nearly 900,000 customers, to the tune of $1.5 billion. Rather than calm markets, panic spread, and hundreds of banks around the country slammed their doors shut. That same year, automobile production plummeted to 1,331,860, a level not seen since 1916. Ford Motor Company's Detroit plants employed over 128,000 people in 1929; two years later, the number was only 37,000, and about half of those people worked only three days per week. For thousands, bread lines replaced the assembly lines. The massive unemployment sent a ripple effect throughout the city; approximately one-third of all families owning homes were delinquent in their property tax payments, putting a crimp in city services.

The misery reached a horrifying degree on March 7, 1932, when thousands of demonstrators marched on the Ford Rouge Plant in Dearborn. Comprised mostly of laid-off autoworkers ("with Communists in their midst"[5]), the crowd carried banners proclaiming GIVE US WORK and WE WANT BREAD NOT CRUMBS. A melee ensued between protestors, police, and Ford security guards. Rocks were thrown, police fired shots, four demonstrators were killed, and 50 others were wounded. Henry Ford's public image took a beating. At the massive funeral parade for the four dead, a banner read FORD GAVE THEM BULLETS FOR BREAD. The Ford Hunger March was Detroit's day of infamy.

The team that Mickey Cochrane took over won 75 games and lost 79 in 1933, good for fifth place in the American League, a distant 25 games behind the Senators. Detroit had some promising young pitchers; their team earned run average of 3.95 and 731 runs surrendered were both the third-lowest figures in the junior circuit. Detroit's big problem, however, was hitting. Lacking home run threats in the lineup (Hank Greenberg and Charlie Gehringer had tied for the team lead with 12), they mustered only 4.66 runs per game, far below the Yankees' 6.10, which topped the circuit. Goslin, of course, was expected to give a big boost to the offense.

Looking over his roster in December, Cochrane planned to bat himself third, with Goslin in the cleanup slot. Goslin, Pete Fox (7 home runs, 58 runs batted in, and a .288 batting average in 1933), and Gerald "Gee" Walker (9, 63, .280) were the established outfielders. Players like Frank Doljack, Bill Lawrence, and Ivey Shiver were spare parts with scant experience. Cochrane reportedly felt highly of Walker's potential. A fleet runner, he led the Tigers with 26 stolen bases in 1932, only one behind the Yankees' Ben Chapman, who topped the majors.

Cochrane expected to catch roughly 120 games a year (he averaged 130 games per season while with the Athletics). Ray Hayworth, Detroit's first-string catcher for the past couple seasons, would be relegated to backup. The infield consisted of Greenberg at first, Gehringer at second, Billy Rogell at

Arriving on the scene in 1934, Mickey Cochrane transformed the culture of the Detroit Tigers (courtesy Ernie Harwell Sports Collection, Detroit Public Library).

short, and Marv Owen at third. Cochrane had tried to make a deal for the Yankees' Tony Lazzeri, one of the hardest-hitting second basemen in the game, but to no avail. He heaped great praise on Greenberg, the 23-year-old kid from the Bronx who was coming off his first full big league campaign. Cochrane gushed, "He had a great season for a recruit. He has power at the plate, is a fine hustler and should be even better next year." He added, "As to Gehringer, there is nothing to be said. He is the class of the American League. Rogell was as good a shortstop as any, except Joe Cronin, and Owen should improve."[6]

The budding strength of the Tigers, however, was the pitching staff, and Cochrane, being a catcher, was delighted at the prospect of helping to develop its youngsters. He went so far as to say that Detroit could have the best mound corps in the league, now that the Athletics had traded away the great Lefty Grove. Firpo Marberry, who won 16 games in 1933, was the dean of the staff at age 34. Along with 26-year-old Tommy Bridges, winner of 14, Detroit was solid at the top of the rotation. After that, however, a lot depended on a couple of kids named Schoolboy Rowe (23 years old) and Elden Auker (22). "If Schoolboy's arm is all right again," Cochrane pointed out, "he will be one of the best pitchers in the business." Rowe had suffered a shoulder injury that kept him out for most of the second half of the 1933 season. Cochrane added, "I believe we can look to Vic Frasier for winning service, too, and I am sure of Marberry." His faith in Frasier may have been a case of misdirected optimism; in three seasons with the Chicago White Sox and Tigers, he went 22–34 with a 5.56 earned run average. "Of course, we could use another pitcher. Who couldn't? I tried to get Ted Lyons from the White Sox, but [manager] Lew Fonseca wanted too much."[7]

The Tigers, in fact, were planning on bringing a sizable contingent of other pitchers to spring training, including veterans Carl Fischer, Vic Sorrell, and Elon "Chief" Hogsett, believed by many to be Native American because of his swarthy complexion and jet black hair. "Am I really Indian? Well, I'm one-thirty-second Cherokee on my mother's side. Maybe more, but whoever figured that out quit checking. Probably afraid of what they might find."[8] Among the youngsters vying for roster spots were names like Orlin Collier, Isidore Goldstein, Luke Hamlin, Roxie Lawson, Charles K. "Buck" Marrow, Truett Sewell, Steve Larkin, and Joe Sullivan.

Before the calendar year was out, Cochrane had signed a new two-year contract (terms were not divulged). Del Baker, the interim manager for the final two games in 1933, was retained as a coach. Cochrane also brought on Cy Perkins, his former backup catcher in Philadelphia, to join his coaching staff.

In early January, Cochrane headed to Detroit to confer with Navin about plans for the upcoming season. To no one's surprise, Cochrane threw himself wholeheartedly into his new job, accomplishing much in those first frigid days in the Motor City.

His initial order of business was a sartorial one. Not only did he request that the team's uniforms be lighter in weight, he also oversaw the return of the Tigers' Old English "D" logo. It had been used, with slight esthetic variations and infrequent lapses, since the late 1800s. One of the first known references to the team's classic font appeared in the *Detroit Free Press* on February 29, 1896, when the Tigers were still a minor league team: "[The Tigers] will use the old blue uniforms for games abroad and will have white uniforms with black trimmings for the home games. Instead of the word Detroit on the shirt front there will be a German letter 'D' on one side."[9] Less than a month later, the same newspaper swapped the lettering's provenance, dubbing it an English "D." Whether German or English, it quickly became iconic.

The Tigers, however, removed the logo from jerseys following the 1929 season in favor of a blue script "Detroit" (pinstripes were even added the following year). In 1931, the Old English "D" was taken off the caps as well, in favor of a plain block "D." The block lettering was not a particularly noxious look, but Cochrane preferred a Tigers uniform that hearkened back to the team's glory days. Thus, the pinstripes and script lettering were ditched, the Old English "D" was brought back to both the home jerseys and the caps, and it has remained there, with the egregious exception of 1960, ever since. Along with the Yankees' interlocking "NY," it remains a masterpiece of design, simple yet elegant, and impervious to the fickle winds of fashion, even across a sometimes gusty century.

Cochrane got together with Gehringer and Rogell to assess the strengths and weaknesses of the Tigers' roster. He asked Navin to bring Schoolboy Rowe up from his home in Arkansas so that physicians could see if his injury had healed. The new manager also went on a kind of media blitz, giving newspaper and radio interviews and talking baseball with fans wherever he went. Between it all, he found time to go house hunting with his wife, Mary. The couple took in a Red Wings hockey game at Olympia Stadium one evening. A photographer, spotting them in their box seats, asked permission to snap a picture, and this quickly drew a crowd. An ovation ensued, and Cochrane stood to acknowledge the cheering.

Unlike his predecessor Harris, Cochrane had an outgoing nature, and public speaking came easy to him. Overcoming the fan apathy that had become entrenched after so many years of mediocre baseball was no easy task, but by constantly putting his face before the public and extolling the virtues of his team, Cochrane succeeded at getting fans excited about 1934. "I do not mind telling you," he intimated to guests at a dinner reception, "that in the last five or six years there has been very little color on the so-called

Tigers. They have been more like pussycats that had been out all night in a downpour. It will be my job to inject color, dash and spirit into the club."[10]

A special night was planned in honor of Cochrane at the Statler Hotel on January 16. Organized by the Kiwanis Club, it hosted members of the Tigers' front office and baseball dignitaries from around the American League. Previously, Cochrane had hedged his bets when asked where he thought the Tigers would finish. But that evening was the closest he came all winter to making a prediction. "I played with the Athletics for nine years," he said in a speech, "and in that time we never finished out of the first division and I do not intend to start now."[11] Before 900 members of the Detroit Yacht Club, he qualified this bold statement by urging fans to "expect no miracles at Navin Field," but promised that Detroit would display "as much fighting spirit as any college football team you ever saw." Gone were the days when the Tigers could be accused of not laying it all out on the diamond. "We'll have a hustling, colorful club if nothing else."[12]

If Cochrane was careful to refrain from making a bolder prognostication, Goose Goslin was not. From his home in Salem, New Jersey, he predicted to a reporter that the Tigers would finish no lower than third. Not stopping there, he went on: "And I wouldn't be a bit surprised if we won the pennant. I look for a three-cornered race, with Washington, New York and Detroit battling for the top all the way." As for his hitting, he noted, "I always liked to hit at Navin Field, and am happy over the chance of playing half my games there. I'll get my share of base hits. Don't worry about me."[13]

It was the beginning of a new era of Tigers baseball in another respect: Spring training, scheduled to begin March 4, would be in a different locale. After a peripatetic existence in springs past, enduring inadequate facilities and unreliable schedules, the team was looking forward to its move to the tiny Florida town of Lakeland, just outside of Tampa. For that, they could thank Al Lang, a promoter and visionary who had spent years touting the benefits of Florida as a spring training site.

Lang was a transplanted Pittsburgher born in 1870. While still a young man, he received the bad news one day that he had cancer of the stomach. Told by his doctor that he could hope for only six more months to live and that he should enjoy them in a climate better suited to his condition than the Steel City, Lang made the fateful decision to heed the advice. He sold his laundry business, and he and his wife made their way south to Florida, settling in St. Petersburg. Lang had a robust constitution to begin with, and the sun did wonders for his health. With his tall, bony physique and shock of white hair, he looked like a cross between Connie Mack and baseball Commissioner Kenesaw Mountain Landis.[14]

He fell in love with his adopted town and wound up serving two terms as mayor. One fine spring afternoon, Lang was sitting in front of Budd's drugstore in downtown St. Pete, reading over the latest news about his beloved Pittsburgh Pirates. He came across a dispatch indicating that the team, which at the time was training in Hot Springs, Arkansas, had had their practice rained out for the third consecutive day. This was a mystifying turn of events to Lang, who recalled that he hadn't seen rain that lasted more than ten minutes since he'd stepped foot in Florida.[15]

It was at that moment that he first got the notion of luring major league teams to train in the Sunshine State. With his boundless energy, he set to work pumping up Florida's benefits to any teams that would listen. In 1914, the Yankees laid out a rudimentary spring training camp in St. Pete, and, one by one, more teams followed in other towns.[16] Lang was a booster at heart; to him, spring training in Florida meant more money in city and state coffers. The plan was that players and the press (and their wives and kids) would stay in the state's hotels, eats in its restaurants, and play on its beaches. For a month or so every year, it would be a steady income, giving the economy an injection of tourists as well, perhaps. Lang played the promoter for numerous towns throughout the state.

The Tigers believed in Lang's dream and set their sights on Lakeland. It is no mystery how the town got its name, with 13 natural lakes in the area. Dotting the landscape were numerous other lakes, which were really only abandoned phosphate mines filled with water. Lakeland was famous for its large population of white swans, who graced its waters and lent the town its tranquil flavor. What more idyllic place, thought Lang and the Tigers, for a team to prepare for a baseball season?

Negotiations between the Tigers and the city began in November 1933, and when a team representative toured Henley Field, he was impressed with what he saw. The park was overhauled (including a complete re-sodding), and the city forked over $1,500 to the Tigers as an inducement.[17] How long the club would continue to train there, however, was anybody's guess. As writer Sam Greene of the *Detroit News* noted at the time, "It's getting to be a habit for the Tigers to change camps every season."[18] The club arranged for the players to stay at the Terrace Hotel in downtown Lakeland. Near the end of January, Cochrane made a stop in the Quaker City before heading down to Florida a few weeks later.

It was a bitterly cold day in Moscow when Kliment Voroshilov, the Soviet Commissar of War, took to the podium at the All-Union Communist Party Congress on February 3. The central issue of his strident address was Japanese saber rattling. Despite Soviet diplomatic efforts, the land of the rising sun appeared unconvinced that peace was better than the prospect of war. From now on, Voroshilov insisted, it would be ridiculous to ignore Japan's preparations for invasion. Interrupted frequently by thundering applause, the Commissar boasted that the Red Army was readying defenses on the U.S.S.R.'s eastern border.

Three days later, news from the streets of Paris was not any better. Furious mobs, revolting against the French government, engaged in open battle with police and troops into the morning hours. Rioters tossed torches through the first-floor windows of the historic Ministry of Marine building, setting it ablaze. Machine gun fire raked the front of the American Embassy. Fifteen demonstrators were shot and killed, while hundreds more were injured. Later that month in Austria, socialists who opposed Fascist threats in the government sparked fighting in the country's five-day civil war. Hundreds died and thousands were wounded. In the peak of the turmoil, Great Britain, France, and Italy all warned Hitler that Nazi Germany must not meddle in the situation.

Back home, Labor unrest was roiling America. That same week, nearly a thousand striking New York City taxi drivers descended on Times Square "just as after-theatre crowds were at their height in the mid-town section." Among their demands was the formation of a taxi drivers union and a minimum wage. "Disorder on a widespread scale flared last night…. Bands of the striking drivers paraded the streets, halting cabs, ousting the passengers, breaking doors and windshields, slashing tires and in some cases wrecking the machines…. In most cases the passengers were told with rough good humor to use the subways."[19]

In Detroit, there were signs that things were improving. The *Associated Press* reported that the number of men at work in Detroit factories of any type had doubled in just over three months. The report called it a "comeback" for a city that "was literally 'flat broke' 10 months ago."[20] Meanwhile, 20,000 production employees at Ford Motor Company's Rouge Plant received pay raises.

If nothing else, 1934 promised to be more pleasant in one respect: The same day as Voroshilov's address in Moscow, saloons in Detroit resumed the legal sale of liquor by the glass, after nearly 16 years of Prohibition. Beginning at precisely six o'clock that evening, bartenders were free to open the taps and pop the bottles. The manager of the cocktail lounge at the Book-Cadillac

Hotel confirmed that Martinis were the most popular drink that night, followed closely by the Manhattan and the Old Fashioned. For the average working class stiff who could not afford the prices at the Book, Detroit had plenty of neighborhood bars. Some of the more popular ones were the Moesta Tavern at Jefferson and East Grand Boulevard, the J. B. Cocktail and Liquor Bar on Bates Street, and the Dolph Saloon. Baseball fans could drop in at Nemo's Bar on Michigan Avenue for a cold beer on the way home after a game.

While Detroiters imbibed at their favorite watering holes, another long-awaited piece of progress was very much in doubt. Early in March, the State Public Works Administration Board all but put the kibosh on a proposed $87,000,000 subway project for the city, citing it as a financial pie in the sky. Harold Ickes, Secretary of the Interior, also denounced the plan as unsound. With everything that was going on around the globe, however, the most sensational news in America was the breakout of notorious gangster John Dillinger from a supposedly escape-proof county jail in Crown Point, Indiana. Brandishing a wooden pistol he had whittled in his cell, the desperado made his way past the guards and fled to an unknown locale somewhere outside of Chicago, setting off a massive manhunt.

Against this backdrop, Tigers pitchers and catchers arrived in Lakeland, with position players streaming in over the course of the next two weeks. There had been rumors that Goose Goslin would be a potential holdout, but he arrived on time with the ink barely dry on his new contract. As per the Tigers' policy, terms were not disclosed, but Goslin himself put it thus, "Mr. Navin treated me fine. I hope I can hit .400 for him."[21]

Chapter Three

"The tumult
and the shouting start"

Cochrane immediately began the process of distancing himself from Bucky Harris. He implemented a far more strenuous and exacting regimen than the Tigers were accustomed to. Sliding pits were brought in. He placed an emphasis on calisthenics, apparently a novel concept to the team. Cochrane believed such activity to be essential for ballplayers who needed to remain supple in order to withstand the grind of a 154-game season.

Off the field, he established a midnight curfew, and players had to be out of bed and ready to go by nine o'clock in the morning. He even went so far as to consult the hotel chef regarding the players' menu. Cochrane's biggest culinary bombshell bade that no man be permitted more than one steak per day. Practice sessions began at 10:30 a.m. sharp and lasted for three hours, including a 20-minute calisthenics warm-up session. Drills ran the full gamut of fundamentals, from sliding, to bunting, to baserunning, to holding runners on. Fielders practiced situational plays repeatedly until they became second nature. Cochrane wanted the Tigers to play a more aggressive, heads-up brand of baseball, and players were coached on the basics of the double steal and suicide squeeze. In essence, Cochrane instilled a fresh attitude into his Tigers. Instead of waiting around for the opposition to make mistakes, the Tigers would now force the issue, putting pressure on the other team in order to create their own luck. Spring training of 1934 was a kind of baseball laboratory for the young Bengals. Physical and technical improvements were attained by experimentation, with the result that every player could realize his full capabilities on the diamond. The excitement over the new season had rubbed off on Frank Navin, who made his first trip down to training camp in four years. Walter Briggs also put in an appearance and immediately gave his stamp of approval to Cochrane's new workouts.

Early in March, former Tigers skipper Bucky Harris, by then the new manager of the Boston Red Sox, created a stir. Detroit, he predicted in a newspaper interview, did not stand much of a chance in 1934. Said Cochrane in response, "I'm going to put that clipping on the bulletin board and have every one read and remember it. Harris and his Red Sox will be very much surprised when they meet us, for Harris is managing one team that we're going to beat."[1]

One of the big questions of the spring was the pitching shoulder of Schoolboy Rowe. In order to strengthen it, he had spent the winter chopping wood at his Arkansas home. Cochrane had wanted him to travel up to Detroit for a physical, but later it was decided that Rowe would head directly down to Lakeland from Arkansas. Rowe was not a fan of the frosty temperatures of early spring in Detroit, having gotten a cold the first day he ever set foot in the city in April 1933. He insisted that his wintertime lumberjack routine had done the trick, and he did not need the attention of doctors.

Once Rowe arrived in camp and began throwing, however, it became clear that not everything was okay. When pain flared up in his shoulder, Cochrane prescribed a few days of rest followed by calisthenics. Trainer Denny Carroll tried to massage out the kinks, but nothing worked. The young pitcher, whom Detroit was banking on so heavily to turn them into a contender in 1934, was finally sent to a specialist in Miami. The pain persisted. Cochrane hinted that Rowe might be forced to start the season at the Tigers' Beaumont (Texas) farm club.

Cochrane also had the pleasant problem of deciding who would bat cleanup: Greenberg or Goslin. After swinging the trade with the Senators back in December, Cochrane had intended to bat Goslin in the fourth slot. Greenberg, however, gained some bulk over the winter and began the spring by tearing the cover off the ball every day in practice. Whichever candidate won the cleanup duties, the other would bat fifth. The leadoff position was a battle between Billy Rogell, Pete Fox, or Gee Walker. Gehringer would bat second, while Cochrane would pencil himself in the third slot. Writer John Kieran called Gehringer a "practically perfect second baseman, except that he isn't wired for sound. Charlie is one of those strong, silent men."[2]

Every spring has its promising young rookie, and 1934 was no exception for the Tigers. Herman "Flea" Clifton quickly earned the praise of both Cochrane and Navin. After a .301 season in the Texas League in 1933, the Tigers felt they had their third baseman of the future. When Cochrane was a member of the Athletics, he was never overly impressed with Detroit's third baseman, Marv Owen, who he felt lacked aggressiveness. Clifton hustled all throughout camp, however, and Cochrane was eager to bring him north with the big club, even if only as a backup utility infielder.

Once Grapefruit League competition got under way, the Tigers' bats were cold. While that was not unusual for any team in the early spring exhibition season, Cochrane nevertheless told his men to take a day off and go fishing, in hopes that the relaxation would clear their heads. Greenberg, in particular, fell into a deep slump and was held hitless in four consecutive games. It even reached the point where Cochrane pondered starting 26-year-old Harry Davis at first base once the season opened. Davis was not known for his bat, and it looked like the first base position might be a weak one for Detroit, unless Greenberg began to hit consistently. The Tigers broke out of their offensive lethargy in a game against the Newark Bears, a 10–6 win in which Goslin and Marv Owen both homered. "The Tigers certainly seem to have found their batting eyes," said the *Free Press*.[3] Owen began fielding and hitting better as the spring wore on. That, coupled with the highly touted Clifton's apparent inability to hit, made it look more and more as if Owen would retain his job at the hot corner.

The Tigers arranged for Schoolboy Rowe to receive treatment from a bone specialist, which initially improved his condition. He threw off a mound in practice and looked strong, but the pain returned even worse following a bullpen session on March 26. An examining physician gave a diagnosis of torn muscles and advised Rowe to refrain from throwing a baseball for at least a month. This did not sit well with the young pitcher, who feared the long layoff would do more harm than good. Rowe went on record as saying he likely would not be physically able to pitch in 1934.[4]

In a few days, however, he began throwing again on the side and reported no soreness. Cochrane may have harbored thoughts that Rowe's issues were all in his head, that he was afraid of cutting loose for fear of re-injuring his shoulder. The pitcher made his spring debut on April 6 against the minor league Montreal Royals. "Pitching easily and making no effort to bear down,"[5] he gave up only two scratch hits in three innings of work. It was Rowe's first time facing live hitters since being shelved the previous July. Cochrane liked what he saw in the brief stint, however, calling Rowe's fastball as good as Lefty Grove's, his former Philadelphia batterymate.

Two days later, the Tigers were trailing the Royals by a run with two outs in the ninth, when Owen's homer tied it up. In the 12th inning, Elden Auker, who had come on in relief in the fifth, proclaimed as he strode to the plate, "This thing has gone far enough. I'm going to put one over the fence and end it."[6] Which he promptly did, picking up the win in the process. On April 10, Detroit broke out for 13 tallies against the Birmingham Barons of the Southern Association, with Goslin and Owen homering again. They racked up 18 runs against the Barons the next day; before the game was half over, Cochrane had pulled most of his starters.

Rowe's final exhibition appearance was against the Cincinnati Reds at Redland Field on April 15. He impressed Mark Koenig, the Reds' third baseman and a former Tiger. After being tied in knots against Schoolboy, Koenig quipped, "Is that the guy that's supposed to have a sore arm? Well, if he's pitching with a sore arm I'll pay $10 to watch him pitch when his arm is right. He's got so much stuff out there now that you can't see the ball."[7] It was a costly victory for the Tigers, however. Goslin suffered a "nose injury that is expected to keep him out of the opening game against the Chicago White Sox," according to the *Associated Press*. "Bleeding profusely, Goslin was taken to Good Samaritan Hospital, where attendants said they did not believe his nose was fractured."[8]

In the end, Rowe would not be going to the minor leagues; Beaumont would have to wait. Cochrane wanted to keep a close eye on his young pitching prodigy. When the Tigers boarded a Chicago-bound train to begin the regular season, Schoolboy was with them.[9]

To most prognosticators, the 1934 pennant race was going to be a case of déjà vu. The Washington Senators and New York Giants were both expected to make a return engagement to the World Series.

It looked like a safe bet. Despite the loss of Goslin, Washington still could put some runs on the board. Joe Kuhel, Buddy Myer, Joe Cronin, and Heinie Manush led a potent offense, and the pitching staff of General Crowder, Earl Whitehill, and Lefty Stewart was strong. The Yankees, who still had the aging Babe Ruth in their stacked lineup, were viewed as the second-best team in the American League. Their mound corps, however, lacked the depth of years past; starters Lefty Gomez and Johnny Allen won 16 and 15 games, respectively, in 1933, but after that, there was a big drop-off. Wrote John Kieran, "Pitching will be important in the Bronx—If the Yankees get it."[10]

The most improved team figured to be the Boston Red Sox, who had acquired the great Lefty Grove from the Philadelphia Athletics in Connie Mack's fire sale. In mid–March, however, the 34-year-old Grove complained of a dead arm. Conventional medical wisdom of the time traced the problem to his bad teeth. Grove visited a dentist, who discovered three abscessed molars. The teeth were pulled, and fans in Boston crossed their fingers and hoped for the best.

As for the Tigers, most experts tabbed them for fourth. If Grove's dead arm lingered, however, they could nudge Boston out for third place. Either way, nobody outside of Cochrane and Goslin gave them a shot at a pennant. An improved team, for sure, but not ready to play with the big boys just yet. "Mickey Cochrane, the fiery backstop," one journalist wrote, "has steamed up Detroit fans as no one has done since the heyday of Ty Cobb."[11]

"Detroit, on paper," wrote H. G. Salsinger, "does not deserve better than third place but paper means nothing in actual competition, a fact that is given fresh proof nearly every season. To win the pennant of 1934 Detroit must not only get breaks in its own competition but it must have the benefit of breaks going against New York and Washington."[12] An *Associated Press* reporter noted, "Mickey Cochrane not only has electrified the Tigers with his aggressive spirit but has brought to Detroit the best catching in the league."[13]

Opening Day always dawns with fresh hope in every major league city. Wrote John Drebinger in the *New York Times*, "With a feeling of tenseness not at all surprising when it is recalled that six weeks of intensive training have just been completed in preparing for it, sixteen major league baseball clubs stand poised today to launch a new championship campaign. All appear strangely confident and, with an utter disregard for what the future may hold in store for them, all are fervently hoping for clear skies and a brilliant sun in order that the business at hand may be set in motion without delay."[14]

Grantland Rice, known as the "Dean of American Sportswriters," penned this of the upcoming campaign: "The tumult and the shouting start, the captains and the camps are back, and there'll be many a silent drama in the daily box scores for those who read between the lines."[15]

Paul Gallico admired what he viewed as the game's pastoral niceties: "How soft and fragrant is the air and how green the grass. Is there a lovelier sight on a spring day than nine men spread out on a baseball field and the pitcher, all in white, making slow graceful motions? There is a sight for you."[16]

Baseball was back, but that was not the only good tidings in Detroit. On March 13, responding to Democratic President Roosevelt's call for increased wages and shorter working hours, the Ford Motor Company announced it was bringing back the five-dollar-a-day minimum wage for production workers. Affecting nearly 33,000 factory employees in the Detroit area, the decision was hailed by Henry Ford, who expressed hope that other industries might see wage increases as well. At the same time, the Board of Directors of the National Automobile Chamber of Commerce recommended reductions in workers' average weekly hours from 40 to 36, with compensating wage increases. An editorial in the *Detroit Free Press* boasted: "Once more the automobile manufacturers of America are demonstrating their capacity for enlightened, broad gauge industrial leadership."[17]

Not all was rosy, however. The next day, the National Labor Relations Board met in Washington to take up the issue of labor problems in Detroit auto plants. The Board had reportedly received several thousand complaints of violations relating to hours of labor and wages. In an executive order, Roosevelt appointed General Hugh S. Johnson to take personal charge of the dispute in an effort to avert a general strike in the industry. After several days of contentious talks, Roosevelt finally stepped into the fray at the 11th hour. On March 20, he wired William Collins, organizer for the American Federation of Labor, all but demanding the postponement of a strike vote. Meeting with the President in the White House less than 24 hours later, eight auto industry executives voiced their discontent with the key point of a settlement plan submitted by Roosevelt: The recognition of the AFL unions. They also rejected the President's call for new elections on worker representation in the auto plants, as well as the formation of an independent board to hear worker grievances. With the discussions going nowhere, the auto executives abruptly got up and walked out of the White House.

That evening, the President made the drastic decision to resort to his licensing powers under the National Recovery Act to forestall a strike. The next day, following a five-hour meeting with Roosevelt at the Washington headquarters of the AFL, labor union representatives voted unanimously to hold in abeyance a threatened strike. More meetings ensued in the following days, and a settlement was reached on March 25. Both sides claimed victory: The factory workers by re-asserting their right to collectively bargain, and the manufacturers by having prevented the AFL from coming into a position where it could dominate the industry. Roosevelt, in a statement from the White House, expressed his hope that

> Out of this will come a new realization of the opportunities of capital and labor not only to compose their differences at the conference table and to recognize their respective rights and responsibilities, but also to establish a foundation on which they can co-operate on bettering the human relationships involved in any large industrial enterprise…. Only in this way can industry and its workers go forward with a united front in their assault on depression, and gain for both the desired benefits of continually better times.[18]

Detroit Mayor Frank Couzens touted the labor peace as the first step in the city's march toward economic revival. Charles Boyd, secretary of the Retail Merchants Association, declared, "The strike settlement undoubtedly was one of the most important things that has happened in Detroit in its process of recovery."[19]

As if on cue, the Detroit Board of Commerce in early April launched its "Speed Recovery Campaign," an extravaganza of civic chest thumping meant to boost public morale. Art-deco posters were prominently displayed on streetcars and in shop and café windows, featuring the slogan "Let's Know Detroit and its 2,494 Industries." It was part of the "Exposition of Progress," a citywide display of all things made in Detroit. It may be called the Motor City, proclaimed the chairman of the expo, but Detroit's factories produced commodities essential and diverse. The list included airplane parts, boats (particularly all-steel pleasure craft), xylophones, artificial limbs, books, pins and roofing nails, cigars, cigar boxes, chewing tobacco, beer barrels, air conditioners (a nascent industry), carburetors, refrigerators, valves, oil burners, shoes, sealing wax, cement blocks, laundry bluing fabricators, cordless electric irons, cleaning products, asbestos pads for dining-room tables, and flags (all nations).

Detroit made dental drills, fireplaces, locomotive wheels, laundry tubs, hair tonic, insecticide, bricks, fur clothing, neckties, bathing suits, corsets, bottle corks, talcum powder, perfume, bath salts, hair wavers, shaving cream, and bells. It also churned out electric sandwich machines, barbecues, stoves, washing machines, vacuum cleaners, sun lamps, elevators, jewelry, mail bags, razor strops, stained shingles, motion picture sound equipment, thermometers, purses, radios, scales, golf supplies, coat hangers, soda fountains, window shades, and caskets.

The city counted 160 producers of foodstuff such as pie fillings, spices, candy, canned eggs, macaroni, Chinese noodles and dumplings, and fruit extracts. There were 66 dairy product companies, 35 makers of nonalcoholic beverages, 13 breweries, and one pretzel factory.

Detroit also had one American League baseball team. The 1934 Tigers' season got under way on Tuesday, April 17, at Comiskey Park in Chicago. "It will be Mickey Cochrane's debut as a manager in charge of an American league competition," wrote Ed Burns of the *Chicago Tribune*. "And the presence of Mickey has much to do with the glowing prophesies made for his ensemble. Maybe this optimism isn't based on Mickey's prospective managerial talents, about which little is known. But there is no speculation about what kind of a catcher this Cochrane is and his batting prowess is well known to one and all."[20] Most agreed that the Tigers would bang out their fair share of hits in 1934. Wrote M. F. Drukenbrod of the *Detroit Free Press*, "When we think of baseball, our mind generally runs to those long drives which crash against the fences or clear them. Pitching may be what some say it is—80 or

90 per cent of baseball—but we will also go for the slugging end. For that reason, until we are shown otherwise, we will continue to believe that the Tigers will be more dangerous this year than they have been for some time because of the presence of Cochrane and Goslin, and the extra base drives which will ring off their bats."[21]

Cochrane had seen a lot of Opening Days, and played in many World Series contests, but he was understandably nervous in the moments leading up to his first game as skipper. "'Oh, oh' he muttered grimly as he paced up and down like a fidgety lion, 'I'll be glad when the first inning is over.'"[22]

Firpo Marberry had the honor of starting and gave up only three runs before Elden Auker took over in the eighth inning. When Cochrane wrote out the lineup card, he had Jo-Jo White penciled in at left field, figuring Goslin wasn't fully healed from his spring training nose mishap. Goslin, however, insisted he was okay to play and talked Cochrane into putting him in the cleanup spot. His nose did not affect his hitting as he banged out Detroit's first hit of the season and scored two runs. Third baseman Marv Owen picked up where he left off in the spring, hitting a double and driving in three runs. A throng of 18,000 patrons, including baseball Commissioner Kenesaw Mountain Landis, braved the chilly weather but went home disappointed. H. G. Salsinger of the *Detroit News* wrote, "Gordon Stanley Cochrane, the new Scotch-Irish-American manager of Detroit, made his debut as a major league pilot yesterday. He received an ovation when he made his appearance on the field, another ovation when he appeared at bat for the first time and a discreet silence when he left the field after the game, for Gordon Stanley Cochrane's debut as a manager was marked by an 8 to 3 victory over the Chicago team.... The debut of Gordon Stanley Cochrane was a distinct success."[23]

Detroit took the next day's contest, with Goslin and Walker both homering. Schoolboy Rowe was rocked in the rubber game, however, giving up six runs in less than three innings. Cochrane could not be faulted for wondering if perhaps he should have sent the kid to Beaumont coming out of spring training.

At League Park in Cleveland on April 20, Carl Fischer shut out the Tribe on five hits. In the eighth inning, with Gehringer on first, Cochrane hit a low line drive to shortstop Bill Knickerbocker. Thinking the ball had been caught, the Tigers' manager halted on his way to first, while Gehringer sprinted toward second. It finally dawned on Cochrane that Knickerbocker had only trapped the ball, and he was thrown out easily. After the 4–0 win, the players held a kangaroo court, presided over by pitcher Firpo Marberry, who informed Cochrane that he was guilty of laxness on the basepaths. Admitting his culpability, Cochrane thus became the first player to fork over the $10 fine that he himself had instituted for players who failed to run out hits. Following a rainout, Detroit headed north for its home opener. Even after only four games, it was obvious this was a different sort of Tigers team. Bud Shaver wrote in the *Detroit Times*, "Two things are responsible for the brilliant type of baseball the Tigers have presented since the bell rang—condition and hustle. The hustling spirit, manifest the day Manager Cochrane led his squad out of the tiny clubhouse at Lakeland, Fla., for its first practice, has continued unabated. If anything, it has gained impetus. The Tigers are the hustlingest club in baseball."[24]

Navin Field, the Tigers' home ballpark, was nestled in the Corktown neighborhood just west of downtown, a short cab ride from the Michigan Central Station. Beginning in the 1840s, an influx of Irish immigrants from County Cork, eager to escape the Great Potato Famine, settled the area and gave it its name. What they built was a working-class district of charming, tightly packed row houses blending Federal, Late Victorian, and Colonial Revival architecture.

A hay market originally sat at the corner of Michigan and Trumbull Avenues; in 1896, the Tigers built Bennett Park at the site. Detroit in those days played in the Western League, a minor circuit led by the imperious Ban Johnson. He eventually re-named it the American League, anticipating his bold vertical move in 1901 to gain major league status. No longer would the stodgy old National League have a monopoly in the world of big league baseball.

Bennett Park was a small, wooden firetrap typical of the era, yet it served the Tigers well through the century's first decade, the years of Cobb, Crawford, and World Series heartbreaks. In 1909, however, with the construction of Shibe Park in Philadelphia and Forbes Field in Pittsburgh, the national pastime inaugurated a golden era of ballpark construction. In this brave new world, hardy athletes gamboled on lush greenswards in awe-inspiring concrete-and-steel stadia that were impervious to fire, termites, and rot. Bennett Park, the intimate playground in Corktown, was suddenly outmoded. If the Tigers were going to face the future, they would need a new baseball plant.

No sooner had the last out of the 1911 season been recorded at Bennett Park than the place was quickly dismantled. Gleaming new Navin Field rose in its place. A "magnificent new stadium," according to *Baseball Magazine*, it was built at a cost of $300,000 and could squeeze 23,000 patrons into its yellow, wooden slat-backed seats.[25] Detroit's modern baseball palace opened for business on April 20, 1912, six days after the RMS Titanic struck an iceberg and sank in the frigid waters of the North Atlantic. Fittingly, Ty Cobb scored the ballpark's first run. Wrote Ralph J. Yonker in the next day's *Detroit Times*, "The crowd was a wonderful tribute to the popularity of the Tigers. The immense stands were packed to the limit like a world's series."[26] On a picture-perfect day for baseball, the Tigers beat Cleveland, 6–5. "Detroit and its Tigers," wrote a correspondent for *Sporting Life*, "have just celebrated the most momentous occasion in the history of Michigan base ball. The opening of the new Navin Field can be adequately described in no other way. For the first time in history, Detroit has a ball yard worthy of its rank among the cities—a worthy setting for the wonderfully successful club."[27]

Now, nearly a quarter-century later, over 20,000 fans made their way down to Navin Field to see the Tigers pull out a 7–3 win over the Chicago White Sox. Goslin and Gee Walker both had two hits and were hitting .409. Marberry went the distance for his second victory of the young campaign. "The park was not packed for the opening in freezing weather but those that shivered through two hours and 12 minutes of play saw the Detroit attack at its best."[28]

Indeed, Tigers fans who had braved the weather (temperatures were in the low 40s, and even started "spitting snow" in the second inning) were generally pleased with what they saw out of their cats.[29] It was a discriminating crowd, from the bleacher patrons to those in the exclusive box seats who had shelled out $1.65 a head. One of them, on seeing a speedy Gee Walker, noted, "He's another Cobb."[30] Another fan, after watching Goslin smash out the Tigers' first single and hustle for an extra base, asserted: "I never saw [John] Stone do anything like that. Guess I'll take another drink on that."[31] Indeed, for the first time in many years, Tigers fans could enjoy a cold beer at Navin Field. Recently, the State Liquor Control Commission had approved a license for a beer garden to Michigan Sports Service Company, which operated concessions at the park. While patrons seated at the garden's tables could purchase bottled beer, the Commission insisted that roving concessionaires dispense brew in paper cups. Joked the *Free Press*: "So the umpires do have a lobby at work!"[32]

Detroit took two of three from the Sox, and Tommy Bridges welcomed the Indians into town by hurling a five-hit complete game against them. At 6–2, everything looked rosy for the Tigers so far in 1934. Strong pitching and timely hitting were carrying the team, and Cochrane had his men playing with a bravura that Detroiters had not seen in a long while.

Just as quickly, the Tigers went into a collective slump. The downward spiral started with a 7–1 shellacking at the hands of the Indians on April 29. Twenty-four hours later, against the St. Louis Browns, Schoolboy Rowe got his second start of the season; he was hit hard again and struggled with his control. In only three innings of work, he allowed four runs on four hits and two walks in a game the Tigers lost, 7–2. "Cochrane's decision to let Schoolboy Rowe, his tall and temperamental young right-hander, make his second start of the season, was the direct cause of the Bengals' defeat," wrote Charles P. Ward of the *Detroit Free Press*. "Rowe looked good in practice Sunday and fooled Mickey into believing he was ready to go the route. But when the Schoolboy went to the hill Monday, he did not look so good. The Brownies greeted him like a long lost brother. He didn't have control and he didn't have much stuff."[33]

With his earned run average at 15.19, Rowe was pulled from the rotation. Cochrane prepared to option him down to Beaumont, but gave him one last shot two days later, albeit in mop-up duty. With the Tigers trailing St. Louis, 5–2, Rowe came on in relief in the ninth inning. As Sam Greene put it, "When Rowe came to the box, he must have felt that he was on trial. Mickey Cochrane had made no secret of his displeasure over the Schoolboy's lack of earnestness. He was told, in effect, to pitch or else."[34] Rowe got three easy outs, gaining a temporary absolution.

Cochrane's biggest quandary was not Rowe, however. It was the Tigers' weak-hitting outfield. Frank Doljack had opened the season as the regular center fielder, with Gee Walker in right and Goslin in left. Doljack never got untracked as a hitter, and Walker cooled down after a sizzling start. With none of his outfielders hitting with any authority, Cochrane felt a shakeup was in order. First, he sat Goslin, his slumping cleanup hitter, for a couple of games at the end of April. He then switched Walker to left. Jo-Jo White, who had only one pinch-hitting appearance in the season's first month, was given a shot in right field. Meanwhile, first baseman Hank Greenberg took over at cleanup.

Goslin's miseries had begun back on April 28, when he hit into four consecutive double plays against the Indians. Tigers fans were beginning to wonder why the team had ever traded away John Stone. All the so-called experts weighed in as to why Goslin suddenly looked like a cream puff at the plate. Among the more common refrains was that his nose injury had not properly healed. "Cochrane decided that the broken nose which the Red Goose suffered before the American League season opened took more out of him than he cared to admit. Therefore Mickey suggested that he take a seat."[35] Others felt that Goslin had put too much pressure on himself to carry the team and justify the trade. Goslin never lost focus, however. He knew he could hit and that he would eventually work his way out of it. "I'll get going," he insisted to reporters.[36]

Cochrane was not finished with his maneuverings. By May 4, Goslin was back in the lineup in right field, and Cochrane announced that he would platoon Pete Fox and White in center against left- and right-handed pitching. These were just the first of many player personnel shifts that would come that season, as Cochrane constantly tried to hit on a batting order and outfield squad that would be most productive.

The Tigers' first big test came on the coast in early May. "How the Tigers will fare on their Eastern jaunt will depend largely on their pitchers," wrote M. F. Drukenbrod of the *Free Press*. "In fact they must get better pitching pretty soon or they are due to drop."[37] Against the Yankees on May 4, Tommy Bridges was highly effective despite surrendering a home run to Babe Ruth. Detroit's bats, however, just could not muster anything against Lefty Gomez. Following the 3–0 defeat, Cochrane juggled his lineup, which helped the offense a bit, but Detroit still lost the following afternoon, 10–6, courtesy of two more homers by the "fat and forty" Babe Ruth.[38] Wrote H. G. Salsinger, "Babe Ruth again demonstrated that Tigers pitchers are his favorite base ball meat. He also demonstrated that the specialists are correct when they pronounce his eye sight perfect."[39] With the two losses in the Bronx, Detroit slipped to fourth place, two and a half games behind the Yankees.

Even Cochrane, at .261, was caught in the hitting malaise; before the game was through, he yanked himself in favor of backup backstop Ray Hayworth. The Tigers' skipper played no favorites in his constant lineup juggling. Cochrane began the season as the number three hitter, a batting position he had enjoyed for years in Philadelphia. When he could not buy a hit, however, he dropped himself down to seventh in the order.

Detroit then headed to Fenway Park for a four-game set with the Red Sox. In the opener on May 6, Goslin tripled off Rube Walberg in his first at-bat of the game. It broke a string of 23 consecutive at-bats without a hit, which saw his average drop to .196. The Tigers lost, 14–4, as the team's defense fell apart, surrendering eight unearned runs.

The following afternoon, with the Tigers trailing, 6–3, with two on and two out in the top of the ninth, Goslin sent a low liner to right field. Moose Solters played the ball hesitantly, and it skipped past him into the corner. Both runners scored, with Goslin chugging around the bases right behind them for a game-tying, inside-the-park home run. In the top of the 11th, Schoolboy Rowe, who had pitched five sterling innings of relief to that point in the game, came to the plate with one out and one on. Right-hander Johnny Welch "gave the Schoolboy one to his liking; he bent his bat on the ball and sent it sailing over the wall in left field for a home run."[40] Charles P. Ward called it a "lazy circuit clout" that Rowe "golfed."[41] This was the first year the 37-foot-high wall had been painted "Fenway Green," although it was mostly covered in advertising signage.[42] Rowe set the Sox down one-two-three in the home 11th for his first victory of the season. Since being demoted to the bullpen, he had pitched ten innings, allowing only five hits and two earned runs, while fanning ten and walking none. "Schoolboy Rowe is quite a ball player. He looks like a regular pitcher, but does not hit like one, unless it might be like 'Babe' Ruth."[43]

The next day, Goslin doubled and batted in two runs as the Tigers won again. Bridges, the team's most consistent starter, turned in a masterful performance for his second win, while lowering his earned run average to 1.24. Detroit dropped the last game of the series despite Billy Rogell's 4-for-4 performance. Goslin, meanwhile, got another hit and seemed to have regained his form.

May 10 marked Cochrane's return to Shibe Park in Philadelphia, the site of his greatest success as a member of the Athletics. He went hitless, lowering his average to .237. Goslin accounted for all the Tigers' runs with a three-run homer, his first of the season, but Schoolboy Rowe was again mostly ineffective and suffered his second defeat. The loss temporarily dropped the Tigers to sixth place in the American League.

On the 11th, the Tigers pounded the Athletics' Sugar Cain for five runs and went on to win, 10–5. Cochrane broke out with three hits, including a solo home run. Detroit took the rubber game, 4–3, behind the fine pitching of Marberry.

After a loss in Washington on May 13, the Tigers' record stood at 11–11. They were tied for fourth place, five and a half games off the pace. The only regular player topping .300 was Charlie Gehringer at .345. The hitters were not hitting, the pitchers were not pitching, and flaws had cropped up in the defense. Cynics were howling that these were the same old Tigers.

The road trip finally ended on a rainy day at Griffith Stadium. Vic Sorrell was pitching a two-hitter through six frames when a drenching downpour forced the umpires to declare it official. With the 5–0 win, the Tigers packed their bags and boarded a train back to Detroit, where they were set to play the next 12 contests, beginning with the Yankees.

Chapter Four

One Hot Goose

At 30 years old, Charlie Gehringer had already been the Tigers' regular second baseman for eight years. A perennial .300-hitter, he had acquired the nickname "The Mechanical Man" because of his reliability at the plate and with the glove. Lefty Gomez, the Hall of Fame Yankees pitcher, once said of Gehringer, "You wind him up in the spring and he goes all summer. He hits .330 or .340 or whatever, and then you shut him off in the fall."[1]

Gehringer could do just about whatever he wanted on a baseball field. While he did not hit many home runs (his career high was 19 in 1932), he banged out a ton of extra-base hits. He once led the American League in stolen bases, and he boasted a high walks-to-strikeouts ratio. He was durable as well, having topped the junior circuit three times in games played. He was the finest second sacker of his generation and started for the American League in the first All-Star Game in 1933.

Raised in rural Fowlerville, about 60 miles northwest of Detroit, Gehringer spent hours as a boy doing the drudgery on his family's farm. He hated it all, the weeding, the hoeing, and the digging, but especially the cow milking in the frosty, early morning hours. He knew that the baseball field suited him more than the cornfield. As was the case with many kids his age at that time in America, his parents did not approve of such nonsense as bats, balls, and bases. Gehringer, however, was not destined for the farm. He was fortunate enough to attend the University of Michigan, where he studied physical education. When not working a few hours a day at a local ice cream plant, he found time to play baseball for the Wolverines, earning a letter as a freshman.

By a fortuitous chance, young Gehringer happened to know a man who happened to know Bobby Veach, who happened to have played baseball for the Tigers years ago with Ty Cobb. The friend talked to Veach, who talked to Cobb, who arranged for a tryout for the college boy at Navin Field. Cobb liked what he saw. The youngster had potential, he thought. The Georgia Peach headed off the field, and, without bothering to change out of his Tigers uniform, made a beeline for Navin's office, where he proceeded to tell the owner that he needed to sign this kid to a contract, and fast.

"I can't remember if I got a bonus," Gehringer was quoted as saying years later. "Maybe five hundred dollars. But I would've signed for nothing."[2] The former farmhand, who used to keep a scrapbook of Tigers greats like Cobb, Veach, and Harry Heilmann, now had hopes of flashing his skills at Michigan and Trumbull.

First, however, the Tigers sent him to the London Tecumsehs of the Michigan-Ontario League, where the 21-year-old hit .292. He raised some eyebrows in a brief September call-up, with six hits in 13 at-bats. Following a .325 season with the International League's Toronto Maple Leafs in 1925, he stuck with the Tigers for good the next season, quickly establishing himself as a bona fide major leaguer.

Charlie Gehringer, dubbed "The Mechanical Man," made it look effortless on the field (courtesy Ernie Harwell Sports Collection, Detroit Public Library).

Fielding a baseball was always something that had come naturally to him. Writer John Kieran dryly wrote, "He [Gehringer] couldn't explain it himself. He just bent over and picked up the grounders that came his way. It seemed the thing to do. It was pleasant and, after a while, it began to pay him well, and he had no regrets."[3]

Having Ty Cobb for a manager was not always easy, however. In the beginning, Cobb treated Gehringer like a surrogate son, giving him invaluable batting instruction. "Then all of a sudden he got upset with me about something," Gehringer remembered. "To this day I don't know what it was. He would hardly speak to me. He wouldn't even tell me what signs I was going to get from the coaches. Weird. But he kept playing me, so it didn't really matter whether he talked to me or not."[4]

The Mechanical Man reached the mantle of superstar in 1929, topping the American League in games played (155), runs (131), hits (215), doubles (45), triples (19), and stolen bases (27), while also driving in 106 runs. A selective hitter, he rarely, if ever, swung at the first pitch. He was one of the smartest players in the game, on the field or off. Kieran also observed, "He is the catch-as-catch-can crossword puzzle champion of the American League, and furthermore, he actually reads the books that certain other professional athletes carry around with them as scenic effects."[5] Charles P. Ward was surprised to discover that Gehringer had a musical bent. "He loves to sit in his apartment of nights and coax soft liquid notes from a saxophone until the neighbors protest."[6] Not the talkative sort, Gehringer was perhaps the worst interview subject in the league.

Despite having reached such highs in his profession, it began to look like Gehringer was wasting his career in Detroit. Here it was, 1934, and he had never experienced a pennant race.

As the Tigers prepared to play the Yankees, Gehringer had been the most consistent bat all season. Goslin and Walker both faded following their torrid pace out of the gate, while Gehringer was starting to heat up. He had batted second for much of April, but was moved to the cleanup slot after Goslin and Greenberg failed to come through.

On May 17, Detroit faced the nondescript slants of southpaw Russ Van Atta. Manager Joe McCarthy's Yankees, winners of nine of their last ten games, had built a nice 4½-game cushion in the standings. New York quickly jumped to a 4–1 lead, but Detroit tied the score with three runs in the fourth, an inning in which Cochrane spiked Van Atta on a hard slide into first base, forcing the pitcher from the game. Frank Doljack led off the next frame with a double over the head of Ruth in left field, and Goslin's single drove him home with what proved to be the winning run. Tommy Bridges, meanwhile, was good but not great. Although he gave up ten hits and walked five in a complete-game effort, only four New Yorkers crossed the plate. Gehringer was the star of the day, going 4-for-4 with a double, while driving in one run and scoring one.

The following afternoon, the Yankees scored five runs in the third inning to take a 5–2 lead, but could not hold on. Goslin's fourth-inning double evened the score. Gehringer banged out two doubles in three official trips to the plate (he also walked twice), drove in a pair of runs and scored another, with Detroit prevailing in a 10–8 slugfest. "It was a knock-down-and-drag-out affair," wrote Charles P. Ward, "which the Tigers won because they kept getting up every time they were knocked down, and going right back to drop the fellows who did the knocking."[7] The two victories guaranteed the Yankees would lose a series for the first time all year. Detroit dropped the third game, but Gehringer went 3-for-3 with another base on balls.

It was an extraordinary display of hitting by the Tigers' second baseman. In 13 plate appearances, he went 9-for-10 with three walks to raise his batting average to .390. Most importantly, Detroit took two of three from New York and was now in second place, only four games behind.

One of the Tigers' most improved areas in 1934 was their fielding. Bud Shaver wrote in the *Detroit Times*, "About half of the games which the Tigers have won this season were won at Lakeland, Fla., before the Tigers ever took the field in an actual contest. And those games must be marked down to the credit of Mickey Cochrane, because he had the foresight and energy to correct some obvious fielding faults in the Tigers."[8]

Cochrane was still not satisfied with his outfield situation, however, and tried to swing a couple of deals to improve things. Dangling Frank Doljack, the Tigers' skipper inquired about the Indians' Dick Porter. Porter, 32, was a solid bat, a four-time .300 hitter with Cleveland, including a .350 campaign in 1930.

The Tribe expressed interested in the trade, which seems surprising. Even though Doljack was six years younger than Porter and hit .386 one year in the minors, he had not proven he could hit every day at the big league level. Cochrane, however, wanted to be rid of the docile Doljack, who rarely hustled and was so often late for practice that he had picked up the nickname "Last Man." He was invariably the final player to hop on the train for an overnight trip, which irked Cochrane no end. The Indians complicated the negotiations, however, when they demanded that the Tigers include Harry Davis. Davis, 25, had been Detroit's regular first baseman as a rookie in 1932, but lost his job when Greenberg arrived the next season. By 1934, Davis found himself back in the minor leagues, at Toledo, where the Tigers wanted to retain him in the event that Greenberg did not develop as expected. Detroit backed out of the deal, and Doljack remained a Tiger.

Cochrane also tried to get Sam West from the St. Louis Browns, again using Doljack as bait. Browns skipper Rogers Hornsby, however, said thanks but no thanks. Even had Hornsby been interested, he would not have settled simply for Doljack. West, still only 28, was already a proven .300 hitter who would retire with a career .299 batting average over 14 seasons, including four All-Star Game appearances. Not giving up, the Tigers tendered Doljack to Chicago for veteran Mule Haas, but White Sox manager Lew Fonseca also wanted pitcher Chief Hogsett, which ended the discussion. Perhaps out of desperation, Cochrane signed George Wilson, a 21-year-old former halfback out of St. Mary's College of California. Nicknamed "Icehouse," the six-foot,

180-pound specimen saw action in only one game in 1934 before being sent down to the minors, where he was never heard from again.

The outfield deficiencies, as well as the batting order's constant state of flux, were not the only issues Cochrane had to deal with. He was quickly learning that the life of a big-league skipper was infinitely more stressful than that of a player. True, Cochrane had been an excellent field general in his days in Philadelphia, but Connie Mack had borne the brunt of criticism when the Athletics lost, and suffered through the most headaches as a result. Now, however, things were different for Cochrane in Detroit. When an outfielder threw to the wrong base, when a hitter failed to deliver in the clutch, or when a pitcher blew his cool on the mound, Cochrane was the one who had to answer to the press and to team management. His personality only heightened his anxiety and worry. The intense Cochrane seemed incapable of leaving losses at the ballpark. Instead, he took them to bed with him, ruminating over decisions and replaying games as he lay awake at night.

The stress had already begun to take its toll on his psyche and may have contributed to his difficulties at the dish. By the third week of May, Cochrane was floundering at .253 with only one home run and 12 runs driven in. The homer had come on May 11, in his return to Shibe Park in Philadelphia. It was one of the few highlights in what had so far been a disappointing season, statistically speaking, for the fiercely competitive man known as "Black Mike."

Detroit was in the grip of an early heat wave. For relief, thousands flocked to Belle Isle, the oasis in the Detroit River. A sign at its bathhouse advertised: "Water 58 degrees; air 88 degrees." Goose Goslin had also begun to heat up. He had himself a nice little 12-game hitting streak going as the Senators marched into town on May 20. Nothing to brag about, to be sure, and he was still batting only .260, but one had to start somewhere. He extended his streak to 13 when he singled off Washington's Bobby Burke. Schoolboy Rowe failed to last the third inning; with nothing on his pitches, the Senators constantly took him deep in counts. He suffered his third loss of the season against only one victory. His earned run average was an unsightly 6.92, and he was the weakest link in the Detroit rotation.

Goslin picked up where he left off the next day, banging out three hits and scoring a run. Chief Hogsett could not protect a 5–4 lead in the top of the ninth, as the Senators tied it. In the home half of the frame, however, Gee Walker hit an infield single and went to third on a throwing error by the pitcher, Ray Prim. Gehringer and Billy Rogell were purposely passed to set up a force at any base. Alex McColl came in to pitch for Washington, and the first man to face him was Cochrane, pinch-hitting for catcher Hayworth. The Tigers' skipper drilled one over the head of Fred Schulte in center field, as

Walker danced home with the winning tally. Goslin's streak reached 15 games when he singled the next day in a 5–2 loss.

Connie Mack's Athletics arrived in the Motor City for three games beginning on May 23. Philadelphia was barely treading water with a record of 13 wins and 16 losses, but they took two games from the Tigers, including an 11–5 walloping in the opener. Billy Rogell went 5-for-5 in the game, raising his average to .301, but the defense was sloppy, giving up four unearned runs. Rowe was shaky in relief, and with an earned run average of 7.14, his future looked very much in doubt. The Tigers still considered sending him down to Beaumont. Cochrane felt he had given Schoolboy a fair trial; the manager was more and more of the belief that Rowe simply was not ready to compete at the highest level.

Marberry's solid pitching helped the Tigers take the second game, but the finale was an ugly display of poor fielding and undependable relief work. Tied at five after seven innings, the Athletics scored four runs in the eighth, added an insurance run in the ninth, and captured a 10–5 win.

Goslin continued his splendid hitting in the three-game series with the Red Sox at Navin Field beginning on May 26. He reached base eight times in 15 plate appearances and drove in seven runs, as the Tigers swept Boston, and his hitting streak reached 21 games. Bridges was not sharp in the opener, walking five batters and hitting another, but he went the distance for his fourth victory. One day later, Rowe pitched his best game of the season to date, keeping the ball low in the zone and going the distance for only his second victory. Although he allowed 11 hits, ten were singles, while he walked three and fanned five in a 9–2 win. The third game was a Detroit rout, as Greenberg blasted two home runs and drove in four runs.

Goslin homered again on May 29 in St. Louis. Walker and Gehringer also hit four-baggers, but Tigers pitchers had no answer for Browns rookie Ray Pepper, who went 5-for-5 with two homers and five RBI in a St. Louis win. Detroit swept a doubleheader the following day, but the Browns ended the series by bludgeoning the Tigers, 11–3.

From there, it was on to Comiskey Park, where Black Mike's men totally dominated the White Sox in a three-game sweep played in scorching heat. Goslin went 8-for-13 with two home runs and six runs scored, as Detroit outscored the Sox, 26–3, in the series. Rowe, in "splendid form," pitched a 3–1, complete-game victory in the opener on June 1, his third win of the year.[9] Chicago's Al Simmons spoiled the shutout with a ninth-inning solo homer. "It was Rowe's day," wrote Charles P. Ward, "and when it is Rowe's day he is a very hard man to beat. And that goes whether he is pitching at a Sunday school picnic … or in a championship game in a big league park."[10]

The next day the Tigers put on a clinic. "The spry Detroit Tigers," reported the *Chicago Tribune*, "were just a bit heartless yesterday in the business of pushing over our poor last-place White Sox. One run would have served their purposes, but the wicked Detroiters were most glutinous. They won, 12–0."[11] Rogell drove in five runs, and Marberry won his seventh game. In the finale, Goslin, Cochrane, Gehringer, and Greenberg all homered, as the Tigers breezed to an 11–2 win, with Bridges notching his sixth victory. "Another brutal plastering from the skilled Detroit Tigers," wrote Ed Burns.[12]

The Tigers then travelled back home for a doubleheader against Cleveland on June 5. Detroit had clawed its way back to within a half-game of league-leading New York, and was just percentage points in front of the Indians. Charles P. Ward gave this assessment of the team: "[The Tigers] have become convinced that the warriors who wear the Detroit uniform are as good as any others and better than some who have been rated their peers.... That might sound a bit cocky, but it must be admitted that the Tigers are cocky now."[13]

In the first game, Goslin went 2-for-3 with two RBI and three runs scored as Detroit slaughtered the Tribe, 20–2. Wrote Sam Greene, "The folks who packed the grandstand pavilions and sun seats will be talking a long time about the afternoon's thrills with principal emphasis on the feats of Leon Allen Goslin."[14]

In the second contest, Goslin went hitless in his first three at-bats before launching his sixth homer of the year in the eighth inning, extending his hitting streak to 30 games. Chief Hogsett, though, could not hold a two-run ninth-inning lead, and the Tigers lost a 5–4 heartbreaker. Nevertheless, Boston trounced the Yankees, 8–3, which put the Tigers in a virtual tie for first place. It was the first time in a decade that Detroit held the top position in the month of June.[15] More than 23,000 fans came out to see the game, the largest weekday crowd at Navin Field in years.

Goslin was finally held hitless the next day, but he played a vital role in the game's outcome. The only Detroit scoring came in the sixth. Goslin drew a one-out walk and quickly stole second. Gee Walker also drew a base on balls, and Gehringer singled Goslin home, with Walker taking third. When Billy Rogell forced Gehringer at second, Walker raced home with the second tally of the inning. Cleveland pitchers Bob Weiland and Mel Harder combined to one-hit the Tigers. Schoolboy Rowe, however, pitched brilliantly in the 2–1 win. He went the distance, giving up only one run, fanning seven and walking none for his fourth win of the campaign. Coupled with the Yankees' 15–3 drubbing at the hands of the Red Sox, Detroit was now sitting alone atop the American League.

Goslin's renaissance was a big factor in the Tigers' offense rediscovering its mojo. In his 30-game hitting streak, he compiled a .376 average, raising his season's mark to .324. "Goslin has become the barometer of Detroit's base ball temperature. 'As Goslin goes, so go the Tigers' has been true since the start of the season."[16] He was still 60 points behind Gehringer, however, who continued to annihilate American League pitching. Detroit then began what promised to be a grueling four-city, 15-game East Coast swing, beginning in Boston on June 12.

Chapter Five

"Get that fellow out of my sight in a hurry"

While the Motor City baked, a cool, brisk, east wind bore down on Fenway Park, and rain had threatened all morning. The Tigers were on a roll, but so were the Red Sox. Boston was expected to be a contender, mostly because of the acquisition of Lefty Grove. Because of lingering arm problems, however, Grove did not make his first start until May 19, and currently had only two wins and a bloated 6.52 earned run average. Boston's record stood at a pedestrian 24–24, although they had won nine of their last 13.

To open the series, Detroit sent Tommy Bridges to the mound. Not a big man, Bridges stood only 5'10" and checked in at a slight 150 pounds. Affectionately dubbed "Little Tommy," he had pitched solidly so far in 1934, but certainly not as good as his 7–3 record would indicate. He was coming off a rocky start in Cleveland in which he had given up six earned runs, but was still credited with the complete-game win.

Bridges, a right-hander, broke into the big leagues with a bang on August 13, 1930. It was a mop-up relief appearance against the Yankees in the Bronx; the first batter he faced was Babe Ruth, who promptly popped to third. Tony Lazzeri, the great third baseman, singled to center, which brought up Lou Gehrig. Facing the third future Hall of Famer in a row, Bridges struck out Columbia Lou, then bore down and got Harry Rice, no slouch at the dish, to ground out to second base. No runs, one hit, no errors. Not a bad way to debut.

It was only later that things got tougher. Bridges, a University of Tennessee product, went through severe growing pains in 1931, his first full season with Detroit. He was frequently behind in the count and walked too many hitters (he issued 5.6 bases on balls per nine innings that season, the most in the league among starters with a minimum of 154 innings). Part of the problem was that he had fallen in love with his curve, which was often difficult to control. Of course, it was an easy curve to fall in love with, capable of dropping off the table at the last split second.[1] Jimmie Dykes, the manager of the Chicago White Sox, once remarked, "It's the best curve in the league and when he has control he'll curve you right back to the bench."[2] Bridges had flashes of brilliance, including coming within one out of a perfect game against Washington in 1932. The consistency, however, was just not there. Then one day in 1933, his manager, Bucky Harris, who was starting to lose patience with his pitching prodigy, told Bridges to stop throwing his curve until he got ahead in the count. The youngster took the advice; he gained more confidence in his fastball and went after hitters, rather than trying to nibble the corners. As his control improved, the fastball became an even more effective weapon. Hitters knew it was coming, but there was nothing they could do about it.

As Bridges warmed up to face the Red Sox, the Tigers' record in 1934 stood at 29–20, one game in front of New York. Keeping the hitters off balance with his curveball, Bridges pitched one of his best games of the season so far. He went the distance, issuing only one walk and two earned runs. With the 4–2 victory, Detroit was now ten games over the .500 mark and increased their hold on first place to a game and a half over the idle Yankees.

The contest was not without incident, as Cochrane was reminded of the pitfalls of his profession. In the fourth inning, Billy Werber tipped a foul ball straight back onto the top of Cochrane's head; it rebounded and landed high on top of the screen. (Although Cochrane was wearing a facemask, this was before the days when a catcher wore a batting helmet to protect his skull.) Wrote James C. O'Leary in the *Boston Globe*: "Cochrane was groggy for several minutes but finally was able to resume play."[3]

The following afternoon featured a good old-fashioned Fenway Park slugfest. Boston looked to have it in the bag with a 15–5 lead after seven innings. But the Tigers applied the pressure, scoring two runs in the eighth. A furious comeback ensued in the ninth, but Detroit came up just short, and Boston was fortunate to get a 15–13 win. The next day's *Boston Globe* described the affair as a "batting orgy."[4] Lefty Grove, who pitched in relief, got only his third victory of the season, despite giving up eight runs in less than five innings. With the Yankees' win over the Browns in New York, the Tigers' lead was shaved to a half-game.

"It is a little early in the race for any club to set up a claim for the pennant," Cochrane said afterward. "It looks as if it were going to be a great race. As to our prospects, you may be sure that we will keep up the fight to the last gasp. Whoever wins this year has quite a chore to perform."[5]

Rain washed out the game on June 14, a day that saw New York shut out the Browns to creep back into a tie for first. But Detroit took the Fenway finale on Friday, 11–4. Showing his stuff in front of the Ladies Day crowd, Schoolboy Rowe picked up his fourth win since rejoining the rotation. Gehringer, with six hits in the three-game series, was hitting an AL-best .415. From there, it was on to New York.

The Tigers' second trip to Yankee Stadium in 1934 did not get off to a good start. On June 16, Bridges was cruising with a 4–2 lead when the wheels fell off in the bottom of the seventh, as the Bronx Bombers scored six runs. Yankees catcher Bill Dickey struck the key blow. Still suffering from flu-like symptoms that forced him to miss the previous game, he came in as a pinch-hitter with two out and a man on board in the seventh. The "wobbly convalescent"[6] sent the first pitch high and far into the right-field bleachers for a two-run homer, and the Yankees never looked back. It was their fifth straight win and put them two games up on Cochrane's cats.

A raucous Sunday crowd of over 55,000 jammed the House That Ruth Built for a doubleheader on June 17. The Yankees drew first blood, taking the opener by a score of 3–2 behind the splendid pitching of Lefty Gomez, who collected his 11th win. In the nightcap, Detroit righted its ship with a 5–2 victory. Bespectacled Vic Sorrell went the distance for his fifth win, but the highlight of the game came from Babe Ruth. "He didn't get a homer—didn't even get a single. But the mighty Ruth gave the crowd its thrill, nevertheless. In the sixth inning, the Bambino made one of the most spectacular catches ever made on a diamond. He raced almost to the right-field bleacher front and, leaping high in the air, with his gloved hand speared Goslin's drive just as it seemed about to drop into the bleachers."[7]

The fourth game was not for the faint of heart. Lou Gehrig homered, his 17th of the year, to put the Yanks up by three runs in the fifth. Down 5–4 in the ninth and facing the prospect of slipping three games back in the loss column, Detroit snatched the lead on a two-run double by Pete Fox, who entered the game hitting .241. The ninth-inning drama continued in the home half of the inning. With the tying run on first and one down, pinch-hitter Ruth "whiffed ingloriously."[8] A single and a wild pitch put Yankees on second and third, but the rally, and the game, ended with a whimper when Gehrig grounded out weakly to second. "It was one of the most dramatic ninth innings of the year," wrote H. G. Salsinger.[9] Final score: Detroit six, New York five. Marberry, despite failing to dazzle, had notched his ninth win for Detroit.

"The whole club is on the move now," writer John Lardner quoted Cochrane after the game. "We got a good ball town and they've been drawing 'em in right along all season. I don't say we're sure to beat out Washington and the Yanks, but it's a good chance. You ought to wait till after the party's over to start handing out those medals. Nobody knows yet."[10]

Perhaps sensing that there had been enough thrills for one series, the weatherman sent a heavy dose of rain, washing out the next day's tilt. The Tigers were able to beat it out of the Bronx with a split of the four games. The newspapers the next day would show that their record stood at 33 wins and 23 losses, with the Yanks breathing down their necks at 32 and 22. As for Ruth, Tigers pitchers had applied the shackles to the Sultan of Swat, holding him to only a solitary single in 12 at-bats. Although hitting over .300, the greatest star the game had ever seen was clearly reaching the end. Wrote Dan Daniel, "If I cannot blow the bugle about the Babe, I am not going to say anything at all, as I think it is a downright miracle for him to be out there day after day."[11]

To that point in the season, manager Joe Cronin's Washington Senators had failed to play up to expectations. When Detroit reached the nation's capital fresh off its exciting series in the Bronx, the Senators were in third place, an uninspiring 32–27. At only two and a half games out, however, Washington was still very much in the hunt. Winners of seven of their last ten, they were poised to make their run.

Detroit's hot bats, however, proved to be too much for the Senators' pitching staff. The Tigers tallied 47 runs in taking four out of the five games, including two extra-inning affairs. "When you can win that kind," observed Cochrane, "and the kind that we closed with in New York, then you've got to conclude that you've got a fine chance to do things."[12] Elden Auker won twice, and Hank Greenberg, who had been gaining confidence as the season went along, hit .414 with 20 total bases and 11 runs driven in. Detroit now had five regulars batting .300 or better. Even if they fell behind early in a game, the Tigers refused to concede defeat until the last out.

By the time the dust settled on June 23, Washington was five and a half games behind first-place Detroit and fading fast. Cronin's men never recovered. The stunning weekend ultimately proved to be the Senators' Waterloo: By the All-Star break, they were nearly ten games behind and effectively finished. Despite his team's thrashing at the hands of Detroit, Cronin was not ready to throw in the towel: "We are not out of the race yet," he insisted. "We are trailing by plenty, I know, but the deficit can be made up if only somebody will come along and beat those Yankees."[13]

The Tigers won two of three from the Athletics in Shibe Park, and then returned to the Motor City for a single game with the White Sox on June 28.

Detroit was in the grip of a scorching heat wave, with the mercury hitting 103 in the late afternoon. Overcoming a late 6–2 deficit, the Tigers sent the game to extras. In the tenth, Gehringer led off with a double, and one out later Greenberg drove him home with a two-bagger of his own. But Detroit was a half-game behind the Yankees, who had been nearly unbeatable since bidding the Tigers *bon voyage* ten days prior.

⚾ ⚾ ⚾

"Music! Laughter! Girls!"

Thus proclaimed a movie poster in May 1934 for a new 19-minute short. It starred the virtually unknown slapstick trio of Moe Howard, his brother Jerome (also known as Curly), and Larry Fine. Entitled *Woman Haters*, the film earned the Three Stooges the sum of $1,000 a week (split three ways) for their Columbia Pictures debut.[14] That same month, fans of the silver screen fell in love with a five-year-old actress from Santa Monica, California, who made a big splash in the film, *Stand Up and Cheer*. While not the first movie appearance by Shirley Temple, it was the one that catapulted her to stardom. Benny Goodman, the jazz clarinetist and bandleader, hit the top of the charts for 15 weeks in 1934 with his version of "Moon Glow." *The Major Bowes Amateur Hour* made its debut in April on radio station WHN in New York. In time it became one of the most popular programs of its era. James M. Cain, meanwhile, rocked the literary establishment with the publication of his violent, now-classic noir novel, *The Postman Always Rings Twice*.

On the political front in 1934, Italian fascist dictator Benito Mussolini gave a thunderous speech in Rome in March. "We prefer to be feared rather than loved, and we care not if we are hated…. In the 21st Century, Italy will have the primacy of the world…. There is only one order: Conquer!"[15]

On May 17 in New York, "with Nazi swastikas dominating the scene and 750 policemen on hand to prevent disorders," a crowd of more than 20,000 descended on Madison Square Garden. Denouncing the "Jewish boycott of Germany," the throng defended the policies of Adolf Hitler, the Reich Chancellor of Germany. On the other side of town, at a meeting of the American Jewish Conference, one bold speaker declared, "The Nazi outburst has brought out the best in the rest of the world. It has surrounded Germany with peoples intent to resist prejudice and intolerance to the utmost. In that sense, Hitler was a fine thing for the world."[16]

In Toledo, Ohio, roughly 1,300 members of the Ohio National Guard were deployed to quell 6,000 strikers at the Electric Auto-Lite Company. Workers had demanded a ten percent wage increase. The two-month-long "Battle of Toledo" resulted in two fatalities and hundreds of injuries. Meanwhile, striking dockworkers in San Francisco were confronted with the "guns and gas" of the city's finest, as "open warfare" flared on the waterfront. Further south, in San Diego, strikers attacked two replacement dockworkers, and 15 policemen were called in to halt the violence. Also among the discontented were the 300,000-strong United Textile Workers of America, who called for a general strike rather than accept an order to drop production by 25 percent.[17] Louisiana Governor Huey Long, tapping into the simmering labor instability and economic doldrums of the Depression, promulgated his "Share Our Wealth" movement.[18] For many Americans, prosperity was something seemingly beyond their grasp.

The exploits of gangsters and bank robbers had a certain perverse fascination for many in Depression-era America. Bonnie Parker and Clyde Barrow eluded capture in a crime spree across a half-dozen states and 15,000 miles. They were finally gunned down on May 23 in an ambush near Arcadia, Louisiana. Meanwhile, with John Dillinger still on the run, the Justice Department placed a $25,000 bounty on his head. In one bank robbery, Dillinger made his getaway in a stolen Ford. Feeling the need to thank Henry Ford for manufacturing such a speedy machine, Dillinger penned a letter to the auto magnate, dated May 16, 1934. Ford received it the following day:

> Hello Old Pal,
>
> Arrived here at 10 AM today. Would like to drop in and see you.
> You have a wonderful car. Been driving it for three weeks. It's a treat to drive one.
> Your slogan should be Drive a Ford and watch the other cars fall behind you. I can make any other car take a Ford's dust.
>
> Bye Bye
> John Dillinger[19]

Ford, who likely did not lack for ad men, declined to respond to the roguish testimonial.

Across the Atlantic, the Nazi Minister of Propaganda, Joseph Goebbels, arrived at the University of Warsaw in June. Under Polish police protection due to heavy protests, Goebbels delivered a lecture "on the aims and purposes of the National Socialist Movement."[20] Not everyone in Germany, however, was swayed by the information campaign Goebbels had been waging. Months earlier, Carl von Ossietsky, a German pacifist journalist, was unceremoniously whisked away to the Papenburg-Esterwegen concentration camp for his dissenting views.[21] Soon after Goebbels' Warsaw speech, Vice Chancellor Franz von Papen, in an oration at the University of Marburg, denounced the "revolution," along with the suppression of speech and the Nazi terror that it had inspired. "It is time," he passionately implored, "to join together in fraternal friendship and respect for all our fellow countrymen, to avoid disturbing the labors of serious men and to silence fanatics."[22] Soon, Hitler instigated the Night of the Long Knives, a bloody purge of nearly 100 party members he deemed liable to stand in his way.[23]

With so much unsettling news around the world and at home, Americans in 1934 looked to the national pastime to give them a temporary tonic from their worries and troubles. That summer, sportswriter Grantland Rice wrote: "[Baseball] means a chance for many millions to lose and forget the drabness of their lives for two hours of an afternoon in the speed, the action and the skill of stars, surrounded by the vocal cataclysm of packed stands watching not only the Hubbells, the Groves, the Ruths, the Foxxes and the Kleins, but also the coming stars from minor circuits who play their part in the drama that runs from April to October."[24]

So far, the American League pennant race was shaping up to be a much-needed cure.

As the season approached its midpoint, Detroit had surprised many critics by hanging close to first place for most of the year. After winning four of seven in a grueling stretch in St. Louis and Cleveland at the beginning of July, including three doubleheaders in four days, Detroit was a mere game behind the Yankees.

Both clubs had distanced themselves from Boston and Washington, and it looked increasingly like a two-horse race in the American League. For the first time in recent memory, fans in Detroit were excited about their team's prospects. Wrote Sam Greene, "The Tigers, leading the league in hitting and exhibiting an aggressive, determined type of ball, are no longer viewed as flowers that bloom in the spring and turn to weeds in mid-summer."[25]

For Cochrane, it was more a case of cautious optimism. He knew Detroit did not stack up favorably with more recent pennant winners, particularly the Athletics of 1929–1931, or the great New York teams of Ruth and Gehrig. But he refused to concede to any rival. If the Tigers could avoid prolonged slumps like the one they had earlier in the year, and if their pitching could continue to improve, he knew they stood an even chance with the Yankees. The biggest issue for the Tigers, in Cochrane's view, was its bench. If anything should happen to big bats like Goslin, Gehringer, or Greenberg, Detroit could be in big trouble. But as long as he could keep penciling in the same players every day, well … but couldn't every manager say the same thing?

Joe McCarthy's New Yorkers were not without question marks, either. They had two top-flight starters in Lefty Gomez and Red Ruffing. Beyond those studs, however, they would have to make do with their two Johnnies,

Broaca and Murphy, who were both untested rookies. They had pitched promisingly so far, but could they be counted on as the summer continued? Starting pitching, Cochrane believed, could prove to be the Yankees' Achilles heel.

The Tigers knew that if they were to make their move, July was a golden opportunity. They would play nearly the entire month in the comforts of Navin Field, whereas the schedule makers had McCarthy's men heading on the road from July 11–29. That played right into Detroit's favor; the Yankees had not shown themselves to be a good team away from the Bronx, while the Tigers played their best at Michigan and Trumbull.

While Cochrane had the Tigers hustling more, they were by no means a wild, hell-bent team at the plate and on the bases. A disciplined, controlled aggression would best describe the way they played the game. Cochrane fined players who made careless base-running mistakes. No one, however, gave Cochrane more gray hairs than did a young outfielder named Gerald Holmes "Gee" Walker.

Gerald Holmes "Gee" Walker was one of the most popular players ever to wear a Tigers uniform (courtesy National Baseball Hall of Fame, Cooperstown, New York).

Actually, Walker had given Bucky Harris, his former manager, fits as well. But when Cochrane took over, he was under the misguided impression that he could harness Walker. "I like Walker as a player and like what I have seen of him personally," Cochrane admitted back in January. "He can hit and he is fast. He can overcome his fielding faults." He then added, in a classic understatement, "They say he is temperamental and I am inclined to think that is true to some extent."[26]

Like every other unmanageable ballplayer before and after him, Walker's faults were forgiven as long as he could hit a baseball. And he certainly could do that. Twice he had hit over .370 in the minor leagues, and he led the Tigers with a .323 average in his first full season in the majors in 1932. Tigers fans weren't completely unfamiliar with the Walker name; Gee's older brother Hub had played with Detroit in 1931. With speed to burn and his reckless style of play, Gee was in many ways a throwback to Ty Cobb, endearing him to legions of grandstand followers.

Walker approached baseball with a football mentality. This came as no surprise; he was a star halfback at the University of Mississippi, once earning All-Southern Conference honors. One incident on the gridiron typified his take-no-prisoners attitude. Walker lost a game for Ole Miss when he fumbled while plowing through the goal line for a potentially winning touchdown run. Walker, so the story goes, was more interested in slugging an opposing defender than in holding onto the ball, which subsequently popped out of his grasp.

In the spring of 1934, the Tigers played an exhibition against the Phillies. Hans Lobert, a notorious bench jockey, tried to rattle the hotheaded Walker by hurling invective his way. Walker responded in kind and topped Lobert by banging the ball around the park in each of his at-bats. "Ho-ho," Cochrane chuckled after one of Walker's hits. "That's what I like to see. They can get him hot under the collar all they please just so long as he talks back to them with his bat."[27]

Cochrane appreciated Walker's raw ability, but the outfielder had a habit of not obeying orders. There were at-bats in the regular season when Walker chose to swing away even though Cochrane had relayed the bunt sign. In the outfield, he did not always position himself the way he'd been instructed, and for all his athleticism and speed, fly balls could be an adventure. At times, Walker lost focus while on the field. Once he got on base, his over-aggressiveness could be a liability. Tigers historian David Raglin phrased it as Walker's "risk-averse approach to baserunning."[28] John Kieran wrote that Walker was a "hot and cold player. Some days he looks like a combination of Ruth, Cobb and [Tris] Speaker and other days he just looks like a Brooklyn outfielder on roller skates."[29]

Cochrane temporarily benched Walked on May 10 after his batting average bottomed out at .233. The *Free Press* reported, "[Cochrane] has soured on Walker's chances to make good. He doubts whether Gerald will hit enough to make up for his fielding lapses and is skeptical about him as a team player."[30] The benching did not last long, however. Walker hit a pinch single late in the game, and the next day went 4-for-5 with a double and two RBI in a 10–5 victory.

Things came to a head, however, at Sportsman's Park in St. Louis on Saturday, June 30. Needing a victory to tie the Yankees for first place, the Tigers trailed the Browns by a run in the eighth inning. After a leadoff single by Greenberg, Walker hit a chopper to third baseman Harlond Clift, whose low throw to second failed to get the force. That made it two on with nobody out, but Walker was immediately caught strolling too far off first base. During the ensuing rundown, Greenberg bolted for third. He was thrown out, but Walker made it safely to second. To add insult to injury, pitcher Jack Knott then picked Walker off second. Just like that, the Tigers had two down and nobody on, and they went on to lose the game. Wrote Charles P. Ward, "The Tigers could have won had Walker not committed his crack pottery."[31]

Mickey Cochrane shows off the form that made him a lifetime .320 hitter (courtesy Ernie Harwell Sports Collection, Detroit Public Library).

Cochrane kept his cool, not saying anything to Walker in the clubhouse afterward. Nevertheless, he spent a sleepless night pondering his next move. After hearing a few whispered grumblings from various players the next day about Walker's sloppiness on the basepaths, Cochrane made the decision to send Walker home. "He cost us the ball game," Black Mike fumed. "It isn't his first offense, either. I've tried talking to him, but he won't listen. I've been as patient as I could be. I'm tired of arguing with him. I'm not going to let him wreck this ball club. It's unfair to the other players, who are hustling all the time, straining every nerve to win."[32] Walker took a train back to Detroit. On Monday, two days after the incident, he worked out for about an hour at the ballpark, spoke briefly with Navin, and went home to await the return of the team.

When asked if Walker would be released or traded, Cochrane pulled no punches in his reply: "All I want is to get that fellow out of my sight in a hurry."[33] Since it was past the June 21 trade deadline, however, Walker would have to clear waivers before he could be dealt. Browns manager Rogers Hornsby had already gone on record as saying his team would put in a waiver claim on Walker if it ever came to that.

On Wednesday, back in Detroit, the manager huddled with Navin, who told Cochrane that he would support him in any decision he made regarding disciplining Walker. Cochrane initially wanted to serve the erratic outfielder with his walking papers, but in an unusual move, he decided to leave Walker's fate up to a player vote. The choice was simple: Should Walker stay or should he go? In a secret ballot, all 24 Tigers voted to allow him to remain with the team. Cochrane abided by the ruling. But Walker was still suspended for ten days without pay. "When he returns I'll be for him again," said Cochrane, "provided he plays the right kind of ball. As far as I am concerned now, the case is closed."[34]

"I guess I had it coming," Walker mumbled contritely.[35]

The incident could not have come at a worse time for Walker personally. After a slow start, he had come on like gangbusters, batting .341 in June to raise his season's mark to .296. Following a closed-door meeting with Cochrane and Walker, Frank Navin was asked what the player had said. "Oh, just what you'd expect any fiery ballplayer to say under the circumstances. Of course he said he was sorry. He said he was going to be careful from now on."[36]

Chapter Six

"They'll never see another game like it"

Very quietly, Schoolboy Rowe had turned his season around. The day after Walker's base-running fiasco in St. Louis, Detroit wasted a fine pitching effort by Vic Sorrell in the first game of a doubleheader, losing 3–2. Rowe went the distance in the late game, and while St. Louis tallied 13 hits, all were singles. The biggest improvement for Rowe, however, was his newfound control. This marked the second consecutive start (both complete games) in which he had not issued a free pass. Rogell and Owen each drove in four runs, as Detroit salvaged the series with a 12–3 win. It was the third straight victory for Rowe, raising his mark on the season to 7–4.

The Tigers headed north for Cleveland, where they played an exhausting five-game, home-and-away series with the Indians beginning on July 2. Bridges pitched a brilliant complete game in the opener, Goslin and Owen each banged out four hits, and the Tigers won, 9–2.

The biggest surprise came the next day, however, when Detroit got another complete game, this time from the unlikeliest of pitchers. Rookie Luke Hamlin was born in Ferris Center, Michigan, and was a resident of East Lansing. He contracted malarial fever during spring training in Lakeland and did not make his first appearance of 1934 until May 29. With five relief appearances so far, and an earned run average of 10.22, Hamlin was only given a start on July 3 due to a string of three doubleheaders in four days. In a 7–2 Tigers victory on his 30th birthday, Hamlin gave up only six hits to the Tribe and picked up his first "W" of the season. Nicknamed "Hot Potato" because of his habit of abstractedly juggling the ball while getting set to pitch, he would win only one more game in 1934.

The series shifted to Detroit for an Independence Day doubleheader. Navin Field was standing room only, as over 40,000 shoehorned their way into the ballpark at Michigan and Trumbull. Among them was a glum-looking Gee Walker, still not allowed to suit up or even to sit on the Tigers' bench.

Instead, he was relegated to a box seat along the third base line, where he tried to stay cool in shirtsleeves and fedora. "Long before the first game started several thousand fans had overflowed onto the playing field. Mounted policemen patrolled the outfield from foul line to foul line and they had their work cut out for them. Every seat in the sunbaked bleachers was filled with sweltering fans."[1]

The first game ended on an unusual play. With the Tigers trailing 8–5 with two outs and nobody on in the bottom of the ninth, Pete Fox launched his second home run of the year to shave the deficit to two. Cochrane kept the inning alive with a double, bringing up Goslin. Cleveland starter Mel Harder, who was still in the game, served a pitch that Goslin launched to deep right. Sam Rice, tracking it, went into the standing overflow crowd, but was unable to come up with the ball. The umpires, claiming fan interference, ruled Goslin out, and the game was over.

In the second half of the doubleheader, Carl Fischer got the start for Detroit but was ineffective. He was pulled in the third inning and replaced by Rowe, who pitched well the rest of the way. Schoolboy got credit for the win, his eighth, in a game called by darkness after eight innings.

The Tigers had enjoyed home cooking all season long, and that trend continued as they swept the Browns in three straight beginning July 6. Bridges kept up his fine pitching with a five-hit shutout in the second game. In the finale, Rowe again came on in relief, this time in the seventh inning with the Tigers trailing, 3–0. By the bottom of the ninth, the score was 4–2 in favor of St. Louis. Singles by Owen and Rowe sent starter George Blaeholder to the showers. Bobo Newsom entered the game and induced Pete Fox to hit a grounder to second baseman Ski Melillo, who booted the ball, loading the bases. Cochrane drew a walk, forcing in a run. Newsom was yanked, bringing on Ed Wells. Up came Goslin, who also hit a grounder to Melillo, who chose to throw home to try to get Rowe. The throw was wild, however, and both Rowe and Fox scored to send the Sunday crowd home happy. Rowe won again, his fifth straight, raising his mark to 9–4.

On July 10, the sport's best and brightest gathered for the 1934 All-Star Game. This was only the second such contest in Major League Baseball history. The first All-Star Game, played the previous year at Chicago's Comiskey Park, was the brainchild of Arch Ward, sports editor of the *Chicago Tribune*. Ward wanted to boost the country's morale during the Depression, as well as generate further interest in the national pastime. The *Tribune* said, "For the first time in history, the greatest players of the American League and the greatest players of the National League, picked by popular vote of baseball followers, will meet in team battle." The newspaper went on to say that, throughout the history of the great American game, "fans kept asking, in their dreamy way, what would happen if the greatest players from all teams, not simply the two best teams, should meet in interleague combat. Unanswered went the question until now."[2]

Timed to coincide with Chicago's "Century of Progress" exhibition, the 1933 All-Star Game was a charity affair, with proceeds going toward the players' benevolent fund to assist former major leaguers down on their luck. Appropriately, Babe Ruth hit the first All-Star Game home run. The event was a success, both financially and in the eyes of the public, so much so that the owners voted to hold another All-Star Game in 1934, this time at the Polo Grounds. On the day of the game, nearly 50,000 fervent folks jammed themselves into the bathtub-shaped ballpark in upper Manhattan. Another 15,000 reportedly had to be turned away. Spectators thrilled to the wonder of so many stars playing together on the same field. Broadcast over both the NBC and CBS radio networks, the game was already being referred to as baseball's midsummer classic.

The Tigers sent three players to the Polo Grounds. Gehringer, who received the most votes of any player in the American League (120,781), started at second base. Cochrane was chosen as a reserve, while Bridges was slated for the bullpen. At .384, Gehringer was second in the American League batting race, behind former Tiger Heinie Manush, who was hitting .403. Gehringer had two singles and three walks in the All-Star Game. Cochrane, who replaced starting catcher Bill Dickey in the sixth inning, grounded out in his only at-bat. Bridges, who boasted ten wins on the season, failed to get into the game. The American League won it for the second year in a row. It truly was a star-studded affair; of the 18 men in the starting lineups, all were future Hall of Famers except Wally Berger of Cincinnati.

Detroit was in second place at the All-Star break, with a record of 47–29, only a half-game behind the Yankees. The Red Sox were a distant third, at six games back. Over in the National League, it was the New York Giants leading the pack, with the Chicago Cubs and St. Louis Cardinals close behind. When the regular season resumed on July 11, the Tigers' bats picked up right where they'd left off, topping the Senators, 13–7, in "an old fashioned slugfest festival."[3] The Yankees, however, won in Cleveland to maintain their league lead. Walker also returned from his suspension that day, but Cochrane was not quite ready to put him back into the lineup yet.

Winning was something the Bronx Bombers were doing a lot of lately, with 13 victories in their last 16 games. Lou Gehrig was the team's biggest offensive weapon in the first half, with 24 home runs, 91 RBI, and a .367 batting average. Bill Dickey and speedy outfielder Ben Chapman were both hitting over .320. New York had concerns, however. Second baseman Tony Lazzeri, who in years past could always be counted on to hit for a high average and drive in over a hundred runs, was mired in a season-long slump. At age 30, and hobbled by an ailing right leg, many were wondering if he was finished. With only a .219 average and 26 RBI, he was one of the biggest disappointments of 1934. Jack Saltzgaver, a 31-year-old rookie third baseman, was a pleasant surprise, hitting .381 since taking over full-time in early May, but he could not be expected to maintain his hot pace for long. Ruth had hit .300 with 13 home runs in the first half, but could his body hold up? The Yankees were still the Yankees, however. Manager Joe McCarthy demanded excellence, and as long as Gehrig and Ruth were around, New York would remain a force.

On Thursday, July 12, the Yankees and Tigers began a highly anticipated four-game series at Navin Field. In a battle of 24-year-olds, Cochrane sent Schoolboy Rowe to the mound, while McCarthy countered with rookie Johnny Broaca. A three-sport star in baseball, boxing, and track at Yale, Broaca had not given up more than three runs in any of his six starts in 1934.

Broaca was shaky at first, giving up three runs in the first three frames, but he settled down and kept the Bengals mostly in check the rest of the way. Rowe was overpowering, striking out 11 in a complete-game, six-hit effort. He was helped by a pair of rally-killing double plays in the fourth and seventh innings. The play of the game occurred in the sixth. Down by a run, New York loaded the bases with two out. Second baseman Don Heffner drove a ball to deep left-center, but Jo-Jo White made a sparkling catch up against the scoreboard to end the inning. Ruth fanned twice and did not get the ball out of the infield. "The Babe seems tired as he goes about his chores," noted the *Detroit Free Press*.[4] The final score was 4–2. Rowe won his tenth game on the season and sixth in a row. Most importantly, the Tigers took over first place in the American League. "With bands blaring," said the *New York Times*, "and seat cushions and straw hats making a veritable shower on the field, more than 20,000 Detroit fans celebrated in world's series style."[5]

The Navin Field faithful were disappointed the following afternoon, as New York pulled out a 4–2 win. The Yankees jumped on the scoreboard in the third inning, when Ruth hit his 700th career home run. "There was a mystical setting," wrote Bud Shaver of the *Detroit Times*, "for the Babe's ascension to the glory of his lost youth. Storm clouds were racing across a sullen sky and heat lightning was playing about the walls as Babe scratched around in the batter's box waiting the offerings of the slim Tommy Bridges, poised on the rubber." Despite his physical decline, Ruth was still the Yanks' biggest drawing card, the player fans paid to watch.

> Age and frustration weighed heavily on the barrel bodied Ruth as he fidgeted in the batter's box. He had not hit a ball out of the infield in two days. Bridges, with his hissing fast ball and baffling curve, had two strikes on him—and the Babe had let three ones go by. [Bridges' next pitch] was not a fast ball and it was not a curve. It was a half speed ball, designed to throw the Babe off his stride. It wasn't slow enough. Babe spotted it for what it was when it left Tommy's hand. He timed his swing perfectly. For that one split second, Ruth shed 10 of his 40 years. The power of his recaptured youth flowed through a buoyant coordinated swing. The fat of the bat met the ball and there was the typical Ruthian "swish" and "swat" as it sailed in a beautiful arc over the right field fences, cleared Trumbull avenue and bounded down the side street to fulfill Babe's cherished ambition.[6]

"The Old Man became Babe Ruth again," noted the *Free Press*. "He swung viciously. The ball soared over the right field wall. It plunked down in Plum Street and went bounding far up the thoroughfare."[7] The two-run shot off Tommy Bridges reportedly carried 480 feet. Number 700 was the Bambino's goal going into the season; now he had finally done it. He gleefully rounded the bases, shouting that he wanted the ball as a memento. A boy on a bicycle retrieved it and brought it back to the park. After the game, with a finder's fee of $20 in his back pocket, he and the Babe mugged for photographers. The game was an entertaining pitchers' duel, with Bridges and Red Ruffing locking horns. Bill Dickey's eighth-inning double scored Ruth and Chapman, and that was all the Yankees needed. With the win, New York was back in first place.

There was concern over Gehrig, however: He had "involuntarily withdrawn" from the game in the second inning with what was reported as a case of "lumbago."[8] To that point, Gehrig had played in 1,426 consecutive games, and it was unknown whether he would be able to return for the rest of the series. On Saturday, July 14, he woke up feeling not much better than he had the day before. He insisted he was okay to play, however. For the only time in his career, he was penciled in at leadoff, playing shortstop; McCarthy intended that the Iron Horse bat only once and then take a seat the rest of the afternoon. Gehrig was still "suffering acutely from a cold in the back that makes breathing difficult and swinging a baseball bat torture."[9] After singling to right to start the game, he was removed for a pinch runner, although his consecutive-game playing streak remained intact at 1,427. Unable to get out of the first inning, Tigers starter Vic Sorrell got lit up for four runs; by the end of three frames New York had a 6–0 lead, and it looked like a laugher.

Detroit got on the scoreboard in the third, when a Gehringer single plated Goslin, who had doubled off starter Lefty Gomez. The next inning, however,

Ruth blasted a three-run shot off Elden Auker, his 701st, to make it 9–1 and seemingly put the game away. Typesetters throughout the land were preparing their papers to show the Yankees with a game-and-a-half lead.

Wrote Sam Greene, "The Tigers of any other year in the last decade would have been beaten then and there. They would have figured that 'It just isn't our day' and begun to think of tomorrow. But this is a different Tigers team that Cochrane has assembled and infused with belligerence."[10]

Against the best pitcher in the American League, the Tigers began a stirring comeback for the ages. They put together a three-run rally in the fourth, putting a slight dent in the New York lead. One more in the fifth made it 9–5 and sent Gomez to an early shower. "Gomez complained of a cold in his precious left arm before the game and pitched as if he had one."[11] It was easily his worst outing of 1934. Neither could relievers Jimmie DeShong and Russ Van Atta stop the bleeding. After the Tigers put up three more runs in the sixth, Navin Field was shaking with the stomps and shouts of the frenzied crowd. Frank Crosetti's two-run homer in the seventh made it an 11–8 affair, and it stood that way until the bottom of the ninth.

The reason for the high scoring was the small, makeshift bleachers that ringed the outfield. Anticipating large walk-up crowds for the series, the Tigers had hastily slapped them together beforehand. Ironically, attendance at Navin Field this day was well below capacity. Perhaps fans simply chose to stay at home rather than fight the long ticket lines and the expected crush of humanity. In any event, the Tigers chose to open the temporary stands, necessitating special ground rules. Any ball hit into those seats was an automatic double. Altogether, the game featured 13 such blows, ten of them by Detroit. This, in the eyes of *New York Times* sportswriter Dan Daniel, turned the game into a farce. "Instead of being a real contest between two clubs fighting for a pennant in a major league, it was a travesty. The fans should have been kept off the field. It was bad enough to have those trick seats on the green without having men and children darting under the feet of the outfielders for those synthetic doubles. Fly balls fell for ground rule doubles. Children were on the field all afternoon."[12]

None of the "synthetic" doubles, however, was bigger than the one hit by Goslin with two on and two out in the ninth inning. It tied the game, and moments later Goslin himself scored the winning run when Billy Rogell singled to left. "It was a wild and wooly game; a free-hitting fray with a comedy touch that at times approached the atmosphere of the old-time picnic baseball feature."[13] Not lost in the hitting barrage was Gee Walker's return to the Tigers' lineup; in six at-bats, he banged out two singles and a double, scored once, and drove in three runs. For the second time in three days, the Yankees "skidded out of first place in the torrid pennant race," and the post-game New York clubhouse "held a thick gloom."[14]

The *Free Press* called it "one of the wildest ball games ever played." It was a dramatic, hard-fought win capable of inspiring a team. "[The Tigers] are very difficult to discourage this season. They kept swinging away and finally fought their way to victory in the riotous ninth, sending 22,500 fans home to tell the folks they'll never see another game like it."[15]

Billy Rogell, the man who had just driven in the winning run in the Tigers' most improbable performance of the season, was enjoying a career

Billy Rogell was the shortstop on Detroit's vaunted "Battalion of Death" infield (courtesy National Baseball Hall of Fame, Cooperstown, New York).

year. A .261 lifetime hitter coming into 1934, Rogell's average now stood at .306. He already had 68 RBI, after totaling only 57 in 1933. The scrappy, sure-handed shortstop was the Tigers' only switch-hitter. He had developed his strength while driving a horse-drawn milk truck as a teenager in Chicago's Rosedale neighborhood. Rogell loved the delivery job; not only was it steady coin, it allowed him plenty of fresh air and sunshine as well. He figured he could stay in shape by lugging milk bottles around all day. On top of that, he could drink as much of the product as he wanted.

Given that history, Rogell's nickname could have been "The Milk Truck." Instead, it was "The Fire Chief." The Yankees' Red Ruffing gave it to him when both were teammates on the Red Sox. The two were fast friends, having discovered one day that their fathers had also been chummy with each other in Berlin before coming to America. A year or so after joining the Red Sox in 1925, Rogell visited Ruffing at his home in Nokomis, Illinois. The town had a volunteer fire company, of which Ruffing was a member. Since Rogell would be hanging around for a couple of weeks with not much to do, he decided to join the outfit, more or less on a lark. A few days later, a fierce house fire broke out while the two pals were relaxing at the station. The alarm sounded, the company scrambled into its gear, and the truck sped clanging down the street to the scene of the action. Upon arrival, Rogell appraised the dire state of affairs and immediately went into action. With the deftness of a seasoned pro, he uncoiled the hose and snaked up a ladder to the roof of the building, accompanied by a resourceful Boy Scout. Ruffing and the rest of the company lost sight of Rogell (and the Scout) in the churning smoke. When the roof collapsed, Ruffing feared that he had lost his friend for good. Once the fire was contained, however, Ruffing and a couple of companions entered the house to find Rogell safe at the bottom of a pile of rubble, along with the Boy Scout. The pair were dazed, but none the worse for wear. It was a tale that Ruffing loved to tell (and no doubt embellish). From that day on, he affectionately referred to Rogell as The Fire Chief, and the nickname stuck.

In the finale of the Yankees series, the Tigers prevailed, 8–3. Schoolboy Rowe, on only two days' rest, pitched six strong innings for his seventh win in a row. Goslin hit his tenth home run. A *Free Press* writer dramatically observed that the last out of the crucial series "resulted in pandemonium, no less, and hats sailed through the air, grandstand cushions struck innocent bystanders and a great roar, greater than the swelling tumult during the progress of the game, resounded in the four winds from Trumbull and Michigan Aves."[16]

Leading up to the four-game showdown, the Yankees had been dismissive of Detroit; Washington posed the bigger threat, they maintained. The upstart Tigers had proven their mettle, however, and the Bronx Bombers shuffled out of town with considerably less swagger. Cochrane's team now sat alone atop the American League by a full length and a half. "Yes, m'lads," wrote the chagrined Daniel, "it will be a race and a hummer. Even the Yankees admit that now!"[17]

It was also the passing of an era. Never again would Ruth appear in a game in Detroit. By the time the Yankees returned to Navin Field in late September, a broken-down Babe would be riding the pine, unable to perform because of injuries. Since his first home run at Michigan and Trumbull way back in 1916 when he was a pitcher for the Boston Red Sox, Ruth had walloped 60 round-trippers in Detroit. Now, in 1934, despite the ravages of time, the Bambino was still as big a draw as ever, especially with kids. Between innings during the series, swarms of children made their way down to the railing near the dugout, calling out for the Babe. Before heading to his position in left, Ruth would take a few moments for yet another round of autograph signing. He was an aging, benevolent god in cleats, ever distributing largesse to his adoring public.

Chapter Seven

Winning Streak

Joe Cronin's Senators arrived for a three-game set beginning July 16. Detroit lost the opener, but took the next two behind fine pitching performances by Carl Fischer and Bridges, who won his 11th game. The reigning American League champions were now 12½ games back. With the Yankees dropping two of three in Cleveland, the Tigers bumped their lead to two and a half games.

Earlier in the season, many observers felt that the Tigers were not going to hang around for the long haul, that they would eventually fade away as the summer heated up. In years past, Detroit was always awed by teams like the Yankees and Senators. Writer Sam Greene maintained that they had had "an inferiority complex."[1] They had proven to be a group that no longer backed down from a challenge, however. They viewed themselves as equals with New York.

Perhaps no player on the Tigers symbolized that new spirit of confidence as much as Marv Owen did. At 28 years old, he was no longer a kid by baseball standards. He had arrived late on the scene, appearing in his first professional game only four years prior. Growing up in San Jose, California, he always had a knack for the game, and his parents encouraged him to pursue his dream of playing it for a living. At his mother's insistence, he attended Santa Clara University, where he was the star of the baseball team. He also majored in Physical Education. "The only reason I took it was because it was the easiest class. I was just there to play ball."[2] Although Owen earned his degree, he admitted he was never a serious student.

Nevertheless, he had a naturally curious, observant mind. In subsequent years with the Tigers, sportswriter H. G. Salsinger wrote of him: "Marvin Owen has the professorial look. You would not take him for anything else. He is quiet and unassuming and he spends much of his time arguing theology and theosophy, biology and psychology."[3] He was innately shy and introverted, but found it easy to express himself with pen and paper. His family and friends could always anticipate long, descriptive letters from Owen while he was on the road with the Tigers. He was also something of a poet. Hardly the image one would expect of a man best remembered for nearly precipitating a brawl in the World Series.

That, however, would come later. Owen's fine play as a collegian earned him feelers from Pacific Coast League teams. He inked a contract with the Seattle Rainiers, and in 1930, his first season, he was the team's regular short-stop. Owen had excellent range and a strong arm, and could have played any-where on the infield. He also had very large hands and liked to show off by holding seven baseballs in each of them. At Seattle, he hit an even .300, which caught the attention of the Tigers, who purchased him for $25,000. The fol-lowing year he became their full-time shortstop and hit over .300 in the first month and a half. He quickly learned, however, that pitchers in the American League were a step above those of the PCL. By the middle of August, his average had sunk to .223, and the Tigers optioned him down to the Interna-tional League's Toronto Maple Leafs.

Owen could have crawled into a shell. Back when he was playing for Seattle, he used to look around at the rest of the players on the field, and he knew in his heart that he was better than they were. It was not arrogance, but simply a confidence that it was in his power to go as far as he wanted in the game. Once he began to struggle in the major leagues, however, his self-assuredness took a beating. In the end, the demotion to Toronto turned out to be the best thing that could have happened. Feasting on inferior pitching, he wound up batting .313. He split 1932 with the Maple Leafs and Newark Bears, hitting a combined .317 with 63 extra-base hits. His great season gar-nered him an MVP Award in the International League, and by the following year, he made it back to the majors.

Once again, however, Owen had a hard adjustment to big-league pitch-ing. Sinus trouble plagued him in 1933, and although he played in 138 games, he lacked the offensive punch expected from a third baseman. Cochrane, speaking to the press in the spring of 1934, admitted to doubts that the tall, freckle-faced incumbent would still be a starter once the season got under way. The rookie manager sat down with Owen in Lakeland and gave him the straight dope: "With your natural equipment and great pair of hands, you ought to be the greatest third baseman living."[4]

Owen took the words of encouragement from Cochrane and stepped up his game. He finished strong in the final few weeks in Florida and was banking on a good start in 1934. It didn't happen. Following another hitless afternoon on May 4, Owen was floundering at .209 with only four extra-base hits. The next day, however, he collected three singles off Red Ruffing of the Yankees, and the hits kept on coming, day after day, week after week. In the three-game series against Washington in mid–July, Owen went 7-for-12, boosting his average to .346, his high-water mark of the season. Cochrane felt that he had even surpassed the Athletics' 25-year-old All-Star third baseman, Pinky Higgins, considered one of the best young players at the position.

Owen and Higgins were on full display as Philadelphia journeyed to Navin Field for a weekend series beginning on July 20. The Bengals dropped a tough one in the opener, 5–4. Schoolboy Rowe was cruising along but gave Detroit a big scare in the fifth inning. Scoring from second on a single by Pete Fox, he accidentally stepped on a bat near home plate, twisting his ankle. He stayed in the game, but Cochrane removed him in the seventh inning with Detroit up, 4–2. The Athletics eventually tied it, and in the top of the eighth, Jimmie

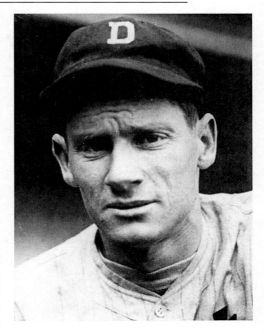

When not scooping up grounders at third base, the erudite Marv Owen "was also something of a poet" (courtesy Ernie Harwell Sports Collection, Detroit Public Library).

Foxx blasted a home run, his 29th of the season. That proved to be the game winner. In the words of *Free Press* writer Jack Carveth: "[Losing pitcher] Luke Hamlin knows today that it is indiscrete to throw a three-and-one ball down the middle of the plate to James Emory Foxx…. It was another ball game that the Tigers should have won but didn't because of their own mistakes."[5]

Elden Auker threw a complete game the next day, winning by a final of 4–1. In the fourth inning, with Detroit up 1–0 and nobody out, Philadelphia's Eric McNair singled, advancing to second on Rabbit Warstler's base knock. Charlie Berry followed with a screaming line drive to first; Greenberg snatched it for the out and stepped on the base before Warstler could slide back safely. He then fired down to Rogell, and the shortstop put the tag on McNair for a triple play.

The following afternoon, the heat wave that had been baking Detroiters finally eased, but only slightly. For the first time in nearly a month, the temperature failed to reach 90; the humidity, however, was still as drenching.

The Tigers were shut out, 1–0, in the first game of a doubleheader. In the second contest, the Athletics teed off on starter Firpo Marberry for six runs in less than three innings. Cochrane called in Rowe from the bullpen. The Schoolboy pitched the rest of the game, giving up only two more runs. The Tigers' bats, meanwhile, came alive, scoring 17 times, and Rowe notched his 12th win of the campaign, and eighth in a row. Greenberg homered, his 13th, and drove in four runs. The battle of third basemen, however, had proven to be a dud: Higgins hit .188 in the four games, while Owen managed only one hit in 13 at-bats.

Later that evening, stunning news emerged out of Chicago: Agents from the Federal Bureau of Investigation had gunned down John Dillinger, public enemy number one, as he exited the Biograph Theatre on the city's North Side. The former Indiana farm boy and ruthless gangster had been watching *Manhattan Melodrama*, a film about, ironically enough, New York gamblers and underworld shysters. Soon after the show ended, Dillinger walked jauntily out of the movie house in the company of two women (one of them an FBI informant). A team of special agents, led by Melvin H. Purvis of the Department of Justice, ambushed the armed criminal, who was gunned down trying to flee. Among the sharpshooters was Herman Hollis, formerly the head of the FBI's Detroit office.

Tommy Bridges took the mound in stifling 104-degree heat on July 23 at Navin Field. In a 7–2 win against the Red Sox, he pitched out of jams seemingly all afternoon long, but went the distance for the 14th time while raising his record to 12 victories against only six defeats. Reported the *Boston Globe*, "Today was 'Ladies' Day' and the girls turned out to cheer their heroes on. Charley Gehringer seems to be their favorite. Charley, you know, is a bachelor. Also a very eligible one."[6] The second baseman went 2-for-4 and was now hitting .390, second in the American League. Every Tiger in the lineup collected at least one hit. Afterward, a reporter buttonholed Sox skipper Bucky Harris and asked him what he felt of his former club's pennant chances. "It will be a tough team to beat. The Tigers have the spirit and the drive and they carry the power."[7]

The next day was even hotter in the city as the thermometer reached 105, the highest since the Detroit Weather Bureau began tracking temperatures 63 years earlier. The Tigers battered Red Sox starter Rube Walberg early and often, garnering a 6–3 win. Lefty Grove was Boston's third pitcher of the afternoon. A major disappointment since coming over from the Athletics in the off-season, Grove gave up a hit in two innings of work, lowering his earned run average to 7.25. "Grove has at least two more seasons of good pitching left in him," insisted Harris. "He'll be pitching and winning his share of games for Boston in no time."[8]

The Red Sox bounced back to take two in a row from Detroit. Coupled with two Yankees wins in St. Louis, Detroit had fallen into a tie with New York for first place. With the Tigers headed to Chicago for three games with the last-place White Sox, however, things were looking up.

On Saturday, July 28, Schoolboy Rowe locked horns with Sox right-hander Ted Lyons, a three-time 20-game winner. The 33-year-old Lyons went the distance, giving up 14 hits and 11 runs, but only three earned, as the Sox made four key errors. As for Rowe, he limited the Sox to one run on three hits in winning his 13th game. Sportswriter Irving Vaughan noted that, "Among the 3,500 in attendance was Rowe's 'girl' from Dallas, Tex. Maybe that's why the Schoolboy turned out an extra neat job of pitching."[9] The identity of the "girl" was not revealed to readers (at least not yet). The complete game marked Rowe's ninth consecutive win; he even banged out three hits and drove in three runs, raising his average to .305. "Pitching with a strong wind behind his back, Rowe handcuffed the Sox throughout the game."[10]

Schoolboy, however, saved his biggest hat trick for the opener of a doubleheader the following afternoon. This time, Comiskey Park's gale-force wind was blowing out, which aided the offense. Sox catcher Ed Madjeski's two-run homer in the eighth put his team up, 15–14. In a desperate attempt to save his bullpen, Cochrane called upon Rowe, who got the last two outs of the inning to escape further damage. In the top of the ninth, Marv Owen led off with a single. Rather than insert a pinch-hitter, Cochrane let Rowe bat. Schoolboy rewarded his manager's faith when he "exploded a homer"[11] into the left-field stands to give the Tigers a 16–15 advantage. In the bottom of the inning, Rowe set the Sox down in order, squeaking by for his 14th win and tenth consecutive. Said the *Free Press*, "The Tigers' Schoolboy was the hottest pitcher in all of baseball. The remarkable feats of the Schoolhouse have contributed more than any other single factor to the surprising rise of the Tigers to the top of the heap."[12]

When Detroiters woke up on Tuesday, July 31, their morning papers showed that the Tigers were a game in front of the Yankees. The Bengals had a record of 59–36. New York had the same number of losses, but two fewer wins. The Tigers had a twin bill at League Park that day against the third-place Indians. In the opener, Cleveland came from behind three times to eke out a 9–7 victory. But Bridges held the Tribe at bay in the second tilt, picking up his 13th win. New York's twin killing against the Red Sox that same day, however, put the Yankees in a virtual tie with Detroit.

The victory by Bridges was the opening volley of a remarkable run. For the next two weeks, the Tigers did not lose a baseball game. On August 1 in Cleveland, Detroit was leading, 10–7, when the Indians loaded the bases with two down in the ninth inning. Unexpectedly called upon in relief, a half-dressed Schoolboy Rowe scrambled for a glove. Unable to find one, he borrowed Elden Auker's. He then went out and fanned Hal Trosky and Odell Hale on six pitches, ballgame over. The next day, Cochrane handed the ball to Auker, who had compiled an earned run average of 7.01 in the month of July. The submariner blanked the Indians and Mel Harder, giving up only four hits in his best pitching effort of the season. On August 3, Rowe had a no-hitter going against the White Sox until Jimmie Dykes singled in the seventh. It was the only Chicago safety of the game, as Schoolboy notched his 11th consecutive decision.

The Washington Senators, meanwhile, buried in fifth place in the midst of a lost season, placed right-hander General Crowder on waivers. It looked like the end of the line for the 35-year-old. Crowder's pitching shoulder boasted a tattoo, a relic from his wilder days in the army. Body art was not something that proper folks displayed publicly in the 1930s, and Crowder made it a point never to bare his shoulder. He was a former stud with the Browns and Senators, a three-time 20-game winner. But his shoulder, tattooed or not, had begun to betray him in 1934, as evidenced by a 4–10 record and 6.79 earned run average. The Tigers initially had no interest in Crowder, but several players on the team, knowing that you never can have enough pitching, approached Cochrane and Frank Navin, urging them to go after the battle-tested veteran. The Tigers' owner liked the fact that Crowder had experienced a World Series with the Senators the year before. On August 4, the General became a member of the Tigers for the waiver price of $4,000. Wrote Jack Carveth of the *Free Press*, "Cochrane expects Crowder to turn in his share of victories for the Tigers before the sites for the World Series are determined. The Tigers' pilot looks for Crowder to reach the form that made him one of the outstanding pitchers of 1932 and 1933."[13] Cochrane also pointed out: "He'll win for us. He's a smart pitcher with speed, a good curve and a deceptive change of pace. Got everything we need."[14]

Rowe started again on August 7, this time against the Browns in Detroit. After giving up a leadoff double to Harlond Clift and a walk to Sam West, Rowe felt what was described as a "stitch" in his back.[15] Wrote Charles P. Ward: "For a few brief moments it looked as if the Tigers had lost their one big hope in the pennant fight. 'Oh, ho!' groaned each man to himself. 'The Schoolboy's injured his pitching arm again. Hell and potatoes! There goes our pennant!'"[16] Trainer Denny Carroll's diagnosis was that the pitcher was suffering from a cold, and he reassured everyone that Rowe would be fit to take his next turn in the rotation. This sounds shockingly reckless by modern standards; today, pitchers are placed on the disabled list at the slightest hint of discomfort. In any event, Auker entered the game in a hurry, threw six innings without giving up an earned run, and got credit for the win. One day later, with temperatures in the mid–90s and a soaking humidity, the Tigers overcame a two-run deficit in the ninth inning to tie the game. They won it in the tenth when Cochrane's single to center plated Goslin, who raced home from second with the winning tally. It was the Tigers debut of Crowder, who pitched a solid five innings before tiring.

Against the Indians on August 10, Rowe extended his personal win streak to 12 games. In the bottom of the 11th, with the bases loaded and nobody out, Schoolboy came to bat in a 5–5 tie with the crowd roaring for a base knock. The Tigers' pitching prodigy blasted a Mel Harder pitch deep to left field. Dutch Holland hauled it in with a leaping catch, but Greenberg was able to trot home with the game-winning run before Holland's throw even made it to the infield. That made it ten straight victories for the Bengals. Auker continued his strong pitching the next day, tossing another shutout against the Browns. On August 12, the Tigers again rallied in the ninth against Cleveland, and won it in the tenth on a Jo-Jo White double. The game featured Detroit's second triple play of the season.

The streaking Tigers followed that up with a rematch with the Yankees in the Bronx. Joe McCarthy, not ready to concede anything to the Tigers just yet, viewed the five-game clash as "just another series. Of course we'd like to win it. But, win or lose, the series won't be in any way decisive. This race is going to last right down to the wire. Too many things can happen between now and the last week in September."[17] For the Tigers, their 4½-game lead seemed anything but comfortable.

"It will be no faint-hearted army which Mickey Cochrane will lead into the east," wrote Charles P. Ward in the *Detroit Free Press*. "Mickey's Merry Men have been under severe pressure since the season began, have gained confidence in their own abilities in test after test and departed for New York promising to give the Yankees 'one hell of a fight.'"[18]

The showdown began with a doubleheader on August 14, a Tuesday. The Yankees were expecting a big walk-up crowd, but even they could not have anticipated the mad rush that descended on The House That Ruth Built. Over 79,000 paying customers squeezed inside, a new Yankee Stadium record. The surrounding streets resembled a mob scene, with an estimated 20,000 sad souls left out. *New York Times* writer John Drebinger called it "the wildest disorder ever seen [outside] the stadium." Crowds "fought with the police mounted and on foot, for over an hour after the first game started before giving up the hopeless struggle and receding from the scene." Not only did fans fight to get inside, they jousted for parking spaces, as automobiles came "honking and piling in, seeking in vain for a space to light, then becoming hopelessly enmeshed in the broiling mass of would-be spectators who couldn't get in."[19]

Inside the stadium was a churning sea of humanity. Wrote Paul Gallico, "You've heard the expression—'Inside, they were hanging from the rafters…' That was no gag either, today. From the press box as you looked right and left down the mezzanines, all you saw was legs dangling from the rear of the top shelf and the runways leading thereto…. It did one's heart good to see such excitement and enthusiasm."[20]

In the first game, New York sprinted out to a 5–0 lead. But just as they had done a month earlier at Navin Field, Detroit sent the great Lefty Gomez to an early shower. Not intimidated by the thunderous Yankee Stadium crowd, the Tigers pounded Gomez for five runs in the sixth inning, and won 9–5. General Crowder struggled, but picked up his first victory in a Tigers uniform. Detroit took the second game of the doubleheader, 7–3. Despite giving up a home run to Gehrig, Rowe prevailed again, outpitching Red Ruffing to gain his 17th win, and 13th consecutive. Gehringer homered in both games.

The Tigers had won 14 games in a row. Playing with the conviction that no one could beat them, they outscored the opposition, 121–47, while racking up four shutouts. Six of the wins were of the come-from-behind variety.

The incredible streak finally ended on August 15, when Johnny Broaca silenced the Tigers' bats. The Yankees lit up Tommy Bridges, who, in the words of the *Detroit Times'* Bud Shaver, "was unable to shake off the Yankee Stadium jinx even on the crest of a winning wave."[21] Bridges gave up five runs in five innings, unable to find any kind of a groove. A rainy forecast kept many folks at home. Only about 10,000 fans witnessed the 8–2 New York win, among them a pair of distinguished visitors in Prince and Princess Kaya of Japan. No record exists of their impressions of the national pastime, whether they ordered hot dogs, or if they clapped when Babe Ruth made a great running catch in right to snuff out a Tigers rally. Noted Joe McCarthy after the game, "The Tigers had plenty of good fortune in running up fourteen straight and may be due for a slump."[22]

A downpour washed out the next day's affair, necessitating a doubleheader on Friday. With better weather, another huge crowd of around 47,000 made its way to Yankee Stadium. In the first game, Gomez showed why he was a great pitcher, holding the Tigers to eight scattered hits in a 5–0 win. Tony Lazzeri's home run was one of the hardest shots ever seen at Yankee

Stadium, banging against the front of the mezzanine facade just inside the left-field foul pole. For Gomez, it was his 20th victory of 1934, making it the third time he reached the milestone. Babe Ruth made a spectacular lunging catch on a liner to right, doing a complete summersault and scraping yards of Bronx turf in the process.

The rubber game of the series was a classic pitching duel between Schoolboy Rowe and rookie right-hander Jimmie DeShong. Rowe narrowly escaped what could have been a serious injury in the second inning. After bunting for a single, he made it to third on Cochrane's base hit to right. Rowe slid awkwardly into the bag, however, and commenced rolling around in agony on the infield dirt. As he described it, "I looked up at [third-base coach] Del Baker when I was about ten feet from the bag. Del held up his arms, meaning that I did not have to slide. I had just started to slide and I tried to switch. I was half up and half down when I hit the bag. The spikes of my left shoe caught in the bag and I fell. The spikes held fast and I twisted my ankle."[23]

After a few minutes of gingerly testing his body out, Rowe judged himself well enough to brave it out. He pitched brilliantly the rest of the way, giving up only three singles and striking out 11 in a complete-game shutout. But it did not come easy. "I never thought I could finish that game. I had to keep walking in the dugout between innings because I was afraid if I sat down I couldn't get started again. By walking I kept up the circulation."[24] There were moments when he limped noticeably while on the mound. "Some times I forgot about the leg when I was bearing down."[25] He added later that evening, "I thought the leg was gone, and I said every prayer I ever knew."[26] Rowe's dominance in that afternoon's game was incredible given his physical condition. One modern sabermetric used to gauge a starting pitcher's effectiveness in a particular contest is Game Score (GSc). Rowe's GSc that afternoon was 87, his highest of the season. It was his 18th victory, and his winning streak now stood at 14. During that run, he had faced Ruth eight times, holding him hitless, including five strikeouts.

The Tigers got out of Gotham having won three of five. They had increased their lead to five and a half games. In the minds of many, Cochrane's Bengals looked like the team to beat in the American League. Back in Detroit, fans swamped the ticket office's mailbox with requests for World Series seats; the Tigers issued a subsequent statement urging fans to hold off until a pennant was assured. Yankees owner Jacob Ruppert, however, remained confident. "We're not out of the race by any means," he vowed. "And the Yankees are best when the going is tough."[27]

Of minor note in the series was the arrival of one Rudolph Preston York in the Detroit clubhouse. The Tigers had just called up the 20-year-old Alaba-

Lynwood Thomas "Schoolboy" Rowe tied an American League record with 16 consecutive victories in 1934, on his way to a 24-win season (courtesy National Baseball Hall of Fame, Cooperstown, New York).

man from Beaumont, where he had developed a reputation as a hitter of awesome power. Rumors had swirled that York, who Cochrane planned to use as a pinch-hitter and utility player, was part Native-American. However, the six-foot, 200-pounder insisted that such claims were exaggerated. "There is a little Indian blood in our family, but it goes a long way back. I never tried to trace it and really don't know what it amounts to."[28] York would play in only three games the rest of the season with Detroit. He was still a few years away from his arrival as a bona fide slugger who would hit 239 home runs wearing the Old English "D."

Chapter Eight

Schoolboy
and the History Books

The month of August had started on an ominous note in Germany. In the wake of the death of President Paul von Hindenburg, Hitler announced himself the country's new absolute dictator. The Fuehrer called for, and received, a sworn oath of allegiance from every member of the army and navy. It was not until a national plebiscite on August 19, however, that nine out of every ten Germans affirmed the new boss.

In Japan, the press threw the first volleys in a campaign clamoring for war against the Soviet Union. At issue was Manchuria, which Japan had seized from the U.S.S.R. in 1931. Since then, dealings between the two nations had strained to the breaking point. Meanwhile in Italy, Mussolini urged his nation to be ready for warfare. Speaking from the turret of an assault tank in front of 5,000 cheering military officers, the fascist dictator declared, "No one in Europe wants war, but the idea of war is floating in the air. We must become a military nation, even a militaristic nation, even—I might add—a warlike nation."[1]

Closer to home, American families were forced to deal with a spike in food prices, a result of the intense drought that had gripped the nation for much of the summer. President Roosevelt, surveying the devastation in Montana, declared that the dire situation required even more than the $525,000,000 in relief recently appropriated by Congress.

In a remarkable display of political audacity, the Louisiana House of Representatives gave controversial Senator Huey Long all-encompassing strength, with "greater powers than those held by Stalin or Mussolini." As the de facto dictator of the Southern state, Long now had the right to regulate taxes, control election machinery, and form a State Constabulary that would supersede municipal police forces. One representative warned of dire consequences of such a concentration of power. "I am telling you now, warning you, that this stuff you are passing here is going to turn Louisiana into a shambles. I warn you that they will overthrow this government, which is getting worse than anything America ever saw or heard of."[2]

Voters in Michigan would go to the polls in September. For now, however, any talk of who would be the next governor or senator took a back seat to the surging Tigers. Wrote David J. Wilkie in the *Detroit Free Press*: "Republican and Democratic aspirants for office—and they run into the hundreds— have made valiant efforts to arouse public interest, only to find that the baseball scoreboards telling of the fight of the Detroit Tigers toward the American League pennant are drawing the crowds and the cheers, while political rallies thus far have been noteworthy for their lack of attendance." It was not just the city of Detroit that had caught Tigers fever. "Michigan is baseball-conscious this year, more than it ever has been, and scoreboards and newspapers that tell of the progress of the Tigers and their newest contenders for the pennant, the New York Yankees, are daily bringing cheers or groans as the fortunes of the teams ebb and flow."[3]

By the time the Tigers arrived in Boston on August 18, the Red Sox, at 14 games back, needed a telescope to see first place. In the opener of a four-game set, Bucky Harris's team was not fooled by the curveball of Tommy Bridges. The Tigers' starter lasted only four frames; eventually, six earned runs were credited against him. Detroit, however, looked like it was going to stage another comeback. Trailing 8–5 in the top of the ninth, the Tigers scored two runs and had Gehringer on third with two down. But Billy Rogell bounced out to end the rally.

"The pennant is by no means clinched," Cochrane pointed out afterward. His bid for a game-winning three-run homer in the ninth had come to naught when Moose Solters hauled in his hard-hit drive up against the center field wall. "There is still a long way to go."[4] The loss did not stop the Tigers from enjoying their stay in New England. "The entire Detroit squad sailed up to Gloucester last evening on the Grand Marshall, after the game, where they were feted at the Riverside Club."[5]

The Tigers were proving to be a major gate attraction. Over 46,000 at Fenway saw them take both ends of a twin bill the following afternoon. Lefty Grove was no mystery to Detroit's bats in the opener, giving up seven runs in only five innings. The Sox mounted a furious comeback in the bottom of the ninth, but the Tigers held on for an 8–6 victory, with Crowder the winning pitcher. Auker tossed a complete game for his 11th victory in the second contest.

With an off day, Cochrane and his men rose early to take in some deep-sea fishing (all, that is, except Goslin, Owen, Greenberg, and Fox; prone to seasickness, the quartet chose instead to brave things out at the team hotel).

Once their chartered boat reached ten miles off Cape Ann, Elden Auker caught the first fish of the day. Schoolboy Rowe's stomach began to feel the effects of the waves, which, according to the locals, were only a light chop. He spent most of the outing below deck, but was his usual self when the Fenway series continued the following afternoon. Looking, in the words of the *Boston Globe*'s James C. O'Leary, like "an unconquerable hero,"[6] and aided by ample offense behind him, Schoolboy was in fine form. Thanks to home runs by landlubbers Greenberg and Owen, Detroit prevailed, 8–4. That made it 19 victories on the season for Schoolboy.

The young Tigers hurler was entering rarefied air. He had not lost a game since June 10, and with 15 consecutive victories, he was one away from the American League mark of 16. It should be pointed out that the record refers strictly to consecutive *decisions* won in a *single season*, whether starting or in relief.[7] It had been accomplished three times before, most recently by Lefty Grove in 1931 when he was with Philadelphia. On the day that Grove tried for number 17 against the Browns in St. Louis, he was out-dueled by journeyman Dick Coffman, who surrendered only three singles in a 1–0 Browns win. Goose Goslin was a member of that St. Louis team; he did not get a hit that afternoon, striking out twice against Grove.

Smoky Joe Wood of the Red Sox and Walter Johnson of the Senators had both won 16 consecutive games in 1912. Wood admitted to being under severe strain as the wins piled up. When the streak finally ended on September 20 against the Tigers at Navin Field, it would be hard to say whether he was more disappointed or relieved. "Defeat," said his manager Jake Stahl immediately afterward, "was the very best thing that could come to Wood. Another week of thinking about his pitching record and he would be fit for a nurse."[8] Johnson's run ended in a controversial loss, but he shrugged it off in his typical mild-mannered fashion: "I lost the game, so what's the use worrying and fussing over it."[9]

There must have been something they were feeding pitchers in 1912, because that was also the year that Rube Marquard of the New York Giants tied the National League record by winning 19 in a row. That equaled the mark of Tim Keefe, also of the Giants, back in 1888. By the time Marquard's streak ended, he was physically and mentally exhausted. After he lost a few games, the *New York Times* offered up the opinion that Marquard had "cracked ... his greatness dissolved into oblivion."[10] That was a premature assessment; Marquard went on to win two games in that year's World Series, giving up only one earned run in 18 sparkling innings.

On Saturday, August 25, before one of the biggest crowds of the year at Griffith Stadium, Rowe went to the mound to try to put his name up there with Lefty, The Big Train, Smoky, and Rube. Opposing him was the Senators' Monte Weaver, a former 20-game winner who had not fared well in 1934. Both men battled, neither giving up a walk, and by the top of the ninth inning, Washington was holding on to a slim 2–1 margin. First up for the Tigers was the right-handed-hitting Greenberg, who walloped a hanging curve long and high to left field, just foul. He stepped out of the batter's box to regroup, but only for a moment. He drove the next pitch, a fastball, over the high wall in right field for a home run, his 20th of the season, tying the game. The fans, having come out mainly to see Schoolboy continue his streak, thundered their approval and tossed straw hats onto the field by the dozens. The Tigers shouted and danced in the dugout.

Marv Owen singled to left, and that was all for Weaver, who handed the ball over to Jack Russell, a 28-year-old right-hander with a lifetime record of 61–110 for Washington. After years of floundering as a starter, Russell had found his niche as a reliever; he was now one of the best in the game and had even made the All-Star team. Right fielder Pete Fox, who already had two hits on the day, lined a fastball into center for a single, Owen hustling all the way to third. With the go-ahead run 90 feet away, Rowe batted for himself. To call Schoolboy a good-hitting pitcher would be an understatement. He was just a fine hitter, period. He came into the game at .309 and had doubled and singled earlier. In a righty-on-righty matchup, Rowe worked the count to two-and-two, fouled a couple of pitches off, and then hit a blooper that fell just beyond the reach of the shortstop for a single. Owen scored, and the Tigers took the lead. As Rowe stood on first base, wave upon wave of applause descended upon him from the D.C. spectators. An error later in the inning brought in another run to make it 4–2.

Rowe trotted to the mound for the bottom of the ninth. Three more outs, and he would be mentioned in the same breath with the greats. Fred Schulte grounded one to shortstop Rogell, who made a bad throw to first, and the tying run was aboard. After a force on Schulte, however, Rowe bore down, striking out the next two pinch-hitters on six pitches. A pouring rain immediately started, but it did not matter. Schoolboy was now a 20-game winner, and with his 16th victory in a row, they would have to find room for him in the American League record books. He had gone 3-for-4 in the bargain, to bump his average to .329.

As he sat in front of his locker after the game, he announced to reporters that he was "going after" Marquard's mark of 19 straight. "Yeah, I think I'll try for it. But, boy, they'll have to come easier than this one."[11]

Back in El Dorado, Arkansas, a certain Miss Edna Skinner admitted that she was "tickled to death" when she heard the news of the win. "I was confident that he would equal the record."[12] And why shouldn't she be? The lovely Skinner was Schoolboy's sweetheart, and had been for several years. The baseball world was about to become very familiar with her name.

Ever since he was a youngster growing up in the liltingly named town of El Dorado, Arkansas, Lynwood Thomas Rowe had been drawing attention because of his athletic prowess, particularly on the baseball diamond. He had always been tall and strong, but his graceful agility set him apart from others. He was born in Waco, Texas, on January 11, in either 1910 or 1912, depending on whom you believe. In the early 1920s, his family moved to El Dorado, as did so many others seeking work in the town's oil boom of that decade. For the rest of his life, Lynwood would consider himself a Razorback.

His brush with greatness came early. In grammar school, one of his teachers was a Miss Mary Blackman, soon to become the wife of Travis Jackson, who at the time was just beginning his Hall of Fame career as a New York Giants shortstop. Much of Rowe's early life is shrouded in hyperbolic mystery, perpetuated (perhaps even created) by sportswriters thirsty for tales of a Paul Bunyan–like figure. With Schoolboy Rowe, fact and fiction were often interchangeable.

His childhood athletic feats were the stuff of myth, and probably have some basis in fact. The exact origin of his "Schoolboy" nickname is a historical quagmire. It testifies to a sporting wunderkind who amazed onlookers with his ability to compete with, and against, players much older than himself. According to one story, apocryphal or not, he was already such a fabled pitcher (and slugger) at age 14 that he was recruited to play in a local adult church league. One day, young Lynwood was on the mound for the Methodists, trying to protect a fragile one-run lead. Facing the Baptists' biggest slugger, he heard a cry cascade down from a hostile fan: "Don't let that Schoolboy beat you!" Rowe beat the Baptists, anyway, and a legend (and a nickname) was born.[13]

Like all great high school athletes in those days, he was a multi-sport star. He was only an average student, although he did receive a prize for penmanship. When not at school or on the athletic field, Rowe could usually be found caddying at Oakhurst Golf Club or hawking newspapers on a downtown street corner. Rowe loved the competition of sports, whether it was football, basketball, or track and field. He excelled in all of them. He was even a talented golfer and boxer. One writer referred to him as a "one man All-American athletic team," in high school.[14] He had excellent eye-hand coordination and was a crack bowler and pool player. The sport that Rowe loved most, however, was baseball, and the irony is that El Dorado High did not field a team. He began building his star reputation on the city's sandlots, however, and the Detroit Tigers eventually got wind of his exploits.

They dispatched scout Eddie Goosetree to El Dorado to see what all the fuss was. Goosetree located the Rowe homestead and knocked on the front door. When an undersized, middle-aged man opened it and acknowledged that he was Lynwood Rowe's father, Goosetree's heart sank: Thomas Rowe resembled nothing so much as a bank teller. He did not look like the type of man capable of siring a progeny worthy of the legends making the rounds.[15] In truth, Goosetree misread the Rowe patriarch, who had been a circus trapeze performer in his younger, more vigorous days. Schoolboy, for his part, always insisted that his Pop had been an architect.

Mr. Rowe told Goosetree that Lynwood most likely could be found down at the firehouse. Not expecting much, but figuring he had already made the long trip and might as well see it through, the scout headed for the firehouse. Goosetree took one look at Rowe, who was big for his age, and decided he might make good, especially since the kid should continue to grow (Rowe eventually topped out at six feet four inches, although some claim he was a bit taller). Using the persuasive powers of a $250 bonus, Goosetree got the (supposedly) 16-year-old Lynwood to sign a Detroit Tigers contract. "Eddie wrote out the contract on the back end of the hook and ladder truck in the El Dorado fire house," Rowe explained years later.[16] Of course, he was not yet of legal age to put pen to anything, so the elder Rowe had to cosign the document. Schoolboy's professional baseball odyssey was about to begin.

According to legend, he refused to report to the Fort Smith (Arkansas) Twins of the Class C Western Association. That resulted in his being suspended by Organized Baseball. Since he was still in high school, however, he was forced to hide his professional status if he wanted to continue to play extra-curricular sports. With his high school still without a baseball team, he continued to play in local leagues for the next two summers. Beginning in 1929, he wandered around in semipro baseball, in cities as far north as Utica, as west as Wichita, and as south as Bastrop, Louisiana. All the while, he was still contractually bound to the Tigers, and when he again refused their minor league assignments to Little Rock in 1929, and finally to Evansville, Indiana in 1931, he remained in a state of suspension by Organized Baseball.

One possible explanation for Rowe's failure to report to the minors comes from J. Alva Waddell, one of his high school coaches. The way Waddell told the story in 1934, Rowe believed "he had made a mistake casting his lot with an outfit like the Tigers, who 'probably never would win a pennant.' He thought he should have gotten into an organization like the New York Yankees or Philadelphia Athletics."[17] In a possibly self-serving account, Waddell claimed to have eventually talked Rowe into sticking it out with the Detroit organization.

It sounds plausible enough. In any event, Rowe was not without an alternative; he had reportedly received a football scholarship from the University of Southern California. Whatever the reason for Rowe's mystifying refusal to go where the Tigers sent him, we do know that he finally agreed to report to the Beaumont Exporters of the Texas League. He was the victor in the first game he pitched, hitting the go-ahead home run in the process. Initially, he had designs on being an everyday hitter, but his manager, Del Baker, quickly rid him of that notion, insisting that he would be more valuable as a pitcher. Wasting no time, Rowe made mincemeat of the circuit's hitters, compiling a 2.30 earned run average and racking up 19 wins against seven defeats. He also showed his prowess at the plate, hitting .295; of his 33 hits, ten were home runs.

Perhaps Rowe's biggest booster was Frank Navin, who practically demanded that the young stud be called up to the Motor City in 1933. Fans in Detroit had been hearing a lot of chatter about the Schoolboy, and eagerly awaited his major league debut on April 15 that season against the White Sox at Navin Field. Using an easy pitching motion, Rowe threw a complete-game, six-hit victory. Afterward, he immediately wired one of his old high-school coaches: "Dear Coach. Beat Chicago, 3 to 0. Allowed six hits. As ever, Schoolboy."[18] He confided to reporters, "The one ambition of my life always has been to win my first big league game."[19] With that now out of the way, what would he do for an encore? There was discussion that perhaps manager Harris would try Rowe in the outfield, where the Tigers needed offensive help. Everyone knew the kid wielded a strong bat, and the temptation was there. If Babe Ruth made the conversion from stud pitcher to slugger, could not Schoolboy do the same?

After only his fourth career start, however, Detroit's prized prospect was shelved with what was diagnosed as a sore arm. Following two weeks of inaction, he returned seemingly his old self, winning five in a row at one point. But the injury bug hit him again on July 15 at Shibe Park. Locked into a pitchers' duel with Lefty Grove, Rowe fielded a bunt off the bat of Cochrane, Philadelphia's catcher at the time. On the throw to first, Rowe "twisted his arm," forcing him to come out of the game.[20] He tried to return too soon, and finally, after an ineffective performance in late July, Detroit made the decision to shut him down indefinitely. For weeks, he carried his arm in a brace, and Bucky Harris noted dolefully, "I honestly don't think he will be able to pitch again this season."[21] He wasn't, and he didn't. The Tigers detected a muscle tear in his right shoulder, and Rowe spent the rest of 1933 worrying about his future.

That all seemed like ancient history. Rowe had always experimented with an assortment of pitches, including a knuckleball, usually from a side-armed or "cross-fire" delivery. Beginning in 1934, Cochrane insisted that he simplify and focus on his overpowering fastball. Rowe also altered his pitching motion to more of a sweeping overhand manner. With his enormous stride, Schoolboy appeared to hitters as if he were on top of them when he released the ball. Noted for always pitching in a sweatshirt under his jersey, he had pinpoint control. In time, he developed a sharp, late-breaking curveball so good that it often fooled the umpires, robbing him of strikes. It was his heater, however, that set him apart: Charlie Gehringer called it "one of the finest fastballs I ever stood behind."[22]

As the summer of 1934 wore on, and win followed win, reporters grew more and more attracted to Rowe's eccentric personality. So did the public. Like many athletes of his time, he smoked, and his preferred meal was a thick, juicy steak. He also broke with convention, however, by ordering large plates of spinach in restaurants, a gastronomic choice that automatically pegged him as an oddball among his meat-and-potatoes teammates. Baseball players have always been a superstitious lot, and Rowe was no exception. On days that he pitched, he filled his pockets with talismans, amulets, and tokens, and the righty always made a point of picking up his glove with his left hand. Among his other good-luck charms were "a Canadian penny, some Belgian and Dutch coins, a United States ten-dollar gold piece, and a jade elephant."[23] Rowe also talked to the ball while on the mound, engaging in chatter meant to convince the orb of the necessity of landing in the strike zone. He called the ball his "Edna," in honor of his girlfriend. "C'mon, Edna," he would cajole, "we got this guy Foxx right where we want 'im." The ball took on a life of its own in Rowe's mind. "Careful, now, Edna. Don't let Ruth get those arms extended." The fact that Rowe had a sweetheart back home was bad enough for the female throngs who stormed Navin Field on a typical Ladies Day. That he was serious enough about the girl to name a baseball after her ... now *that* was doubly devastating. Rowe's dark hair, penetrating eyes, and chiseled jawline had caused many a swoon among his admirers. Even his gold-capped front tooth, the result of a high school football injury, lent him a certain air of roguishness.

Rowe's sense of showmanship drew comparisons, once again, to Ruth. Near the end of the 1934 season, sportswriter James C. Isaminger commented that the Tigers' pitcher had for the moment, "replaced Babe Ruth as baseball's biggest drawing card."[24] Rowe loved nothing more than pitching against the Yankees. He reveled in the big stage, the pressure-packed situation. There was electricity in the air whenever he took the mound. Fans flocked to see him wherever he was, either at the ballpark, on the street, or in hotel lobbies. Like Ruth, Rowe understood the adulation for what it was and did not try to hide from it. Wrote Sam Greene, "Schoolboy has a full understanding of his importance to the baseball public."[25] After other players had already ducked into the locker room following a game, Schoolboy could be seen signing autographs for the flocks of kids who had descended on him *en masse*. At the Seward Hotel, where he stayed during the season, the occasional fan would pop out from behind one of the lobby's potted plants, pen and pad in hand. "Firpo Marberry told me never to get a swelled headed," he pointed out, "and believe me, I never will. I sign all the autographs asked for and am nice as I know how to be to fans, newspaper men, and autograph hunters alike. I figure in my business you got to be a diplomat."[26] The hero worship did not go to his head, however. Rowe soaked it up but kept it in perspective. He was aware of the greats who had come before him. The 16-game winning streak did not change things. He understood that he had a long way to go to justify the comparisons to Johnson, Mathewson, Alexander, and Grove.

Bud Shaver of the *Detroit Times* wrote,

> Schoolboy Rowe, catapulted into sudden fame by his slingshot arm, gets a naïve delight out of the stir he has caused, but is slightly dazed by it all. He is amazed that merchants of whom he never has heard are eager to give him suits, neckties and shoes. Strange vistas of radio and newspaper syndicate articles are beckoning with a golden gleam. Most any 22-year-old boy might be dazzled into giddiness by it all, but the Schoolboy is kept on a fairly even keel by that homely brand of wisdom which is the product of small towns, called "horse sense."[27]

On Wednesday, August 29, in the second game of a doubleheader, Schoolboy pitched against the Athletics in Philadelphia, gunning for his 17th victory in a row. Shibe Park's normally sparse crowds that summer had turned the stadium into a dull, dreary place. Nevertheless, a throng of more than 33,000-strong shoehorned its way into the park that afternoon, intent on witnessing history. Police reserves were brought in to hold back those without tickets. Hundreds of freeloaders found spots on the rooftops beyond the right-field fence. Meanwhile, back in Detroit, a huge mob gathered at Grand Circus Park to hear the game's radio broadcast amplified through a speaker.

Opposing Rowe was Philadelphia's 24-year-old rookie, John "Footsie" Marcum, sporting a 9–9 record. The Tigers struck quickly, tallying two runs in the first inning. Rowe's every move brought a cheer from the assembled masses; he breezed through the first three frames, giving up only one hit.

The Athletics tied it in the fourth, however, and disaster finally struck the following inning, when Philly lit up Schoolboy for five runs, capped by a two-run homer by Pinky Higgins. They scored one more run in the sixth and three in the seventh, before Cochrane mercifully yanked Rowe. The pitcher received a big standing ovation nonetheless from the crowd, and even from the Athletics' dugout. In came Vic Sorrell to try to put an end to the barrage. The final score was Athletics 13, Tigers 5. Marcum was not spectacular, but he had bested the hottest pitcher in the game.

Rowe simply did not have it. His fastball lacked its customary zip, and his curve was flat. It was by far Schoolboy's worst start of the year (his GSc was a mere seven). Cochrane, while not trying to make excuses, suggested that the consecutive-wins streak had adversely affected Schoolboy. With all the interviews and autograph seekers, his pitcher had simply worn down.

The following afternoon, Rowe was a guest on NBC radio. In an endearing blend of cockiness and guilelessness, he predicted that of course the Tigers would go to the World Series. In fact, they would probably win it in four straight. One of the games would be a shutout, he said, and you could bet he would be the one tossing it. He felt bad about losing the previous day to end his streak, but he guessed he had it coming to him. He had to take some bad breaks occasionally, and better that it happened in Philadelphia than, say, the Polo Grounds. Rowe's implication was obvious, since that was the home park of the Giants, a team with a good chance to reach the World Series. The radio program's host began to wrap up the interview. With only a few seconds remaining, Rowe bluntly whispered into the microphone, "Hello, Ma. Hello, Edna. How am I doin'?"

Radio was still a relatively new-fangled technology in those days, and ballplayers were not exactly the most media-savvy individuals. Even for the 1930s, however, Rowe's off-the-cuff (but on-the-air) aside to his mother and sweetheart seemed like the stuff of a hopeless country bumpkin. Rowe had clumsily broken through the fourth wall; in the process, he created a catch phrase: "How'm I doin', Edna?" For the rest of the season, the opposition shouted it back to him while he was on the mound, all part of an effort to rattle him.

Rowe's streak was over, as were the distractions that went along with it. Holding a five-game lead in the American League, the Tigers were masters of their own destiny. Nevertheless, with one month left in the 1934 season, nothing was assured. Schoolboy and the rest of his team could now focus on finishing what they had started.

Rowe righted his ship five days later, in a rematch with Marcum and the Athletics at Navin Field. In a pre-game ceremony, the Detroit Federation of

Musicians awarded Cochrane an honorary membership, mainly on the strength of his saxophone skills. Unfortunately, his membership card read "Stanley Gordon Cochrane," rather than "Gordon Stanley Cochrane." The Tigers, on the other hand, played a mostly mistake-free game, prevailing 4–2 thanks to a four-run fourth inning. Rowe went the distance for his 21st win, and Detroit bumped its American League lead to six games.

The previous night, Cochrane had appeared on a radio broadcast sponsored by the Detroit Ford dealers. Asked what was holding the Tigers atop the league standings, his answer was definitive: Speed. "We have been using old fashioned baseball methods this year, and that's one of the main reasons why we've been leading ... for many weeks. Yes, we've been sacrificing and squeezing, hitting and running." He was not ready to celebrate yet, however. "There are only 25 playing days left. A lot can happen in that time. We've got a comfortable lead now, but if we let up we're likely to find ourselves behind the eight ball at the finish."[28]

The Athletics won three of the five games, which was significant: It marked the first time the Tigers had lost a series since the Browns had taken two of three at the end of June. Bridges pitched a spectacular four-hitter in the finale on September 8, picking up win number 18, in a contest that took only one hour and 31 minutes. Connie Mack, for his part, was convinced of Detroit's superiority. Speaking at a Knights of Columbus rally in Detroit, the venerable Athletics owner went on record as saying that the Tigers would be the American League champions of 1934.

Chapter Nine

"Phenomena, bordering on the miraculous"

Hank Greenberg was only 23 years old. For Detroit's six-foot-three, 210-pound first baseman, however, 1934 was proving to be a breakout season. His parents, both Romanian-born Jews, meant to name him Hyman. The story goes that the fellow who filled out his birth certificate had never heard of such a name, and simply wrote in "Henry." When Greenberg's family moved from New York's Greenwich Village to the Bronx, he suddenly found himself living across the street from Crotona Park, a 127-acre, municipally owned oasis where young Henry spent countless hours playing baseball with the other neighborhood kids.

Greenberg's best sport at James Monroe High School was basketball, but he was good enough at baseball that the New York Yankees were hot on his trail. Owner Jacob Ruppert was always on the lookout for a great Jewish player, fully aware of the boost in attendance it would provide, given the city's large Jewish population. Scout Paul Krichell invited a teenaged Greenberg to a box seat at Yankee Stadium, where the youngster got an up-close view of Lou Gehrig (whom Krichell had signed years ago) in the on-deck circle. Greenberg was a Giants fan, but Krichell, ever the salesman, leaned closer to him and whispered, "He's all washed up. In a few years, you'll be the Yankee first baseman."[1]

Things did not work out that way, however, but it may have been for the better. With Gehrig entrenched at first base, Greenberg would have had little chance of playing in the Bronx. He signed with Detroit instead and quickly established himself as a rising star within the organization. A solid first season with the Raleigh Capitals and Hartford Senators earned him a promotion to Detroit for the final three weeks of 1930. He quickly found out that he was not welcomed by all. He was subjected to Jew-baiting from the opposition, and even certain of his teammates did not take kindly to having a Jew on the club. Year later, Greenberg recounted how Phil Page, an infinitely expendable

Only 23 years old in 1934, Hank Greenberg was just emerging as one of baseball's all-time great sluggers (courtesy National Baseball Hall of Fame, Cooperstown, New York).

young Tigers pitcher, called him a "goddamn Jew" after Greenberg hit him on the knee with a line drive in batting practice. In the face of the taunts, Greenberg found support from other teammates, particularly Schoolboy Rowe. Billy Rogell, himself a well-known hard-ass who refused to take crap from anybody, also encouraged the youngster. "Go out and outplay the bastards," he once told him.[2]

After two more years of minor league seasoning, including 39 homers at Beaumont in 1932, Greenberg made the Tigers' squad out of spring training in 1933. He had a fine rookie campaign, batting .301 and driving in 85 runs. With only 12 home runs, he was still a raw-boned kid and had yet to discover the power stroke that would make him famous. Greenberg entered the 1934 season determined to improve both his power hitting and his fielding; he did both. He emerged as the Tigers' biggest home-run threat, and by the end of August had already topped the century mark in RBI. The countless hours of infield practice had begun to pay dividends. "Have you been watching big Greenberg around first?" asked Cochrane. "He's the most improved first baseman in the league."[3]

Now, with the season entering the final stretch, Greenberg faced a dilemma: Would it be proper for him, as a Jew, to suit up and play on September 10, which was Rosh Hashanah, the Jewish New Year? Additionally, what about September 19, which was Yom Kippur, the Day of Atonement? According to tradition, Jews were to spend the day in solemn prayer with God, refraining from work, and certainly not cavorting on a baseball diamond. The answer had been relatively easy in 1933; with Detroit buried in fifth place and not much to play for, Greenberg had no qualms about sitting out those two days. This year, with the Yankees breathing down Detroit's neck, it would be more problematic for Greenberg to announce that he was going to take two games off because of his Jewish faith.

In the days leading up to Rosh Hashanah, the debate became a national story. Should he play, or should he pray? Greenberg was hearing it from all corners, some saying he should abide by the tenets of his faith and stay at home, while others argued that the Tigers were in the middle of a pennant race; taking a seat on the bench would hurt the team when it needed him most.

One prominent Detroit rabbi was asked his views. "Mr. Greenberg," he wrote, "who is a conscientious Jew, must decide for himself. From the standpoint of Orthodox Judaism, the fact that ballplaying is his means of living would argue against [playing]. On the other hand, it might be argued quite consistently that his taking part in the game would mean something not only to himself but to his fellow players and, in fact at this time, to the community of Detroit."[4] Greenberg knew that no matter what decision he made, there would be criticism. "I was in a terrible fix."[5]

At Navin Field on September 9, the day before Rosh Hashanah, Greenberg came to bat in the tenth inning of a tie game with the Red Sox. Gehringer was on second, Rogell on first, with one out. Over 28,000 fans erupted as Greenberg laced a single over second, scoring Gehringer. The Tigers had themselves a 5–4 win, with Rowe going the distance for his 22nd victory. Detroit's offense was clicking: The entire lineup, including Rowe, entered the game with plus-.300 batting averages. New York swept a doubleheader over the Browns, so despite the Tigers' victory, their lead was down to four games. Greenberg, Detroit's big gun, was now batting .376 in his last 25 games, with 19 RBI and an on-base plus slugging percentage (OPS) of 1.066.

The Tigers were leaving to Greenberg the decision whether to play on Rosh Hashanah. "Mickey Cochrane told me it was a personal matter that I must handle myself."[6] After a mostly sleepless night in his room at the Detroit Leland Hotel, Greenberg headed down to Shaarey Zedek Synagogue early on the morning of September 10. Immediately afterward, still undecided, he made his way to Navin Field. As game time approached, the Tigers began changing into their uniforms, but Greenberg sat by himself in front of his locker in his street clothes, trying to arrive at a resolution. Finally, just minutes before three o'clock, he announced to Cochrane that he could write his name into the lineup. Hank Greenberg was going to play.

The game turned out to be the signature event of his season. Boston right-hander Dusty Rhodes held Detroit scoreless until Greenberg's seventh-inning solo home run tied the game. The Tigers' slugger wasn't finished. Leading off the ninth, he swung viciously at Rhodes' second pitch and drove the ball on a line over the center-field wall for a 2–1 win. The *Boston Globe* called it "one of the hardest hit balls in the history of Navin Field."[7] It had been an exhausting week for Greenberg, but the victory was worth it. "As Hank crossed the plate to complete his trip around the bases," said the *Detroit Free Press*, "the crowd swarmed around him and thumped him on the back. Hank accepted the congratulations quietly and then walked from the field with his head down. In the 24 hours preceding the game he had waged a terrific battle with himself and he was tired. He wanted to be alone."[8] Elden Auker, who allowed only three hits, got his 13th win, and the Tigers gained a half-game on idle New York.

Peeling off his uniform in the locker room after the game, Greenberg's emotions showed in his words. "I did a lot of praying before the game and I am going to do a lot of it after, but certainly the Good Lord did not let me down today. I was afraid I would be knocked down a couple of times by pitched balls, but once I was in there, I had only one thing to do—keep swinging."[9]

Wrote the *Detroit Jewish Chronicle*, "It was a great day for the Tigers. It was a great day for Henry Greenberg. It was a great day for Detroiters, who got a thrill out of this one-man game by a Jewish boy."[10]

A regular feature of the *Detroit Free Press* sports section was a columnist writing under the byline of "Iffy the Dopester." A civic rooter and unabashed Tigers fan (but also a critical one), Iffy took delight in Greenberg's big game. "I don't know whether Hank Greenberg did anything wrong—I doubt it—in the eyes of the priests of the synagog, but I'm here to testify to the world as a baseball expert that the two hits he made in that ball game were strictly kosher."[11]

Earlier in the month, Frank Navin went before Detroit Mayor Frank Couzens and the City Council to lay forth a plan for the rapid expansion of the Tigers' ballpark. Confident that his team would reach the World Series, Navin knew that additional seating would be necessary in order to accommodate the thousands of ticket requests that had already begun pouring in. With a seating capacity of roughly 30,000, Navin Field was simply too small. The Tigers' owner received permission to close a section of Cherry Street, just beyond the left-field wall, between National and Trumbull Avenues, for the duration of the World Series.

Navin hired local contractor Jerry Utley, a former pitcher for the University of Michigan. Utley's job was to build a massive, temporary wooden bleacher section extending from the left-field corner to the flagpole in deepest center field. The first row of the new stands would begin 20 feet inside the left-field wall, a portion of which would have to be demolished. Slanting steeply upward for 70 rows, and capable of holding 17,000 patrons (at one dollar a head), the bleachers would lie right on top of Cherry Street. At a cost of $25,000, it was a considerable investment for Navin and Briggs. Both, however, were expecting a big return.

Finally, in a meeting in Chicago on September 13, Commissioner Landis gave Navin the thumbs up to begin the process of printing World Series tickets. He also made an official announcement: Should the Tigers win the pennant, the first Series game would take place at Navin Field on October 3.

The same day that Landis uttered his decree, Schoolboy Rowe shut out the Senators in Detroit. Auker pitched nearly as well in a victory two days later; in the series finale, Tommy Bridges did not allow Washington an earned run in notching his 19th win. A furious three-way race for the American League batting title developed between Lou Gehrig, Charlie Gehringer, and the Senators' Heinie Manush. After going only 3-for-16 in Detroit, Manush was batting .354, while Gehringer was at .356, barely behind Gehrig's .358.

With the Tigers 5½ games in front, the Yankees arrived at Navin Field for a four-game set beginning on September 17. New York would need to win at least three to keep its hopes alive. Should the Bronx Bombers sweep, things would suddenly get very interesting. Before the opener, Ruth all but conceded a pennant for Detroit. "I guess the Tigers are in. Nothing but a miracle can stop them now."[12] The Babe, limping badly with what he called a charley horse, would not play in the series, and, in fact, feared he was finished for 1934.

The first game had a World Series atmosphere, as over 36,000 fans squeezed into Navin Field and cheered the Tigers on all afternoon. Acknowledging the contest's importance, the American League dispatched four umpires to the scene, something rarely done in the regular season. A band blared out music between innings, and mounted police kept back the fans ringing the outfield in makeshift stands. The boisterous crowd watched General Crowder, the August waiver-wire pickup, work his magic. He went the distance, striking out five and giving up only six hits, as Detroit beat Lefty Gomez, 3–0. Gehrig and Gehringer both went 2-for-3. When left fielder Goose Goslin caught the final out, a fly ball off the bat of Myril Hoag, he threw it "high into the air to permit a scramble by fans who rushed from the bleachers and the standing sections along the outfield, [and] the crowd let out that long-restrained yelp of victory."[13]

Crowder took particular pleasure in the outcome. After racking up 50 wins the previous two seasons, he got off to a terrible start in 1934. The Senators gave him up for dead, as did nearly every other major league team. Now, however, he was proving to the baseball world that he still had something left in the tank. For the Yankees, this was not how they wanted to open the series. The Tigers' lead stood at 6½ games. Even if New York were to win all of their remaining 11 contests, Detroit could split their final 12 and still win the pennant.

Yankees skipper Joe McCarthy knew it was not over yet. "Certainly we have a chance. A club always has a chance until the standings show that it is mathematically out of it. It was just another ball game. No, you can tell them the Yanks are not down yet."[14]

The *Detroit Times'* Bud Shaver agreed. "Theirs is a forlorn hope, it is true, but not once have the Yankees shown any signs of cracking, although baseball wise-acres have foretold their temperamental collapse a half dozen times this season. The Yankees despite injuries have hung on in a battle with a young, dashing and pennant-mad ball club, and now in the final furlong even the schedule is against them."[15]

Iffy the Dopester, on the other hand, sensed defeat in McCarthy's men. "The Yankees were the ones to proclaim the Tigers champs Monday afternoon at Navin Field. They looked up into the faces of the 35,000 fans who jammed the park and they said as plainly as any Roman gladiator who ever thumbed his nose at an emperor: 'We who are about to die, salute you.'"[16]

New York's bats once again were held in check the following afternoon, this time by Schoolboy Rowe. The Tigers' ace hurled a complete-game, six-hit shutout for his 24th win. In his sterling 1934 season, Rowe had been unbeatable against New York, with five wins, a 1.76 earned run average, and a 0.935 WHIP (walks plus hits divided by innings pitched). Red Ruffing pitched well for the Yankees, but Navin Field erupted in cheers when Greenberg hit his 25th home run in the fourth inning. That was all Detroit needed in the 2–0 victory. Gehrig went 1-for-4, as did Gehringer. "Boy," gushed Billy Rogell, "that World Series dough is sure enough looming up now. You know, I've been kind of afraid to say that out loud until now. I've thought about it plenty. But my share is going right into the old sock for the education of my boys."[17] Iffy the Dopester of the *Detroit Free Press* was on edge all game long. "Of course, I'll admit there were moments when I felt like Frank Navin looks, but Schoolboy Rowe had his Edna ball and he relieved my anxiety often enough so that I didn't freeze solid."[18]

September 19 was Yom Kippur, and Greenberg, at the insistence of his father, did not play. The Tigers missed his offense as they fell, 5–2. It was the only game Greenberg would miss all season. His fill-in, Frank Doljack, singled in three at-bats, but Johnny Murphy stymied the Detroit bats that day. Gehringer and Gehrig both went hitless. Meanwhile, in Cleveland, Heinie Manush went 3-for-5 to overtake Gehringer in the batting race, .356 to .355, with Gehrig still on top at .357.

New York gained a split by taking an 11–7 slugfest in the finale on September 20. Many fans felt the Tigers' loss only served to delay an inevitable pennant for Detroit. Joe McCarthy's Yankees trailed by 5½ games, and the season's final bell had already begun to toll. Gehringer managed only one hit in five trips to the plate, to slip three percentage points behind Gehrig, who went 1-for-3. Babe Ruth did not play in the series, although he took batting practice before the final contest. He drove a few balls beyond the fence, giving early-arriving Tigers fans one final glimpse of the Sultan of Swat.

With their first pennant since 1909 all but a certainty, the Tigers travelled south to St. Louis for four games beginning with a doubleheader on September 22. Indeed, there was nothing like Browns pitching to break a team out of its offensive funk. In the opener, Tommy Bridges became a 20-game winner for the first time in his career, hurling a seven-hitter in an 8–3 victory. It was a moment to savor for Little Tommy. Along with his knee-buckling curveball, he had become one of the best pitchers in the American League on guile and guts. In the second game of the twin bill, Gehringer went 3-for-5, to raise his average to .357, putting him in a dead heat with Gehrig. Goslin went 5-for-5, and the Tigers' bats exploded in a 15–1 laugher. The St. Louis defense fell apart, as only five of the Detroit runs were earned.

After the game, a reporter asked Cochrane which pitcher would get the nod in the first game of the World Series. Black Mike did not hesitate in his answer. "That's easy—Rowe. I don't care who the other manager picks. It may be bad bridge, but it's good baseball to lead your ace and that's what I'm going to do."[19] Not wishing to sound premature, however, Cochrane was quick to add, "If we don't win the pennant, look for me at the bottom of Lake Erie."[20]

In the first game of a doubleheader the next day, Rowe was denied his chance at win number 25, as the Browns pulled out a 4–3 victory. In the second game, General Crowder again showed he was not yet ready for pasture, going the distance and giving up only one run in a 2–1 win. In New York, the Yankees took two from the Red Sox, cutting Detroit's lead to 5½ games.

The Tigers wrapped up the American League championship the following afternoon, September 24. Although Cochrane's men had an open date, the Yankees fell to the Red Sox in the Bronx, 5–0. The unlikely hero of the game for Boston was 24-year-old rookie Spike Merena, who threw a four-hit shutout for his first (and only) big league victory. At approximately five o'clock, and with only 2,000 or so diehards still around to see it, Tony Lazzeri grounded into a 5–4–3 double play to end the game, and the Tigers were officially World Series-bound. The big news of the day, at least for Yankees fans, was the final appearance at the Stadium by Babe Ruth. His departure after 16 seasons in the Bronx was already a foregone conclusion. Still limping badly, Babe started in right field and caught a fly ball in the top of the first that he fortunately did not even have to move on. In the bottom half of the inning, he drew a walk before gingerly hobbling to first base. Unable to carry on, he called for a pinch-runner, exited the field to the cheers of the small crowd, and just that like, the Babe's long and storied career in pinstripes came to a close.

The Tigers, meanwhile, the team that Ruth had almost managed, could do nothing but wait for the result of the game back in Michigan. After its conclusion, a reporter contacted a joyous Cochrane, who said, "Of course I am delighted. But I rather wish we could have clinched it out on the field where we have been fighting all season to win that pennant."[21] Cochrane became only the 12th manager in the history of Major League Baseball to win a championship in his first year at the helm.[22]

Frank Navin, who got wind of the victory while at his club, noted, with his characteristic composure: "I'm glad that's over. Now all we have to do is get ready for the World Series, and I hope we make as good a showing as we have made so far."[23] To mark the clinching of the pennant, Hudson's department store in downtown Detroit unfurled a massive victory banner, "90 feet deep and 60 feet wide," over its main entrance.[24] Six stories in height, it proclaimed "Champions 1934" above a giant smiling tiger. A crowd of thousands snarled traffic on Woodward Avenue in its attempt to catch a glimpse of the huge flag. "We'll win the World Series," a jubilant Cochrane announced. "I've been on four championship clubs, but never have I been so confident of winning the world championship as right now."[25] Of the long, hard pennant fight, Iffy the Dopester wrote in the *Detroit Free Press*, "That [the Tigers] didn't crack under the strain is only due to the genius of Professor Cochrane ... he drove them on with a relentless fury. Nor did he spare himself."[26]

Suddenly, Detroit's offense began clicking again. They pounded White Sox pitchers for 22 runs in a September 26 doubleheader, the Tigers' first appearance at Navin Field since clinching the pennant. Greenberg had one of the best days of his life, with 15 total bases and nine RBI in the two victories. Bridges was roughed up for ten runs in the opener, but Auker pitched well in the second game to capture his 15th win.

The Sox shut out the Tigers in the third and final game of the series, while Schoolboy Rowe surrendered eight runs. Gehringer failed to get a hit, dropping him below Gehrig of the idle Yankees. Finally, Detroit welcomed the Browns to Michigan and Trumbull for a season-ending doubleheader on Sunday, September 30. The bats were alive in the opener, a 10–6 Tigers victory. It was win number 100 for Detroit in 1934, the first time the organization had ever reached the century mark. In the second game of the twin bill, Tommy Bridges won again, his 22nd, to cap the most exciting regular season in Detroit in decades. The only down side was that Gehringer went only 2-for-7 on the day, to wind up second to Gehrig in the AL batting race, .363 to .356.

The hitting star that final day was Jo-Jo White, who collected six hits in the two games, to finish with a batting average of .313. Back in the spring, most everyone figured center field would be the Tigers' weakest link. The platoon of White and Gee Walker, however, had been a pleasant surprise. White's average was hovering in the .270 range at midseason. But Walker played only one game in center after returning from his suspension on August 7, as Cochrane shuffled him between the corner outfield spots. Given the full-time job in center and batting leadoff most days, White went on a tear, hitting .383 in August. He also solidified the defense, making some sparkling plays. White's real name was Joyner, but he had acquired the nickname Jo-Jo because of the way he drawlingly pronounced his home state of Georgia.

His hero growing up was Ty Cobb, who also hailed from the Peach State. The 24-year-old White patterned his style of play after Cobb, perfecting a "kicking" slide aimed at jarring the ball out of an infielder's waiting glove. He was selective enough at the plate to draw 69 walks against only 39 strikeouts, and his speed helped him to steal a team-high 28 bases. White's hustle endeared him to Cochrane and to Tigers fans, and his second-half play was one of the big reasons for Detroit's ascension in the American League.

The 1934 Tigers had one of the best offensive seasons ever. The trio of Greenberg, Goslin, and Gehringer were dubbed the "G-Men," the same nickname as the special agents at the Federal Bureau of Investigation. As a club, Detroit batted a major league-best .300, and their 959 runs also led both circuits by a wide margin (the Yankees were a distant second with 842). They also topped all of baseball in hits, doubles, RBI, stolen bases, and on-base percentage. Their high-octane attack was not predicated solely on the long ball; they only hit 74 home runs, good for fourth in the AL. Greenberg led the team with 26, but nobody else hit more than 13. The excellent defensive infield of Greenberg, Gehringer, Rogell and Owen, known as the "Battalion of Death," combined for 463 RBI. Incredibly, the quartet played every game of the season, the lone exception being when Greenberg sat out Yom Kippur. Outfielders Fox (.285, 101 runs scored, 25 stolen bases) and Walker (.300, 20 steals) also had big years.

Goslin more than justified the trade that brought him to the Motor City; he hit .305, drove in 100 runs, and scored 106.[27] Despite his reputation of thriving at Navin Field, he batted only .279 at home in 1934, compared to .328 on the road.[28]

Cochrane, who hit .320, gave a valuable insight into the philosophy that had made the Tigers a success: "We determined to stick to our course. Your first five hitters in your lineup are your heavy hitters. Why waste them with sacrifices and leave the lower end of the batting order to bring in the runs? We stuck to our system of playing for a big opening in one inning and cleaning up, and we have won a pennant as a result of it."[29] While other players in baseball had better offensive seasons, Cochrane was voted the American League's Most Valuable Player as much for his inspirational leadership as for his bat.

Detroit's four starting pitchers all contributed fine seasons, led by Rowe, who won 24, and Bridges, who totaled 22. Auker was a pleasant surprise in his first full season, winning 15 games, as did the veteran Marberry, who was an effective swingman. Crowder proved to be a valuable pickup, going 5–1 after coming over from Washington in August. In an era of high offense, Detroit's earned run average of 4.06 was second in the AL to New York's 3.76. The Tigers were also second in strikeouts to the Yankees. Indeed, Cochrane had instilled in his men the importance of throwing strikes: Detroit issued the fewest bases on balls in the junior circuit.

Physical aches and pains are part of the grind of a long baseball season. The team that does not lose key players for extended periods considers itself extremely fortunate. That was the case with the 1934 Tigers, whose roster remained intact throughout the season. Good fortune aside, Detroit's winning campaign was not a mere fluke. In the words of sportswriter Shirley Povich, "Mickey Cochrane had the kind of team that helped to make its own breaks. He had the kind of team that is always characteristic of the pennant winner—hustling, smart, powerful."[30] Nevertheless, 1934 was a grueling ordeal for Cochrane, mainly because of the torture his body endured. By his own account, he hurt his left ankle early in the season, and it never fully recovered. By the end of the summer, his arms and legs were covered in bumps, bruises and cuts sustained while sliding into bases, or from the innumerable foul balls that ricocheted off his body. With all the squatting endured in his ten years as a major league catcher, his knees and ankles resembled those of an old man. Moreover, Cochrane's personality did not allow him to relax all season long; by the end, he was emotionally exhausted.

With 101 victories, the Tigers won the American League pennant by seven games over New York. Without question, the turning point in the season for both clubs was July 14, at Navin Field, when Detroit scored four runs in the ninth inning to beat the Yankees, 12–11. Instead of suffering a loss that would have dropped them further into second place, the win catapulted the Tigers into the top spot, and they never relinquished it the rest of the season. It was a defining moment for the team, proving to the baseball world that they were just as good as Ruth, Gehrig, and the rest of the Yankees, maybe even better. At the season's conclusion, one writer called the Tigers "phenomena, bordering on the miraculous."[31]

Despite playing in tiny Navin Field, Detroit led the major leagues in attendance in 1934, with 919,161. Considering the bad economic times, it was a testament to just how much the Motor City loved its Tigers. In the *Detroit Free Press*, Iffy the Dopester applauded the newly minted champions, setting the stage for the team's first trip to the World Series since 1909:

> This is the big, the outstanding thing. We have won the American League pennant. And all the rest is frosting to the cake, the parsley to the fish, the feather on the hat, the sauce to the meat. And even if the lads had not won the pennant it would not have mattered greatly. As far as we are concerned 'twas all for the sport of the thing. It has made us forget our troubles, it has cleansed our souls with the joy of laughter, it has been a recess from our woes, a surcease from our worries…. Detroit will remain as it is, the dynamic city of the unsalted seas.[32]

Chapter Ten

Heartbreak and Garbage

Back in January, a group of reporters had huddled around New York Giants player-manager Bill Terry at the team's annual business meeting. In a relaxed, bantering style, Terry gave his impressions of the senior circuit's contenders for the upcoming 1934 season. Someone asked him what he thought of the Brooklyn Dodgers. Looking nonplussed, Terry replied, "Brooklyn? Haven't heard much about them lately. Is Brooklyn still in the league?"[1] The flippant comment would come back to haunt Terry and his team.

For much of the summer, it looked like the Giants were once again the best squad in the National League. With batting stars Terry, Mel Ott, Travis Jackson, and Jo-Jo Moore, along with Carl Hubbell and Hal Schumacher on the hill, they were the odds-on favorite to win their second consecutive World Series. By early September, the poised and experienced Giants had built a seven-game lead over the St. Louis Cardinals.

Then New York suddenly went into a swoon. By the time they faced off with Brooklyn for a season-ending, two-game set, the Giants had fallen into a tie for first with streaking St. Louis. Dodgers fans, having waited all year for revenge for what they perceived as Terry's disrespect, invaded the Polo Grounds *en masse*, eager to root on their Bums. Brooklyn won both games, proving to Terry that they were, in fact, still in the League. The Cardinals, meanwhile, took two in a row from Cincinnati to capture the pennant in improbable fashion.

Today, we remember the 1934 St. Louis Cardinals as the "Gas House Gang." While baseball historians cannot agree on exactly when the team picked up the moniker (or who initially bestowed it upon them), it is nevertheless a fitting one, indicative of their rowdy, take-no-prisoners attitude toward the game. When America was looking for heroes in the midst of the Depression, the Gas House Gang provided picturesque characters who were also exceptional talents on the field. Assembled by their Bible-quoting, cigar-chomping general manager, Branch Rickey, they were, like the Tigers, a mix of veterans and youngsters who possessed that often cited but hard-to-define quality called "chemistry."

Dizzy Dean was the Cardinals' answer to Schoolboy Rowe (although fans in St. Louis no doubt believed that Rowe was the Tigers' answer to Dean). Both were 24 years old, grew up in Arkansas, had blazing fastballs, and possessed charismatic personalities. No two pitchers shined brighter than Rowe and Dean in 1934. The latter won 30 games and led the league in strikeouts

There were no two bigger pitching stars in 1934 than Schoolboy Rowe and the St. Louis Cardinals' Dizzy Dean, seen here at that year's World Series (courtesy Ernie Harwell Sports Collection, Detroit Public Library).

for the third straight season. Was he the best hurler in the game? He sure thought so; all you had to do was ask him. Such swagger came naturally to Dizzy. "It ain't braggin' if you can back it up," was perhaps his most enduring *bon mot.*

Dizzy's younger brother, Paul, was also on the St. Louis starting staff. Back in spring training, before Paul had ever thrown a pitch in a big-league game, the brash Dizzy boasted, "How are they going to stop us? Paul's going to be a sensation. He'll win 18 or 20 games. I'll count 20 to 25 myself."[2] Dizzy turned out to be a prophet, as Paul won 19. Unlike his voluble brother, Paul never said much, which led sportswriters to wonder how two such radically different apples could have fallen from the same tree. Searching for a sobriquet for Paul, the scribes settled on Daffy, mostly because it sounded similar to Dizzy. Paul, understandably, did not appreciate the nickname. Hungry for copy, sportswriters ate up the Deans. Iffy the Dopester, however, was not buying into all the flimflam just yet. "If [the Deans] were sports writers, or lawyers or doctors or truck drivers or peanut vendors their oddities would not attract any attention. But when a fellow can get a four-column cut of himself on any sport page because he caught a ball or hit one or did something else with it, why naturally he is of such importance that every time he kisses his wife, or fails to, it takes on a national—if not worldwide—significance."[3]

Frankie Frisch was in his first full campaign as manager of the club, having taken over midway through the 1933 season. Frisch, who was also the team's second baseman, was a 16-year veteran with a lifetime .319 batting average with the Giants and Cardinals. Like Cochrane, he was extremely energetic, with a fiery, competitive streak that rubbed off on his players. He had attended Fordham University, where he excelled as a track star and majored in Chemistry (hence, his nickname, the "Fordham Flash"). He also showed early on to be a fine leader of men, captaining the football, basketball, and baseball teams.

The biggest cog in the St. Louis offense was slugging first baseman "Ripper" Collins, who topped the National League in 1934 in both home runs and practical jokes. Twenty-two-year-old Joe Medwick walked like a duck, but did not hit like one. "Ducky" banged out 40 doubles, 18 triples, drove in 106 runs, and averaged .319 in 1934. The Cards could manufacture runs like no other team. At third base was Pepper Martin, "The Wild Horse of the Osage," who could hit for average and was one of the best baserunners in the game. Frisch's double-play partner was 28-year-old Leo Durocher. The Massachusetts native did not carry much of a bat. Babe Ruth, in fact, once called him "The All-American Out." He was, nevertheless, a cocky, scrappy player who refused to back down from a challenge. Durocher was "Old School" before there was "Old School." Nicknamed "The Lip," he was an irrepressible chatterbox on the field. Off it, he was a playboy who appreciated the perks that came with being a professional athlete. He was also a hustler who never met a rule he didn't break.

"It's the gamest team I ever saw," remarked Frisch of his Cardinals. "The gamest, best bunch of fighters that ever won a league title."[4] On paper, the teams matched up evenly, although the Cardinals possessed the experience that could swing things in their favor. Cochrane and Frisch were intelligent, forward-thinking skippers and excellent strategists. It promised to be one of the most colorful World Series in many a year.

A festive crowd of 42,505 braved the cold and wind for Game One at Navin Field on Thursday, October 3. Among the luminaries in attendance were Mr. and Mrs. Henry Ford, humorist Will Rogers, comedian Joe E. Brown, and Hollywood actor George Raft. Babe Ruth, in the press box taking notes for his nationally syndicated World Series column, could be forgiven for casting a wistful eye down on the field below and regretting that it was not *him* managing the Tigers. The Babe also had some unfinished financial business: In the spring, he had laid a $100 wager with Goslin that he would outhit the Goose in 1934. Ruth finished with an average of .288 to Goslin's .305. During batting practice, The Sultan of Swat went down to present Goose with a check.

Gathering with reporters at the stately Book-Cadillac Hotel before the game, baseball Commissioner Kenesaw Mountain Landis declared succinctly, "It'll be a fire-eating series. That's enough for me to say."[5] Iffy the Dopester was not making any predictions: "So, who's going to win the World Series? And I say right back: I don't know and neither does anybody else."[6]

Also taking in the game were five members of the 1909 Detroit team, the last group to reach the Series: Donie Bush, Davy Jones, George Moriarty, Charles O'Leary, and Oscar Stanage. Navin Field appeared different from just a few days ago; the recently built bleachers in left field had necessitated the scoreboard's relocation to right. In batting practice, Greenberg delighted the early arrivals by blasting three balls into the new section.

It was the hottest ticket in town. Box seats sold for $6.60 a pop (roughly $118 in 2017), grandstands for $5.50. A general admission entry cost $3.30, while bleachers were a relative bargain at $1.10 (all figures included federal tax). The night before the game, an army of die-hard Tigers fans began forming a line that snaked all the way around the stadium, in hopes of grabbing tickets when the bleacher windows opened in the morning.

In a deal brokered by Commissioner Landis, the Ford Motor Company agreed to pay $100,000 to sponsor the radio broadcasts over the NBC and CBS networks. That meant a bigger financial windfall for the players.[7] Not everybody was happy with the arrangement, however, specifically newspaper editors across the country, who felt that Landis had turned baseball's grandest stage into a commercial. The Tigers were proving to be a popular team nationally, which heightened interest in the Series. Just before the opening, Cochrane appeared on the cover of *Time* magazine. The article was full of praise for the skipper. "Cochrane's arrival in Detroit coincided roughly with the revival of the automobile industry and the first signs of revived prosperity. His determined jolly face soon came to represent the picture of what a dynamic Detroiter ought to look like."[8]

Dizzy Dean was manager Frisch's obvious choice to start for St. Louis. The pitcher spent a charming morning at the home of Henry Ford and was in a fine humor. As he took a few swings in the cage before the game, a bat flew out of his hands and nearly hit a photographer on the head. "I can't afford to cripple one of those boys," he drawled. "They're my best friends."[9]

Cochrane's lineup did not have any surprises. White was the leadoff hitter, playing center, followed by Cochrane, Gehringer, Greenberg, Goslin in left, Rogell, Owen, and Fox in right. He insisted there would be no more outfield platooning; Walker and Doljack would be reserves. "That's the club that won the pennant and if the boys were good enough to do that, they're good enough to win the World's Series."[10]

The start of the contest was delayed about 20 minutes to allow the bottlenecked throng to squeeze its way into the main entrance at Michigan and Trumbull. As a result, both starting pitchers had to warm up twice. The big news was that Cochrane, despite his earlier assertion that he would begin the Series with Rowe, instead went with Crowder, who had World Series experience. Perhaps Cochrane was taking a cue from Connie Mack, his former Athletics manager, who started the seldom-used, 35-year-old Howard Ehmke in Game One of the 1929 Series. Defying the naysayers, Ehmke fanned thirteen in a 3–1 Philadelphia win over the Cubs.

Crowder was no Ehmke on this day, but he pitched solidly. The problem was the Tigers' infield; noticeably jittery, it made an error in the first, two in the second, and two more in the third. By that time, St. Louis had staked Dizzy Dean to a 3–0 lead. True to their reputation, the Cardinals exhibited smart, aggressive baserunning. In particular, Ernie Orsatti set the tone early when his hard slide into second knocked the ball out of Gehringer's glove on a potential force play. The Tigers' sloppy defense came as a surprise; as a team, Detroit had committed the fewest errors in the American League (156), and tied the Senators for the highest fielding percentage (.974). Pitching on only two days of rest, Dean's command was not sharp in the early innings. The Tigers tried to capitalize by taking him deep in counts, but Dean grew stronger as the game went along.

It would be unfair to say that Cochrane's decision to go with Crowder over Rowe had backfired. Crowder's defense had simply let him down. Of the four tallies he was charged with, only Medwick's homer in the fifth was earned. Behind 4–1 and needing baserunners, Cochrane was forced to pinch-hit for Crowder in the fifth inning. Firpo Marberry came on in relief in the sixth, but Dean, the first batter he faced, stroked a double, and St. Louis quickly plated four runs to break the game open. The final was Cardinals 8, Tigers 3. Greenberg hit the Tigers' only home run, a solo shot in the eighth. With better defense, the day's storyline may have been decidedly different. "The Tigers' crack infield cracked wide open here this afternoon," wrote the *Detroit Times'* Bud Shaver, "kicking away whatever chance Alvin [General] Crowder had of beating the Cardinals' pitching ace, Dizzy Dean."[11]

This was St. Louis's fifth trip to the World Series in nine years, while the Tigers had played like a gaggle of greenhorns. The Cardinals, Dean and Durocher in particular, hurled endless invective at the Detroit bench all game long. Greenberg's religion made him a primary target. If the goal had been to rattle the Tigers, St. Louis was successful. Cochrane, while not pleased with the score, refused to second-guess his decision to go with Crowder. "It's gone. Tomorrow's another day."[12]

Dean went the distance for the win, despite what he called his "lousy" pitching.[13] He was not far off in his self-assessment. Laboring all afternoon, he fell behind in the count to 12 of the 36 batters he faced. In an era when starting pitchers expected to finish what they started, Dean threw 150 pitches by one count, "altogether too much for even a youthful arm," said the *St. Louis Post-Dispatch*.[14] That total included 34 called strikes, 41 swings and misses, 22 fouls, and 53 balls, hardly an efficient tally. He walked only two, suggesting the Tigers had been done in by their own impatience at the plate. Journalist Westbrook Pegler penned as wonderful a description of Dizzy on the mound as we are likely to find:

> He was slinging the ball at the Tigers as though every man of them had done him some great personal wrong. You should see Brother Diz pitch one of his good ones sometime. He is big and full of bone and side-meat without a morsel of fat in his carcass and he can fling the ball so fast it seems to climb over itself in the rush. It takes sudden crazy shoots which are so sharp and wide that even the customers can see the breaks and it is plain that he gets a joyous emotional let-go when the ball obeys him well. He has a habit of tucking his glove under his right fin after each hitter has had his dose, to hitch up his pants with one hand and reach inside with the other and stuff his shirt-tail down. He throws so hard that the force of each pitch bows him low. The

scarlet beak of his cap almost grazes the dust, his right leg comes up waving above his head and it always takes him some time to sort himself out for the next throw.

Pegler's next words were eerily prescient, to a degree: "Brother Dizzy sums up as quite a pitcher at this writing, although another year or two may find him poor and forgotten with his arm squandered and his living gone."[15]

Perhaps channeling Ring Lardner's Jack Keefe character of literary fame, Iffy the Dopester complained that Dean was ... well, *fortunate.* "This Dizzy Dean person is a lucky stiff. He didn't have a thing but a fast ball, a change of pace and good control. And he was lucky in putting the ball just where he wanted to all through the game—nice and low, just above the old knee caps. The lucky stiff!"[16]

At the conclusion of the game, Branch Rickey wired to congratulate Dean and to invite him to a get-together the following night. Dizzy hurried off a reply: "Many, many thanks. This American League is a pushover. Breezed through today with nothing but my glove. Tell everybody hello. Henry Ford will be my guest in St. Louis on Friday. Cook a good meal for all of us—sandwiches and everything. Will Rogers and Joe E. Brown coming too. Thanks again. Dizzy Dean."[17]

For Tigers fans, hope had given way to gloom. Wrote Jack Weeks of the *Detroit News,* "Corktown, thrust suddenly into the very center of the sporting world's attention, lived through an aeon Wednesday afternoon, experiencing in a few hours joy, sorrow, triumph, defeat, hope and finally despair."[18]

The night of his Game One victory, Dean made a radio appearance (sponsored by Grape-Nuts) in which he conversed across the continents with Rear Admiral Richard Byrd. Byrd at the time was manning a meteorological station in Antarctica. The Cardinals' pitcher, at ease with princes and paupers, hailed the famous explorer with a "Howdy there Dick Byrd down at the South Pole!"[19] Dean commenced to explaining to Byrd how he had won the game, even though he was not in his "usual shutout form."[20] The Tigers, he insisted, were not worthy competition. "I just staggered through without a thing on the ball. I'd be tickled to death if they'd let me pitch the second game. I'd have my stuff back and probably shut the Tigers out."[21]

Game Two was pivotal; Detroit did not want to fall into such a deep hole heading into St. Louis. The 43,451 fans in attendance hoped Schoolboy Rowe could deliver in a big way. While he was warming up, Dean waltzed over to stand behind him and offer advice on how to pitch to the Cardinals. When Cochrane complained about Dizzy's antics, the latter made his way to the Tigers' dugout, picked up a couple of bats, and headed across the field to the visitors' bench. "You fellows don't know what bats are for, anyways," Dean blurted.[22]

Rowe got off to a shaky start. The Cardinals mocked him from the dugout with a constant bark of "How'm I doin,' Edna?" With one out in the second, St. Louis catcher Bill DeLancey hit a grounder that scooted past the pitcher. The ball then bounced off the shin of Gehringer, who made a valiant effort to come up with it behind second but was unable to make a play. On Rowe's next pitch, Ernie Orsatti sent one high to left field between Goslin and the foul line. It kept carrying away from the Goose and landed in the corner for a run-scoring triple. Rowe bore down and got Durocher to pop out to Greenberg at first, and right fielder Pete Fox caught Bill Hallahan's low liner for the third out.

The next inning, Pepper Martin worked Rowe for a three-two count. Rather than walk the leadoff man, Rowe grooved one down the middle, and Martin banged it over second base for a single. Jack Rothrock bunted him over, and one out later, Medwick sent Rowe's first pitch on a line to left. Goslin charged the ball on one hop as Martin rounded third; his throw was wide of the plate and Martin scored, with Medwick taking second. Up next was Ripper Collins, who stroked another single to left, but this time Goslin's throw was on the money. Cochrane, blocking the plate, caught the ball with time to spare. Medwick's hard slide sent Cochrane spinning, but the catcher held on to the ball, and umpire Bill Klem called the runner out. The two clutch plays by Goslin and Cochrane saved Rowe; instead of Detroit being down by three, the score remained 2–0. Cochrane sustained a spike wound, but he remained in the game.

On the mound for the Cardinals was 31-year-old portsider William Anthony "Wild Bill" Hallahan. He threw hard, but had led the league in walks three times, befitting his nickname. Pitching in his fourth World Series with the Cardinals, he was three years removed from a 19-win season. Hallahan struggled in 1934, with only eight victories and a 4.26 earned run average. He pitched great down the stretch run, however, and Frisch valued his experience. Hallahan cruised through the first three innings, when controversy reared its head in the bottom of the fourth.

Goslin led off the frame by grounding out. Rogell lifted a high fly to center field, which, on a normal afternoon, would have been a sure out. But Orsatti was fighting the strong wind blowing in all day from the east. Misjudging the ball, he dove for it at the last second, but it dropped for a double. Orsatti's sunglasses shattered when his head banged into the turf; his eyes were spared damage from the flying bits of glass, but he sustained a cut just above his left cheek. Marv Owen then grounded to second, with Rogell scampering over to third. That left it up to Fox, who was hitless so far in the Series. The right-handed batter pulled a hard drive down the line, which third-base umpire Brick Owens called fair. While the ball rolled around in the corner, Rogell raced home, with Fox making it to second.

The Cardinals swarmed around Owens, arguing long and loudly that it was a foul ball. The call stood, however, and Rowe struck out to end the inning. It settled into a pitchers' duel from then on. The Cardinals could do nothing against Rowe. Detroit's best chance to tie it came in the sixth, when leadoff batter Rogell reached second on a throwing error, but he never scored.

With the Tigers down 2–1 in the bottom of the ninth, Fox opened with a single to right. It was only the fifth hit off Hallahan, who appeared to be tiring. Cochrane faced his most critical decision of the Series so far, if not of the entire season. Rowe was due to bat next. Should the manager yank his starter and send up a pinch-hitter? Rowe, of course, was a great hitter, but had not been able to do anything against Hallahan all afternoon. To take him out of the game at this point was a big risk, given the way he was pitching. Cochrane sent him up to the plate but took the bat out of his hands, calling for a bunt. Schoolboy laid down a beauty; Hallahan fielded it and threw to first for the sure out. Fox stood on second, the tying run.

The next scheduled batter was Jo-Jo White, who also was hitless off Hallahan, but this time Cochrane was not going to take any chances. He sent up pinch-hitter Gee Walker, who promptly popped one up between first base and home plate, near the line. In a classic case of "I–Got-It-You-Take-It," catcher DeLancey and first baseman Collins let the ball drop in fair territory between them, while Walker, racing down the line, made it to first. The ball took one bounce, however, and landed in foul territory; Walker had to return to the batter's box to continue the at-bat.

Hallahan was incensed with DeLancey and Collins, and showed it. After the game, Collins claimed he had lost the ball when some fan flashed a mirror in his eyes. The perpetrator, he argued, was sitting in a third-floor window of a garage beyond right field, across Trumbull Avenue. Collins was not the only witness to the flashing: Charles Navin, the Tigers' secretary (and nephew of Frank), vouched that "all during the last four innings the fellow was at work with that mirror. I spoke to several persons about it. It's a dirty shame that anyone would do a thing like that."[23] Whoever it was, he was an equal-opportunity flasher; Cochrane attested that he had gotten it in the eyes a few times himself.

Blessed with new life, Walker roped a single to center, and Fox flew home with the tying run. That was all for Hallahan, who was still peeved at the turn of events. He gave way to lefty Bill Walker, the former New York Giants star. A lengthy confab at the mound ensued between Frisch, Walker, and his infielders. Quite possibly, they discussed Gee Walker at first and his history of base-running blunders. Whatever the case, Walker the pitcher kept a close eye on Walker the runner. After the usual cat-and-mouse, Gee Walker bolted for second before Bill Walker had started his windup. The pitcher tossed the ball to Collins at first, a rundown resulted, and Frisch easily put the tag on Walker. Among the collective groans at Navin Field, none was more doleful than Cochrane's, who saw the entire play unfold from the vantage of the batter's box. Cochrane fanned for the third out, and when the Tigers trotted to their positions to start the tenth, Gee Walker was nowhere to be seen. Frank Doljack, he of the .233 batting average, had unceremoniously replaced him in center field.

Gehringer reached on an error to lead off the bottom of the tenth. Two outs later, he stole second, but was stranded when Owen lined out to center. The Cardinals, whose bats had been stymied, finally managed a hit off Rowe when Pepper Martin hit a one-out double in the 11th. Before the hit, Schoolboy had retired 22 consecutive batters, but now he would have to reach back for something extra with the game, and perhaps the Series, on the line. He struck out Rothrock and induced Frisch to hit a grounder to second. The game remained deadlocked.

With one out in the bottom of the 12th, Walker suddenly could not find the strike zone, issuing free passes to Gehringer and Greenberg. The crowd was ready to explode with anticipation. Goslin, the battle-tested veteran brought to Detroit for moments just like this, came to the plate. He took a mighty cut, roping one into center field; Gehringer galloped home, and the Tigers won the thrilling affair. Rowe, who went the distance, could not have pitched any better. He seemingly grew stronger with each passing inning: Of his seven strikeouts, five came in the final four frames. He did not walk a batter all afternoon. It was, in the opinion of Bud Shaver, "one of the grimmest mound struggles in the history of the World Series."[24]

For St. Louis, the loss stung. They stormed off the field and into the visitor's locker room, which Frisch barred from reporters until his men had finished violently throwing their equipment around in anger. "It was just a tough one to lose," he spat afterward. "And you can't take anything away from Schoolboy Rowe, he pitched a great game. Our defense was not what it should have been."[25] Hallahan was particularly bitter. "Ain't that brutal. There you have a game won, and what happens. But there's nothing you can do about it now. It's just baseball, I guess."[26]

It was a stark contrast to the Detroit clubhouse, which was full of back-slapping and whoops of joy after the hard-fought victory. "So we couldn't beat them, eh?" asked a jubilant Rowe. "Well, we did, didn't we? For the first

Goose Goslin (right) shows Mickey Cochrane the bat that drove in the winning run in the 12th inning of Game Two of the 1934 World Series (courtesy Ernie Harwell Sports Collection, Detroit Public Library).

few innings, I felt there was something funny inside of me. I didn't feel right. Mind you, I wasn't scared. I've never been scared in my life. But after I got over that third inning, I had every confidence that we would win."[27] Rowe admitted to pitching the entire game with a sore arm. Still, he added, nothing would have kept him from the mound that day.

"Rowe's exhibition in the last nine," wrote Herman Wecke in the *St. Louis Post-Dispatch*, "was one of the finest exhibited in the World Series in many years."[28] Sportswriter Alan Gould lent further perspective: "Lynwood [Schoolboy] Rowe stands today alongside the pitching giants of World Series history, towering as mightily and casting as big a shadow now across the chances of the St. Louis Cardinals as Jerome [Dizzy] Dean did in his jungletown debut two days ago."[29] Paul Gallico summed up the moment: "This fellow named Lynwood Rowe and nicknamed Schoolboy took that pitching hill as a boy, and, unless I miss my guess, he walked off it a man."[30]

Immediately after the game, both teams made their way down to Union Station on Fort Street. Awaiting them were six gleaming trains designated "Tigers Special," "Cardinals Special," "Rooters' Special," "Sportswriters' Special," "Chamber of Commerce Special," and "Coach Passengers." Thousands of gleeful, exuberant well-wishers packed the platform to see off their heroes. At precisely eight p.m., the "Cardinals' Special" was the first of the cars to roll down the tracks, heading southwest to St. Louis for a highly anticipated Game Three.

⚾ ⚾ ⚾

With the Cardinals' Paul Dean facing off against Tommy Bridges, the 34,000-plus at Sportsman's Park anticipated a close pitching duel. It was a picture-perfect afternoon for baseball, shirtsleeve weather in the parlance of the day. Paul Dean pitched even better than his big brother had two days earlier. Setting the tone in the first inning, Daffy buzzed Cochrane with an inside fastball that sent the Tigers' catcher sprawling in the dust. If it was a purpose pitch, it did the trick: Detroit's batters looked tight throughout. The Cardinals struck immediately in the first, on a leadoff triple off the bat of Pepper Martin and a sacrifice fly by Rothrock. At the plate, Dean helped his own cause with a sacrifice fly in the second to make the score 2–0.

The Tigers had their share of runners. Through the first six innings, they left a whopping 12 men on base. In the tight spots, however, Dean made the right pitches and took advantage of the anxiousness of Detroit's hitters.

Bridges didn't have his best game and was pulled with nobody out in the fifth following a leadoff double by Martin, a triple by Rothrock, and a single by Frisch, making it 4–0. The Tigers' only run of the game came in the ninth, when Greenberg's triple with two down scored Jo-Jo White. For Detroit, it was a game of lost opportunities: They were 0-for-10 with runners in scoring position and left 13 men stranded. Performances like that are bad enough, but are even more demoralizing when they put you down two games to one in a World Series. It was an impressive feat of pitching by Dean, whose poise belied his 21 years. His catcher, DeLancey, himself only 22, called a great game.

After the win, Frisch taped a poster on the Cardinals' clubhouse door with the words, "They cannot beat us." When asked about it by a reporter, the manager shouted, "Boy, they ain't going to do it, either!"[31] Even though he threw 155 pitches, Paul Dean maintained that the Tigers had not given him much trouble.

Cochrane's spike wound on his leg, a result of Medwick's hard slide in Game Two, by now was inflamed and swollen. Two multi-colored, grapefruit-sized bruises had also appeared alongside it. Trainer Denny Carroll insisted, however, that the skipper would be okay for Game Four. Cochrane seemed more frustrated at his team's offensive struggles that afternoon. "You can't win without runs," he sighed.[32] Bob Murphy in the *Detroit Times* marveled at Cochrane's fortitude. "Not a word has been uttered by Cochrane as to the great physical handicap under which he is playing this World Series. This Tiger manager is from the mould which never complains, but plunges doggedly and gallantly ahead."[33]

Schoolboy Rowe, in a ghostwritten newspaper column the next afternoon, opined, "I'm glad the Deans aren't triplets, or better."[34]

⚾ ⚾ ⚾

Before the next morning, word got out that Cardinals president Sam Breadon had ordered a police escort to keep an eye on Dizzy Dean. After Game Three ended, Breadon had spotted Dean getting into an automobile bearing New York license plates. In an odd leap of logic, Breadon figured it might be the car of a kidnapper, and he quickly sent someone over to order Dean out of the vehicle. The pitcher protested that the auto belonged to a couple of fans who had volunteered to drive him home. Nevertheless, Breadon could not unburden himself of his peculiar notion: Someone *might* try to kidnap his most valuable commodity. As a precaution, two of St. Louis's finest followed Dean's every move that evening and kept a sentry over him while he slept.

Cochrane, meanwhile, was correct when he said the Tigers were not hitting. As a team, they were batting only .207 in the three games. Culprits included Cochrane himself, at .091 with no runs scored or driven in. Leadoff man Jo-Jo White was not much better at .182. Marv Owen was hitless. Greenberg, the club's cleanup hitter since early September, looked like he was feeling the pressure. Despite his triple in the ninth inning of Game Three, he was not having a good Series, going 1-for-9 with men on base. Cochrane decided to drop Greenberg down to the sixth spot in the order for Game Four, hoping to relieve him of some of the pressure. Goslin, batting .357 in the Series, would take over the cleanup position, and Rogell moved up a notch to fifth.

For the fourth consecutive game, St. Louis scored first. In the second inning, the Cardinals loaded the bases with nobody out against Elden Auker. But the submariner escaped potential disaster, giving up only one run. It would be a battle the rest of the afternoon for Auker, whose sinker wasn't sinking and curve ball wasn't breaking. He would have to depend more on his fastball, which was not his normal *modus operandi*.

Facing 16-game-winner Tex Carleton, another side-arming right-hander,

Auker led off the third with a bid for his first career home run. His long smash drove Orsatti to the base of the wall in right-center field, where he finally hauled it in. Then, after a Jo-Jo White strikeout, Carleton suddenly lost it. Cochrane doubled. Gehringer and Goslin both drew walks to load the bases. Rogell, who had struck out earlier in the game, followed with a single to center, which scored two runs and sent Goslin to third.

Frisch, deciding to cut his losses, yanked Carleton. He brought in the 43-year-old right-hander Dazzy Vance. In his heyday with the mediocre Brooklyn Robins, Vance was one of the fastest pitchers in the game, a three-time 20-game winner who led the league in strikeouts seven times. The only thing missing on his resume was a World Series appearance. Now that he had it, he faced the unenviable task of pitching to Greenberg. The Tigers' slugger got fooled on an outside pitch, hitting a slow roller to the right side. He beat it out for an RBI single; just like that, the Tigers had a 3–1 lead.

Auker ran into trouble in the third inning. He quickly retired the first two batters, but a single, a walk, and another single produced a run to pull St. Louis to within one. Detroit answered right back in the top of the fourth, without the benefit of a hit. After drawing a one-out walk, Jo-Jo White attempted to steal second. Catcher DeLancey's throw sailed into the outfield, and White tried to make it to third. Orsatti, playing a shallow center, retrieved the ball and threw a peg to third that had White dead to rights. Pepper Martin dropped the ball, however, and White was safe. He scored soon after when Vance threw a wild pitch, making it 4–2 Tigers.

Auker hit another bump in the road in the bottom of the fourth. Orsatti led off with a single. Durocher grounded to Owen at third, who threw down to Gehringer to get a force and possibly a double play. But Orsatti slid hard into the bag, and Gehringer dropped the ball as he hit the ground. The official scorer charged the Tigers' second baseman with an error, and the Cardinals had runners on first and second with none out. Spud Davis, pinch-hitting for Vance, blooped a single to right, scoring Orsatti and sending Durocher to third. With the score 4–3 in favor of the Tigers, St. Louis had a chance to do even more damage.

At that point, Frisch rapidly scanned the bench for a man who could run for the lumbering Davis at first. He sent in Dizzy Dean (some accounts claimed that Dean volunteered for the duty), to the delight of the home crowd, which let out its biggest roar of the day. The move, while unusual (not to mention risky), was not unprecedented. In his career so far, Dean had pinch-run five times. He was, in fact, one of the speediest runners on the Cardinals, which was saying a lot. Either way, the fans loved it, and as Dean reached first and patted the departing Davis on the back, the cheers began anew.

What followed remains one of the most bizarre plays in World Series history. Pepper Martin hit a sharp grounder to Gehringer, who scooped the ball and flipped it over to Rogell to get the force. Dean, high-stepping it to second, jumped up in the air as he approached Rogell, rather than attempting to slide. Rogell's strong relay struck Dean right smack on the forehead. The ball ricocheted high into the outfield, while Dean dropped as if he had been shot. Second-base umpire Bill Klem called him out. Durocher scored on the play, tying the game, but a sudden hush fell over Sportsman's Park. Dean lay sprawled on the ground near second base, "out as cold as a mackerel,"[35] in the words of John Drebinger, as teammates (and Tigers) gathered round to check on the status of the world's most famous pitcher.

Dean revived slightly, although not enough to walk off the field on his own power, much less remain in the game. "As (Dean) was being lugged off the field in the arms of his brother and other comrades," wrote J. Roy Stockton in the *St. Louis Post-Dispatch*, "it was easy to see the Cardinals' championship chances vanishing with the bearers and their burden."[36] Sportswriter Damon Runyon quipped that the Cardinals "handled [Dean] as gently as if he were a sack of eggs."[37] The uncertainty regarding their star pitcher cast a gloom over the Cardinals and popped their rally balloon. Auker retired Rothrock on a short fly to left, and Frisch grounded into a force to end the frame. Meanwhile, Dean was rushed to St. John's Hospital.

The game remained tied until the top of the seventh. Bill Walker gave up a leadoff single to Gehringer, and Goslin bunted him to second. Rogell followed with a ground ball right to Durocher at short. Gehringer, instead of holding at second to see if the ball would make it through the infield, motored down to third at the crack of the bat. It was a rare mental mistake for The Mechanical Man, and he would have been hung out to dry at third, but Martin dropped Durocher's throw, his third miscue of the afternoon. It gave the Tigers runners at the corners with one out.

That brought up Greenberg, who drove a long fly ball to center. Tracking it, Orsatti reached out his glove, but he could not hold on to the ball; Greenberg cruised into second with what was ruled a double. Gehringer scored, and Rogell took third. Walker pitched out of the jam, however, and Detroit had to settle for a one-run lead.

By that time, an announcement was made that Dean had not suffered any serious harm; this tidbit brought another loud cheer from the crowd. The close, exciting game was broken open by Detroit in the eighth. The big blow was Rogell's bases-loaded, two-run single. Greenberg hit a ground-rule double that just missed being a home run, and later swiped home on the front end of a double steal. Indeed, it was a game of redemption for the man they called "Hammerin' Hank," who went 4-for-5 with two doubles, three RBI, and a run scored. Auker settled down and went the distance in the 10–4 victory.

St. Louis played sloppy baseball, making five errors and using five pitchers, none of whom was effective. Frisch felt the Cardinals had played like a sandlot team. Reporters demanded to know why he used Dean as a runner, risking serious injury when he had other position players, most notably the fleet-footed Burgess Whitehead, on the bench. Frisch insisted it was a wise move, given Dean's speed. "This sort of accident will not happen once in the next 20,000 times, if at all," he added, an estimate that seemed like little consolation.[38] Cochrane liked his team's chances to go all the way, now that his bats seemed to have woken up. "We're off now. The Cards won't win another game."[39]

For the *Detroit Free Press*, Iffy the Dopester wrote, "They beat better ball clubs in the American League because they out-nerved them. If they win the World Series—and psychologically they now have better than an even chance—it will be the old story all over again—beating a better ball club because they didn't quit even though they did stagger under a new kind of fire."[40]

Dean was asked how he felt after the game. "You can't hurt me, hitting me in the head," he affirmed. "I never knew I was hit until I woke up on the ground. I didn't see the throw start. All I saw was a lot of stars and moons and cats and dogs. Sure, I'm gonna pitch tomorrow. I've been dyin' to get at them Tigers again. I'll beat 'em, too."[41]

Cardinals shortstop Leo Durocher was ready to move on from the shoddily played contest. "If we win every other day, we're bound to cop the Series."[42]

Decades later, Billy Rogell recounted the play that nearly brought down baseball's most flamboyant pitcher. "It really bothered me. That poor sight being carried off the field. Of course, it was Dizzy's fault. He threw up his head in the way intentionally. Even said so. He wanted to break up the double play. And to tell you the truth, I never saw the play because I was coming to the bag at an angle. I caught the ball and threw. Actually, if I'd have known his head was there, I would have thrown the ball harder."[43]

If a wallop in the head by a baseball was supposed to get in the way of Dean's pitching the next day, somebody forgot to tell him. Dean was his old self in Game Five, allowing only six hits and two earned runs over eight innings and 108 pitches. But Tommy Bridges, despite having pitched just two days prior, was even better. In a complete-game effort, he walked none while fanning seven. Detroit prevailed, 3–1, to take a commanding three-games-to-five lead in the Series.

Detroit opened the scoring in the second inning when Pete Fox hit a two-out double to drive in Greenberg from first base after he had drawn a base on balls. A mild hullabaloo erupted in the bottom of the third with two out. Switch-hitting Jack Rothrock was at the plate, batting from the left side against Bridges. Pepper Martin, the runner on first, broke for second. "Cochrane," wrote the *St. Louis Post-Dispatch*, "taking the inside pitch, found Rothrock in his way and threw. The ball hit the bat and caromed to the second baseman's position."[44] Home-plate umpire Brick Owens immediately called Rothrock out for interference, and the threat was over. Frisch put up a long protest, but to no avail.

In the sixth inning, Gehringer ran the count full before Dean grooved a fastball down the middle. The Tigers' second baseman crushed the pitch for a long home run that landed on the roof of the pavilion in right field. Three batters later, a run-scoring fly ball by Greenberg made it 3–0, and that was all the Tigers would need.

Bridges had St. Louis flailing away all afternoon. When they did make contact with his wicked curve, all they could do was chop the ball into the ground or pop up weakly. In a remarkable display of pinpoint control, he pounded the strike zone and was constantly ahead of hitters. Only twice did he go to three balls in a count, and both at-bats ended in strikeouts. The Cardinals' only tally came on a solo home run by Bill DeLancey in the seventh inning. Pepper Martin made a bid to tie it in the eighth when, with one on and one out, he drove one to deep left-center. It looked like a sure double, possibly an inside-the-park home run given Martin's speed. But center fielder Jo-Jo White, racing madly back, made a fine grab just a few feet from the wall. Goose Goslin called the catch "one of the greatest in any World Series."[45]

In a pressure-packed bottom of the ninth, St. Louis had runners at the corners with only one out. But Bill DeLancey, in the words of Grantland Rice, "took three over the plate with a squawk that is still reverberating through the Osage and the Ozarks, on its way to the Rio Grande."[46] Bridges then induced Ernie Orsatti to ground into a force at second to end it.

It had been an unexpected and risky move on Cochrane's part to go with Bridges, rather than the more rested Rowe. But Little Tommy always pitched well at Sportsman's Park, while Rowe had been less successful. The Tigers' skipper knew that he was opening himself up to a heap of criticism if Bridges were to falter. Now, he looked like a genius, with Rowe primed and ready to go in Game Six in Detroit. "Rowe will start sure tomorrow," Cochrane said in the clubhouse after the game. "We have the Cardinals on the run and I'm anxious to get it over."[47]

Fans back in Detroit could smell victory. A trickle of them began forming a line near the box office at Navin Field before Game Five had even ended. As the late afternoon turned into early evening, an eager multitude descended onto Michigan and Trumbull. All reserve seats had been sold long ago, but Tigers worshippers were hoping to snare the 20,000 or so bleacher tickets that would go on sale at 9 o'clock the next morning, just a few hours before Game Six. With Rowe on the mound, the long-elusive world championship at last seemed within the Tigers' grasp.

Rumors swirled before Game Six that Cardinals owner Sam Breadon was prepared to put the team up for sale. Among the names floated as potential buyers, the most intriguing was Henry Ford. Breadon quickly squelched such talk, however. "If somebody would come along and offer me an attractive price for my holdings, naturally I would sell. But nobody has. There has been no offer from anybody to buy the club. There has been no offer by anybody to sell the club."[48]

The brilliant Indian summer day began with a bad omen for Schoolboy Rowe. While puttering about in his hotel room in the morning, someone (it was never mentioned exactly who) had accidentally slammed a bathroom door on Rowe's pitching hand (or so he claimed). Despite a mild swelling, he doubted it was serious, but that was not the end of the matter. Later during pre-game warmups, Rowe was yacking it up with Joe E. Brown, the Hollywood comedian and baseball fan who was a perennial presence at the World Series. (In 1932, Brown had actually appeared as a member of the St. Louis Cardinals in the Warner Brothers film, *Fireman, Save My Child*.) When photographers asked Rowe to shake hands with Brown, the funnyman squeezed a bit too hard, aggravating the swelling. Rowe, however, shrugged it off and stepped into the cage for some batting practice, which, by his own account, made the hand even worse. He headed back to the locker room, where he soaked it in water as hot as he could bear. Not surprisingly, that did not help much, and the pain persisted. But throwing caution to the wind, he made his way to the field to start the game.

The Cardinals got on the board in the first inning, when Rothrock hit a one-out double and scored on Joe Medwick's single. Paul Dean had no trouble with the Tigers the first time through the lineup, but Detroit capitalized on a Cardinals miscue with two out in the fourth. Jo-Jo White walked and would have been thrown out on an attempted steal, but he slid hard into second, bowling over Frankie Frisch, who could not hold on to the ball. With Frisch lying on the ground and the ball rolling away, White dashed down to third.

That brought up Cochrane, who had yet to drive in a run in the Series. After fouling off one pitch after another, he hit a slow roller to first baseman Ripper Collins. Cochrane beat it out for a single, scoring White, but he half-slid and stumbled awkwardly over the bag. Dean, who was covering first, accidentally spiked him near the left kneecap. Cochrane came up limping but stayed in the game.

St. Louis sought retaliation for White's belligerent slide the next inning. Following Medwick's leadoff single, Collins grounded one to Gehringer, who tossed to Rogell to start a double play. But a charging Medwick slid in with spikes flying. Rogell was upended, narrowly avoiding a slashing.

In the top of the fifth, Durocher legged out an infield single, and Dean's bunt sacrifice sent him to second. Pepper Martin, hitting .348 in the Series, lined a single to left. With Durocher rounding third and heading home, Goslin made a wild throw to the plate. Durocher scored, and Martin raced all the way to third. Rothrock bounced out to Rogell, as Martin scored to make it 3–1.

Dean set Detroit down in order in the bottom half of the frame, but in the sixth he committed the cardinal sin (no pun intended) of walking the leadoff man, in the person of Jo-Jo White. Cochrane's single put runners on first and third with nobody out. Gehringer ran the count to 3–2 before hitting a dribbler to Dean, a perfect double-play ball. Bending over to field it, the pitcher took his eye off the ball and it rolled through his fingers. White scored, Cochrane suddenly represented the tying run at second, and the Tigers had the makings of a big inning.

In a classic example of how baseball strategy has changed since the 1930s, Cochrane then entrusted Goose Goslin, his cleanup hitter, with the task of bunting the runners over. The plan went awry; Goslin's bunt was gobbled up by the catcher, DeLancey, who threw to Marin at third to nail Cochrane. The Tigers' manager put up a verbal protest, arguing he had slid in under the tag, but umpire Brick Owens wasn't buying it. Photos seemed to indicate that Cochrane indeed was safe.

Runners remained at first and second, but now with one out, up strode Rogell. He lofted one to center field for the second out, but Gehringer tagged and reached third. Dean was almost out of the woods, but he still had to face Greenberg. With the crowd praying for a hit, Greenberg banged one into left, scoring Gehringer to tie it up. Marv Owen, with only two hits in the Series, stood in against Dean, hoping to give Detroit its first lead of the game. As

Goslin danced off second, Owen hit a chopper to Durocher, who threw to first to end the frame.

Paul Dean made amends for his costly error the next inning, this time with his bat. After Durocher's one-out double, Daffy laced a single to right, and Durocher scored easily, giving St. Louis the lead, 4–3. In the home half of the seventh, it looked as if the Tigers would catch a break. Fox led off with a high pop fly to left that fell between the backtracking Durocher and the onrushing Medwick and Orsatti. Fox made it all the way to second, and Rowe bunted him over to third. With a drawn-in infield, White bounced to Durocher, whose quick throw home beat Fox by a slight margin. Cochrane was up next, but did not get a chance to hit, as White was promptly thrown out stealing, ending a frustrating inning for Detroit.

The Bengals threatened again in the eighth with runners at first and third with only one out. But Dean got Rogell to hit a short fly to center, as the runners were forced to hold. That brought up Greenberg, with a chance to be a hero.

Many of the great hitters acknowledge that a smart pitcher will throw you only one good pitch to hit in every at-bat. Greenberg was expecting a fastball right in his wheelhouse, which was exactly what Dean threw him. Inexplicably, however, the Tigers' slugger watched it go by for a called strike. It was an opportunity wasted. Greenberg had lost the battle within the battle; the at-bat ended when he popped out to first base. "I often wondered," Greenberg recollected decades later, "what would've happened if I'd jumped on that fastball."[49]

In the ninth, with two outs and nobody on, Rowe gave the Navin Field crowd one final thrill, driving a ball to deep center field, but Orsatti hauled it in to seal the St. Louis win. "That boy has got ice water in his veins," Leo Durocher praised Paul Dean in his ghost-written column the next day.[50]

It was the best game of the Series from a competitive standpoint. Both Rowe and Dean had pitched valiantly. It did not appear that Rowe's bruised pitching hand bothered him; he did give up ten hits, but walked none and struck out five. For Paul Dean, who threw 127 pitches, it was his second win of the Series. The Cardinals had withstood the Tigers' ace and were feeling good about their chances in Game Seven. To many observers, the turning point of the game, and indeed the Series, was Brick Owens calling Cochrane out at third to dampen the seventh-inning rally. Certainly, Frank Navin thought so. "I've been waiting 35 years to see Detroit win a championship here," he growled after the game, "and when we've got one in our grip, some guy blows it for us."[51]

Both Cochrane and Rowe were treated at Providence Hospital following the loss. Whether from the effects of throwing nine tough innings, or from Joe E. Brown's handshake, Schoolboy's swelling had gotten worse. Whatever chance there was of him being available for Game Seven, even to face a batter or two, it now seemed a highly unlikely prospect. As for Cochrane, he could barely walk up the hospital steps without assistance, as his knee was stiffening up and nearly impossible to bend. He spent several hours with it immobilized under a heat lamp. X-rays revealed no serious injury to the kneecap. In the words of Dr. Keane, the Tigers' team physician, the cartilage had been "pulled." When reporters asked for a midnight update, the doctor hedged his bets. "There is no way of determining until tomorrow noon whether Mr. Cochrane will be in any condition to play. I most certainly will not consent to his going in if it means a permanent disablement risk."[52]

The Tigers' long, long, grinding baseball season, which had begun in Lakeland back in February, came down to a World Series Game Seven at Navin Field on October 9, 1934. Cochrane, despite his aches and pains, decided he was well enough to play. But who would his starting pitcher be? Having used Rowe the previous day, and with Bridges coming off a complete game in Game Five, the most logical choices were Crowder or Auker. In somewhat of a surprise, Cochrane again passed on Crowder's experience and handed the ball to Auker, the right-hander who had pitched effectively in the Game Four victory.

The 24-year-old Kansas farm boy had one of the more unusual deliveries in the major leagues, a slinging, sidearm motion that was born out of necessity rather than any desire to be different. In his first football game for Kansas Agricultural and Mechanical College (the forerunner to today's Kansas State University), Auker separated his shoulder, making it impossible for him to throw overhand. He was forced to completely alter his mechanics and throwing motion, even in football, where he played quarterback.

As a semipro pitcher in Manhattan, Kansas, Auker once squared off against the Kansas City Monarchs and the great Satchel Paige, who had ridden into town with a 33-game winning streak in tow. The only tally Auker surrendered in the 2–1 victory was a home run by catcher T. J. Young. Once out of college, Auker was scouted by the great Bronco Nagurski, who apparently thought a side-arming quarterback could make it in the National Football League. The Chicago Bears offered Auker $6,000, but he chose baseball instead, signing with the Tigers for $450.

Bob Coleman, his manager at Class B Decatur, recommended that Auker go from a side-arming delivery to a completely underhanded one. He fash-

ioned his windup after that of Carl Mays, who won over 200 games in the
big leagues with a delivery that went so low his knuckles almost scraped the
dirt. Auker caught a lot of ridicule about his unorthodox style, but it produced
results: He won 16 games with Beaumont in 1933 and three more with the
Tigers after being called up in August. Auker always believed that were it not
for his gridiron injury, he never would have reached the major leagues.

With Dizzy Dean gunning for his second Series win, the Tigers had their
work cut out for them. It soon became apparent that it was not Auker's day.
He retired Durocher on a fly ball to lead off the third, but after a double, a
single, a stolen base, a walk, and another double, he looked up to see Cochrane
plodding out to the hill to give him the heave-ho. In an act of desperation,
the manager called for Rowe, bruises and all. Schoolboy faced three batters,
surrendered a single and a double, and could not be blamed for vowing never
again to shake hands with a comedian.

Before the nightmare inning was over, Chief Hogsett and Tommy
Bridges were also thrown into the fire. The Cardinals batted around, scored
seven runs, and the city of St. Louis began preparing for a World Series
parade. With little hope of coming back against the nearly unbeatable Dean,
the Tigers played the rest of the game listlessly, a team beaten in body and
spirit.

The excitement was not over, however. In the top of the sixth, Ducky
Medwick and his .357 Series average came to the plate with Pepper Martin
on second. Medwick cracked a long drive off the center-field fence. Martin
scored easily to make it 8–0, while Medwick ploughed his way around second
and headed for third. At the bag, Marv Owen awaited a throw from the outfield as Medwick slid in hard.

At that point, the firestorm began. In a cloud of dust, Marv Owen's right
foot came down violently on Medwick's legs. Was it deliberate or accidental?
Many of the writers perched in the Navin Field press box agreed that Owen's
act was a cheap shot. He had blocked the runner's path to the bag as if to
make a play, even though the relay throw was obviously going to be too late.
They insisted that Owen's stomp had come while Medwick was on his back,
defenseless. The Tigers' third baseman conceded that his spikes had inad-
vertently landed on Medwick's foot. In Owen's view, Medwick had been the
aggressor, kicking him three times and cursing him out. To Owen, it was a
dirty slide with bad intent. To Bud Shaver of the *Detroit Times*, Medwick
"deliberately slashed at Owen … a vicious and unprovoked attack."[53]

Whatever the specific details, and without knowing with certainty who
kicked whom or when or why, what is clear is that Owen and Medwick nearly
came to blows then and there. Third-base coach Mike Gonzalez and umpire

Bill Klem quickly intervened. The Cardinals rushed out of the dugout, led by Dean, sporting a towel around his neck. The umps shooed them back to their nest. Medwick claimed he extended his hand to Owen to show there were no hard feelings, but Owen apparently rebuffed the gesture. The outbreak of bitterness was inevitable. All Series long, the two teams had been at each other's throats.

A tenuous truce was restored between Owen and Medwick. The first pitch by Tommy Bridges to Ripper Collins was a duster that sent him to the dirt. Picking himself back up, Collins laced the next pitch into center, scoring Medwick to make it 9–0. More boos rained down from the grandstand.

When the inning ended, and Medwick headed out to his position in left field, he received a rude welcome. The denizens of Navin's new-built bleachers bombarded Medwick with bottles, fruits, vegetables, and other sundries. At first, Medwick took the onslaught in stride, playfully picking up peaches and pears and pretending to take a bite. When the blitzkrieg failed to subside, and a few projectiles narrowly missed his head, he backed up to the infield, while members of the grounds crew gathered the litter. Even a few Cardinals, including Dizzy Dean, participated in the housecleaning.

With things seemingly settled down, Medwick resumed his position, only to face a fresh barrage of garbage. He went back to second base, waited a while, and returned to left again. But it was clear that the bleacher fans did not appreciate his presence. More rubbish was thrown. Westbrook Pegler called it "one of the most disgraceful and delightful incidents ever witnessed" in a World Series.[54] Finally, Cochrane emerged from the Tigers' dugout to plead for peace from the mob, with little success. The umpires requested that Medwick be removed from the game so that play could resume, but Frankie Frisch would have none of it.

Watching all this from the vantage point of a front row box seat was the cigar-chomping, eagle-eyed Commissioner Landis, in fedora and topcoat. With crooked finger, the judge beckoned Klem, Owen, Medwick, and the opposing managers over for a deliberation.

Landis asked Medwick what had happened on that slide. Medwick answered plaintively that a lot of things can happen on a slide. Landis, that old grandstanding magistrate, theatrically raised his right arm, thumb pointed upward, and ordered Medwick out of the ballgame. His sentence in tow, Medwick was escorted off the field by a posse of police (and a refrain of boos from the bleachers).

Landis then whirled on Owen. Had the third baseman done anything untoward to instigate the fracas? If Owen's memory served him well, he had done no such thing. Satisfied with that defense, Landis pounded his proverbial gavel and allowed Owen to remain in the contest. A befuddled Frisch then proceeded to rush at Klem, who apparently had neglected to tell the Judge of Owen's offense. Frisch's objection, however, was overruled.

Chick Fullis replaced Medwick in left. The Tigers went down in order in the sixth. St. Louis tacked on two more runs in the seventh to make it 11–0. Dean dominated, and when Owen grounded into a force for the final out in the ninth, the Cardinals mobbed their flamboyant hero on the Navin Field mound.

It had been a bitterly contested Series. The heroics of the Brothers Dean, each of whom won two games, stood out for St. Louis. "To the nation's baseball followers," claimed the *St. Louis Post-Dispatch*, "it was a drive of the Deans. And to the same fans, the World Series triumph was a triumph for the two slender boys from the cotton fields of the South, who in a few brief years have become national figures."[55]

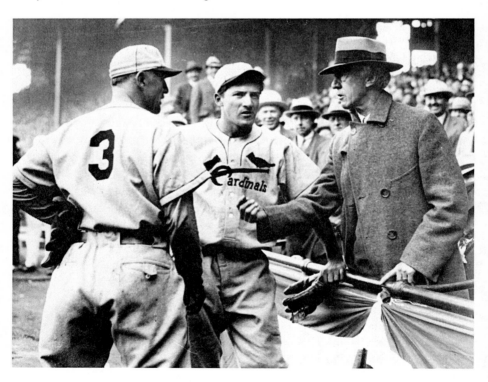

Cardinals left fielder Ducky Medwick huddles with his manager, Frankie Frisch (left), and Commissioner Kenesaw Mountain Landis (right). Medwick is about to be removed from Game Seven of the 1934 World Series for his own safety (courtesy Ernie Harwell Sports Collection, Detroit Public Library).

As for the Tigers, they hit only .224 as a team. Greenberg and Gehringer were the sole regulars to hit over .300. Cochrane had driven in one measly run. After the sun had set on Game Seven, he made the obligatory shuffle across to the visitors' locker room, to congratulate Frisch on a job well done. "We had our best chance Monday and blew it," Cochrane conceded to reporters. "We should have sewed up the series then but we didn't and it's no use crying about it now."[56] Black Mike took a deep breath, as if an influx of oxygen would lend him the strength to undo the past three hours. "Everything happened to us today," he sighed.[57]

Cochrane took the loss hard, harder than any he ever had before. When his Athletics lost the World Series back in 1931, and he gave up all those stolen bases ... well, that was one thing, but this was a different animal altogether. As the field general of this team, the man entrusted with the job of leading it to the mountaintop, he knew he would spend the rest of the winter wondering what went wrong at the end.

The Tigers' clubhouse had a funereal quality. Before the game had even begun, newsreel technicians, anticipating a Detroit victory, had taken over the cramped space, setting up Kleig lights, huge motion picture cameras, and assorted wiring for sound. It was all for naught. A dapper-looking Graham McNamee, radio personality extraordinaire, would not be asking Cochrane how it felt to be a world champion manager. In fact, he would not be asking him anything. Cochrane, in no mood to chat further, fended off the press. The picture of defeat, he sat slumped on a trainer's table while a doctor tended to his mangled knee.

Paul Gallico wrote, "The Cardinals were the roughest, toughest, hardest, slam-bangingest club I have ever seen, and the nearest thing to the old-time baseball nines that the present generation has seen."[58] The Cardinals had capitalized on Detroit's inexperience. With the eyes of the world on them, the Tigers lacked their customary aggressiveness at the plate, which had served them so well during the regular season. The infield defense, one of the team's strengths in 1934, looked tight, particularly in the first game. Trying to strike a positive note, General Crowder remarked, "Well, we had to be better than seven other clubs to get into the Series. That's something."[59]

Down through the ensuing decades, the common refrain has been that Medwick was removed from Game Seven for his own safety. That is mostly true, as far as it goes. But Judge Landis insisted that his taking out Medwick was not merely an act to appease the crowd. "I saw Medwick kick at Owen," he explained after the Series was over, "and his act warranted punishment. That is why I ordered him out of the game."[60]

As entertainment, the World Series had delivered as promised. Gushed *The Sporting News*:

> The stirring events that brought to a close the 1934 playing season established the game still more firmly as the national sport—first in the hearts of the American people—a dashing, vivid, pulsating, brilliant and clean sport, representative of the American spirit.... The St. Louis Cardinals and Detroit Tigers have paved the way for the building up of a new courage among the people of the nation by their example and have lifted baseball to a new pinnacle, where it proudly stands as a symbol of a country that never yields to odds.[61]

⚾ ⚾ ⚾

Iffy the Dopester's poignant column the day after Game Seven of the 1934 Series was one of his most memorable. It echoed the sentiments of a city not yet ready to bid adieu to a splendid summer, nor welcome the winds of winter:

> There are no regrets in the hearts of real sportsmen, Mickey.
>
> You fought the fight; you did your damndest.
>
> You gave a tired and jaded old town the thrill it needed, the call to battle and high courage.
>
> You took a green young ball club and you led them to the American League pennant. By all the laws of baseball and by the gods of chance you should have been beaten but you never sounded retreat.
>
> Three things make baseball the great American sport: Base hits, errors, and the breaks of the game.
>
> They epitomize life itself. We advance by hits and the errors of our opponents in baseball as in business. And over all are the breaks in the great game.
>
> In that sixth game the Cardinals got the breaks. And in the seventh the Tigers got Dizzy Dean. Kismet, selah, and all that sort of rot.
>
> And so now, Mickey old lad, don't take it too hard to heart. We know you to be a tough loser, as any game fighting man is, but you can find surcease from your sorrows in this: You gave them everything you had and that is all anybody can ask of any man.
>
> We'll be with you when the robins nest again, Mickey, me boy.
>
> And O what a team we'll have next year![62]

Chapter Eleven

"You can't keep
a gang like that down"

After the dust settled on the 1934 World Series, Frank Navin immediately tore down his temporary bleachers, the site of such ignominy in Game Seven. The Tigers retreated to their off-season lives. One of the first to leave the city was Goose Goslin, who headed to Salem, New Jersey, where he would make much-needed improvements to his farm. Two days after the Series ended, Schoolboy Rowe and Edna got married in a private evening ceremony at the Detroit Leland Hotel. The pitcher did not reveal the whereabouts of the honeymoon, but hinted that the newlyweds planned a motor trip. Pete Fox, who was one of the groomsmen at the wedding, made his way back to Evansville, Indiana, following the ceremony.

Jo-Jo White headed to College Park, Georgia. Gee Walker would first go home to Hattiesburg, Mississippi, and then he and his wife would journey south to Florida to hit the beaches and the links. Frank "Last Man" Doljack, who had, as per his custom, shown up late for a mandatory workout before Game One of the World Series, was not tardy in catching a train home to Cleveland. Hank Greenberg had plans to spend part of the winter in sunny Miami, but also in the Bronx. He signed with the Brooklyn Jewels of the American Basketball League at a pay rate of $20 a game. Ray Hayworth hurried off to High Point, North Carolina, where he and his brother had a dairy farm. Marv Owen, meanwhile, hung around Detroit for a week before hopping on a Pullman bound for San Jose. He apparently held no grudge against Ducky Medwick, insisting that he would shake hands with the Cardinals left fielder should their paths cross again.

General Crowder had a homestead in Winston-Salem, North Carolina, where his dogs were awaiting him for what promised to be a fine hunting season. Vic Sorrell returned to Raleigh for some good fishing; Fred Marberry to Corsicana, Texas; Carl Fischer to Medina, New York, in time for the pheasant season. Tommy Bridges beat it back to Tennessee.

Elden Auker and Chief Hogsett both set out for their Kansas homes. Heinie Schuble and Flea Clifton were a couple of utility infielders who barely played in 1934, but had been placed on the World Series roster as insurance. Schuble now went to look for an off-season job in his native Houston. Clifton planned a hunting trip in northern Michigan before making his way back to Cincinnati. Luke Hamlin looked forward to getting back to his gas station in Lansing. Only Billy Rogell, The Fire Chief, stuck around to brave the Detroit winter. Before they dispersed, each of the Tigers received $4,313, their individual loser's share of World Series spoil (the Cardinals' booty was $5,941 per man).

As for Cochrane and Gehringer, both were to join Connie Mack and Babe Ruth, along with a touring team of all-stars, on a steamship bound for Asia (or "The Orient" in the parlance of the day). Scheduled to sail from Vancouver on October 20, the *Empress of Japan* would first take the squad to Hawaii, then on to Japan, before quick stops in Shanghai, Hong Kong, and Manila. Ruth, the manager of the team, hailed it as a goodwill voyage to promote baseball, a sport that the Japanese, in particular, wholeheartedly embraced. Previously, Cochrane was a member of an all-star team that made a similar tour in 1931. That year, the Americans beat the Japanese in all 17 exhibitions they played.

For now, Black Mike simply wanted to forget about the seventh game of the 1934 World Series. "I'm tired. I'm just going to stay around Detroit for a while and loaf."[1] As for any improvements he planned to make to his team, he would only say that he would not even begin to think of that until he was in Hawaii.

When Frank Navin had acquired Cochrane back in December 1933, he signed the former Athletic to a two-year contract, so there would be no swirling rumors this off-season as to who would manage the Tigers. That did not mean, however, that it was a winter free of trade speculation. Navin headed south to Louisville for the annual minor league meetings, where he sold the little-used and underachieving outfielder Frank Doljack to the Milwaukee Brewers of the American Association. If nothing else, the transaction underscored the fact that the Tigers expected to be successful in their quest for another fly chaser.

Al Simmons of the White Sox, a favorite of Cochrane from their days in Philadelphia, was reportedly headed to the Motor City. A lifetime .354 hitter, Simmons had blasted 240 home runs in his 11-year career. Among the names of Tigers potentially to be sent packing were Ray Hayworth, Vic Sorrell, Gee Walker, and possibly a minor league pitcher or two. Simmons, a left fielder, would be an upgrade in the outfield, now that it looked like Walker was expendable. But Navin denied the rumors, saying all he knew was what he read in the papers; White Sox manager Jimmie Dykes said the same. To Tigers fans, the prospect of Simmons slugging it out at Navin Field must have been mouth-watering.

The rumor was given additional credence when Mr. and Mrs. Cochrane, along with Mr. and Mrs. Al Simmons, were spotted together at a restaurant in Agua Caliente, Mexico, just across the border from San Diego. Following a relaxing stay at Hot Springs, Arkansas, the couples were on the final leg of their trip before heading north to catch the Hawaiian-bound steamer along with Ruth's all-stars. Reporters, naturally, took the hobnobbing as a sign that the Tigers had all but bagged Simmons, which was not the case. There was also speculation that either the Indians' Earl Averill or the Browns' Sam West were on Navin's short list.

One far-fetched story had Charlie Gehringer heading south to Cleveland to be the Indians' player-manager. But Navin squelched that rumor as well. What he really needed, he insisted, was a reliable left-handed starter. In 1934, the only southpaw in the rotation was the veteran Carl Fischer, who would never remind anybody of Carl Hubbell. Also in demand was a dependable infield reserve.

One obstacle Navin faced in his quest was that the Tigers were not particularly deep and had few spare parts to offer in way of a trade. Harry Davis, the slick-fielding first baseman who had lost his job in Detroit to Hank Greenberg, had hit .317 at Toledo in 1934 and could prove enticing. The Red Sox, for one, were looking for a first baseman, and were perfectly willing to offer Rube Walberg, but the lefty starter was past his prime, and Cochrane likely would take a pass on such a deal.

Another possibility was Earl Whitehill, who had won 133 games for Detroit before they traded him to Washington in December 1932. Senators owner Clark Griffith had made it known that the lefty, winner of 14 games in 1934, was on the market. Cochrane and Navin viewed Whitehill as a definite upgrade over Fischer or Hogsett, but the Tigers did not have much that Griffith would be interested in. The Indians' Bob Weiland, a southpaw with a 21–55 career mark, was also available. Ed Wells, another former Tiger now toiling for the Browns, was another name being floated about. As the off-season progressed, however, it became increasingly apparent to Cochrane that he might have to make due with such young lefty prospects as Joe Sullivan, Jake Wade, Paul Sullivan, and Ray Fritz.

The Gehringer to Cleveland rumor, however, was not going away. No sooner had Cochrane alighted from the steamship *Mariposa* at San Pedro, California, having completed his tour of the Orient, than he was buttonholed by reporters wanting his opinion of the buzz. "I haven't heard anything about it," Cochrane shrewdly replied. "If it's true, it's the worst news I've heard since they told me Dizzy Dean was going to pitch the seventh game of the World Series."[2] Gehringer also pleaded ignorance. As far as he knew, he was still going to be with the Tigers. At least he hoped so.

His trans-continental travels at an end, Cochrane arrived back in Detroit on December 7. Huddling with the press at the train station, he dispelled any lingering notion that the Tigers were going to bag Al Simmons. When pressed about other potential deals, he simply shrugged before being whisked away in a taxi.

Two days later, he and Navin, along with coach Cy Perkins, headed for the winter meetings at the Commodore Hotel in New York. The trio was approached by Browns player-manager Rogers Hornsby, who still had a keen interest in Gee Walker. Hornsby viewed the absent-minded outfielder as a potential superstar. All he needed was the right potter to mold him, which, in Hornsby's view, was himself. No deal materialized, however. There were rumors of a three-team package involving the Browns, Red Sox, and Tigers, which would have sent Walker to St. Louis, but talks never gained much traction. The Yankees were also interested in purchasing Walker if he was for sale. "I have a hunch that Gerald Walker can be calmed down and turned into a worthwhile outfielder," said New York manager Joe McCarthy. "They say he is a crazy man on the bases, but you can't be crazy on the bases without getting on. In other words, Walker can get to first and that's a lot more than can be said for some of the other flychasers drawing salaries in our league."[3] But when the Tigers asked for light-hitting outfielder Sam Byrd in exchange, McCarthy looked the other way. Navin and Cochrane were in a bit of a quandary when it came to Walker. He had been *persona non grata* in Detroit for some time, and while the Tigers had made no secret that the outfielder was available, a part of them remained reluctant to give up on him so soon. The team still held out hope that Walker could develop into a great player.

If it was any solace to Cochrane and Navin, no other American League team made a big splash in the off-season, either. While in New York, reporters asked the Tigers' manager his thoughts on the 1935 season. For what it was worth, he predicted Detroit would repeat, followed closely by the Yankees and Indians. Despite the lack of player movement, however, the winter meetings did not lack for interesting storylines. The National League voted to allow night baseball for the first time. Each team was allowed seven contests under the lights for 1935. Only the New York Giants, Brooklyn Dodgers, and

Pittsburgh Pirates voted no on the measure. The American League, meanwhile, eschewed the experiment. Senators owner Clark Griffith bemoaned night baseball as "only a step above dog racing."[4]

Returning home from Hawaii, Cochrane found a good omen waiting for him in his mailbox. It was a letter from the Michigan Secretary of State. Earlier, while still on the islands, Cochrane had sent in an application requesting license plate number 101. The implication was obvious, since the Tigers had won 101 games in 1934. The letter informed him that the number was already taken; the Secretary's office, however, had gone ahead and reserved number 102 for Cochrane. "That's all right," he figured. "That will give us a new goal to shoot at next season."[5]

Tigers pitchers and catchers were scheduled to report to Lakeland, Florida, on March 3, to be joined in a week by position players. Cochrane was betting that, unlike in previous years, they had kept up an exercise regimen over the winter and would need less time to round into shape. The Tigers' brass clearly liked its spring training digs enough to return for a second season. The *Detroit Free Press* reported, "The Lakeland training camp is one of the best in the citrus belt. The climate is ideal, the grounds large and well kept and the location all that could be asked."[6]

Navin was confident of success in 1935, but he knew the competition would be tougher. "The Yankees are the team to beat," he remarked in January. "The records show that last year they had the best pitching in the league and pitching is, of course, the main requirement. I also understand that the Yankees have some first class material coming up from the minors. They are going to give us plenty of trouble, but I think we will finish ahead."[7]

Although he did not give names, the "first class material" Navin was referring to was Joe DiMaggio, whom the Yankees had purchased from the San Francisco Seals of the Pacific Coast League back in November. DiMaggio, however, would not be spending his summer in the Bronx; New York insisted that the 20-year-old remain with the Seals for one more season, in order to prove his full recovery from a knee injury. The Yankees were a team in transition. With Ruth gone, Lou Gehrig would be the big man at Yankee Stadium in 1935. The days of DiMaggio, however, were looming just around the corner.

From his home in El Dorado, Schoolboy Rowe made headlines in February when he refused to return his signed contract for 1935. In those days before the empowerment of players, before the collapse of the reserve clause and the arrival of sports agents, team owners held all the cards when it came to salaries. A player's standard contract would arrive in his mailbox every winter, with the salary already filled in by ownership. The player was expected to sign dutifully, even if his salary was reduced. If the player did not like the terms, his options (unless he was a big star), were limited: Either sign or find some other line of work. Holdouts, forced to bargain from a position of weakness, were portrayed negatively by the press, which often was no more than a mouthpiece for ownership. Players found little sympathy from the public, especially during the Depression when millions were already out of work.

Nearly every other Tiger had already signed and returned his contract, making it all the more conspicuous that Rowe had not yet put pen to paper. He insisted he was not a holdout in the strict sense of the word. In his view, the terms of the contract were simply not satisfactory. "I will talk with Mr. Navin at Lakeland next month and I am sure everything will be all right." He added cryptically, "There are a few things I want to find out about before I sign." Schoolboy headed off to visit his mother in Dallas, where he re-affirmed his stance to scribes, without getting into the specifics of what it was he wanted to "find out." He boasted that all the hunting he had done over the winter had kept him in tip-top shape. He predicted that he would win 25 games in 1935. As for Navin, he conceded that every player had the right to make the best deal possible for himself. Until the owner received word that Rowe would not report to Lakeland, he was not considering him a holdout and remained confident the two parties would come to terms.

On February 17, Navin headed south for a brief vacation in Miami before rendezvousing with Cochrane in Lakeland. The two planned to discuss the upcoming campaign; no doubt, Schoolboy Rowe would be one of the topics of conversation.

⚾ ⚾ ⚾

A lot had happened to Babe Ruth since nearly being offered the Tigers' managerial post a little over a year ago. He had hit his 700th home run in Detroit in July. He had played before legions of adoring fans on the post-season all-star exhibition tour of the Orient. He had parted ways with the New York Yankees. And on February 26, 1935, he officially became a member of the National League's perennial doormats, the Boston Braves.

He would be more than just a player, however. Judge Emil Fuchs, team owner and president, had lured The Bambino back to Beantown, where he had begun his career, by promising him the title of vice-president and assistant manager. Ruth was also given a three-year contract at $20,000 per, along with a portion of profits. The Sultan of Swat saw it as his chance for one final hurrah and a stepping-stone to his dream of managing a big league team one day. The Yankees, on the other hand, were thrilled to have gotten rid of the aging slugger, whose waistline had increased while his power had decreased. No longer would Ruth pester Jacob Ruppert about wanting to manage the Yankees. No longer would he try to undermine Joe McCarthy's authority. From now on, Ruth was Judge Fuchs's problem.

⚾ ⚾ ⚾

No sooner had the Tigers begun the trek down to Lakeland than they received some unfortunate news: East Lansing resident Luke Hamlin had crashed his automobile into a tree on the campus of Michigan State University. He had survived, but his left (non-pitching) arm was fractured in two places, and doctors were saying it would be two or three weeks before he could start heading south.

Hamlin had won only two games in 1934 with a 5.38 earned run average, and he was a longshot to make the team. Still, many viewed his mishap as an omen that Detroit's incredible injury-free run was about to end. An additional red flag flew when Marv Owen underwent surgery for a recurring sinus infection, delaying his Florida arrival. All winter long, the baseball Jeremiahs had predicted that bad fortune would finally catch up with the Tigers in 1935. Hamlin and Owen, they now believed, would be just the first dominos to fall.

In February, the Tigers signed Dixie Howell, a 22-year-old fresh out of the University of Alabama. An All-American at halfback, he had recently starred in the Crimson Tide's victory over Stanford in the Rose Bowl. Howell was also a promising baseball player. Eddie Goosetree, the Tigers' scout who had signed Schoolboy Rowe, had been hot on Howell's trail for nearly a year. The kid could run down fly balls with the best of them and reminded Goosetree of Tris Speaker. Howell also played short and third at Alabama, and that's where the Tigers wanted to test him out, figuring he still lacked the offensive power required of an outfielder. Howell, blessed with movie-star looks, had ventured to Hollywood for a series of screen tests. Universal Studios liked what they saw and wanted to sign him up for a new, football-themed serial based on the Frank Merriwell stories. Howell opted to give baseball a chance first. He showed up in Lakeland to much fanfare, which made him nervous from the start. "I didn't know my arrival would create such fuss. I came here merely to learn."[8] Howell was nothing if not raw, prompting Cochrane to make a few adjustments to his left-handed swing. "He looks like a fellow who will be hard to fool," the manager beamed. "He probably won't knock the cover off the ball, but he should get plenty of hits.... He'll give pitchers many a headache."[9] The hope was that Howell was talented enough to make the jump from college straight to Detroit.

Schoolboy Rowe's arrival also made big news. He felt better than he ever had in his life. "If I win 25 games, I'll be quite satisfied."[10] As for his contractual holdout, it ended with a whimper. On his first day in camp, Rowe huddled with Navin for all of two minutes, and the owner emerged with a 1935 contract displaying Rowe's signature at the bottom. Terms were not divulged, but Schoolboy conceded that he was pleased with the outcome. Cochrane, as well, had some unfinished financial business. Early in the 1934 season, when the team was struggling, he had promised to buy every player a new pair of baseball spikes if they won the pennant. The promise had been overlooked during the exciting closing weeks of the season, but now that it was back to the business of baseball, he remembered to fulfill his vow.

The Tigers won four of their first eight exhibition games and were daily tearing the cover off the ball. "They believe in themselves," wrote W. W. Edgar of the *Detroit Free Press*. "They're actually boasting of what they'll do. And that's a great change from the condition that existed only a year ago."[11] Against the Boston Braves at Lakeland on March 21, Tigers pitching held Babe Ruth hitless for his new team, as Detroit scored two runs in the bottom of the ninth to win, 5–4. Nevertheless, Cochrane sensed that the team was not putting forth its best effort. The evening of the Boston game, he called a meeting at the hotel and lit into his men. Accusing them of loafing, he warned that if they thought they could roll to the American League pennant by playing the type of lackadaisical baseball they had shown so far, they had another thing coming. The show of disapproval achieved its desired effect, as the Tigers pounded the reigning world-champion Cardinals the next day, 12–5.

Goose Goslin was the biggest recipient of Cochrane's tongue-lashing. After the old war-horse had mailed it in during a few games, Cochrane felt it was time to call him on the carpet. The manager benched him for a few games, which bewildered Goslin, who took pride in his reputation as a hustling player. Cochrane understood that Goslin was simply trying to avoid overexerting himself before the season began. He pulled Goslin aside in private and explained to him that it was important to maintain discipline. The younger players on the team needed to see that loafing would have consequences, even for established stars. Goslin was satisfied with that explanation.

After the victory over St. Louis, however, Detroit was trounced on successive days by Casey Stengel's Brooklyn Dodgers. With an open date in the schedule, Cochrane made his charges run through exhausting drills in the sweltering Florida heat. To add to their penance, the regulars were forced to sit in the stands the next game as the reserves beat Rochester, 11–1.

The Cardinals proved to be a good tonic for the Tigers. On March 27,

Detroit gained sweet revenge on the Brothers Dean, 13–8. Goslin hustled in the field and drove in three runs, while Greenberg tripled with the bases loaded and later singled in a pair. Jo-Jo White, homerless in 1934, hit one against Paul Dean. Detroit took special pleasure in routing the loud-mouthed Dizzy. One Tiger reportedly crowed, "That guy'll find out he can't talk his way through baseball. Paul's all right—he's a swell kid, but that Dizzy doesn't go with us."[12]

The beauty of spring training is its boundless hope. Every year, it seems, a young, unheralded player comes out of nowhere, banging out hit after hit and looking like a potential all-star. The 1935 Tigers had that player in Chet Morgan. It was not as if nobody had heard of Morgan. In 1934, the outfielder had won the batting title at Beaumont, hitting .342 with 216 hits, 120 runs scored, 42 doubles, ten triples, and six home runs. Most agreed, however, that he was a long shot to make the Tigers in 1935. He got off to a blistering start in the spring exhibition games, with 12 hits in his first 25 at-bats. Unfortunately, Morgan was an even worse outfielder than Dixie Howell, and an atrocious baserunner to boot. Still, there were whispers that Cochrane would have no choice but to bring him north.

Clyde Hatter, a 26-year-old lefty who had a 37–61 record in five minor league seasons, was looking like a world-beater. With a good fastball and curve, Hatter was cool under pressure and fielded his position with grace and agility. Cochrane banked that he was the left-handed starter he had been looking for. If not, there was Joe Sullivan, a highly touted prospect who won 25 games for the Hollywood Stars of the Pacific Coast League in 1934.

A mini-controversy flamed up in New Orleans, where the Cleveland Indians trained. The Tribe was expected to be a serious contender in 1935, but Cochrane apparently was not of that opinion. During an interview, Black Mike was asked what he thought of the Indians' chances in the American League. He supposedly replied, "The Indians? Who are they?" This flippant remark did not sit well with Cleveland manager Walter Johnson or his team. Cochrane had no desire to give the Tribe any motivation, *a la* Bill Terry the year before ("Is Brooklyn Still in the League?"). The Tigers' skipper rapidly penned a letter to Johnson, claiming that his words were misrepresented and he meant no disrespect. He asked Johnson to post the letter in the Cleveland clubhouse for all to see. The former pitching legend, however, did no such thing. Johnson tore up the letter, throwing peace and pieces to the wind. Let the Indians read about Cochrane's repudiation in the papers, he proclaimed. Johnson, for one, was not about to quench any spark that might light a fire under his team. When Cochrane got word of Johnson's reaction, he was visibly miffed. "All right, if they want to be that way, we can take care of ourselves."[13]

Ed Bang, sports editor of the *Cleveland News*, huffed: "Of such mole hills are baseball's mountains made."[14]

The Florida weather had been cold and damp, which made it hard on the pitchers who were trying to loosen up their arms. The rain resulted in muddy, slippery playing conditions. When the Tigers finally broke camp and headed north on April 3, Cochrane was happy to have all his charges ready, able, and vertical. Detroit journeyed with the Reds to play a dozen exhibition games in Florida, Georgia, the Carolinas, and the Virginias. The bad weather followed them everywhere they went.

Cochrane was less impressed with Dixie Howell the more he saw of him. The ballyhooed Alabaman with the leading-man looks was awkward at the plate; whether he would make the big club appeared very much in doubt. On April 11, the Tigers and Reds were practicing one morning in Lynchburg when Howell was struck in the face by a batted ball. He suffered a broken right cheekbone, with the fracture extending into the eye socket. Howell was fortunate not to have suffered greater injury; he would be out for at least three weeks, according to doctors. The unlucky ball had been struck by Johnny Mize, a 22-year-old Reds minor leaguer, who later went on to a Hall of Fame career with the Cardinals, Giants, and Yankees.

The Tigers and Reds concluded their northerly jaunt in Cincinnati, where they unlocked the gates to Crosley Field on April 14 in a final warm-up before the regular season. Detroit bagged Cincinnati, 3–2, with Auker giving up only four hits in eight innings. Over 10,500 fans showed up at the ballpark at Findlay and Western that afternoon, capping an exhibition season in which the Tigers had continually played to packed houses. Cochrane's men looked primed for the defense of their American League title.

Perhaps the biggest surprise of the team was the re-emergence of Gee Walker. In the final week in Florida, he had hit and fielded well, and looked like a new man on the basepaths. Cochrane unhesitatingly chose him as his starter in right field over the incumbent, Pete Fox. Chet Morgan, the spring-time hitting phenom, was slated for reserve outfield duty. But Cochrane was concerned about Marv Owen, who still had not rounded into the proper playing shape.

The Tigers expected big things from Greenberg, who went on record as saying his personal goal in 1935 was to swing for the fences more. "That's the thing that makes stars," he noted.[15] He approached Cochrane at the end of spring training with his desire to be the everyday cleanup hitter. It was an indication of Greenberg's growing confidence. He batted mostly sixth in 1934, although by September Cochrane was penciling him into the fourth slot nearly every day. In the Series against St. Louis, Greenberg had batted cleanup the first three games and sixth thereafter. Now, heading into 1935, Cochrane agreed that his slugging first baseman was a candidate for full-time cleanup duty.

Many prognosticators believed the Tigers had been a very good team in 1934, but that they were only a key injury or two from falling back to the pack. The Yankees, Red Sox and Indians were expected to give Detroit a good battle. Would the Bronx Bombers still have the same swagger without Babe Ruth? They possessed possibly the best starting staff in the American League, with Lefty Gomez, Red Ruffing, Johnny Broaca, and Johnny Allen. They had also purchased some pitching insurance in Pat Malone, winner of 115 games in seven years with the Cubs. A big question mark was 35-year-old Earle Combs. Could he come back from a skull fracture sustained in a collision with the center field wall late in the season? Moreover, what of the young, unproven George Selkirk, counted on to take over for Ruth in right field? Lou Gehrig might have to shoulder most of the offensive load for the Yanks if either Combs or Selkirk faltered.

Offense was something the Cleveland Indians did not have to worry about. Rookie Hal Trosky (35 homers, 142 RBI, .330 BA in 1934) and Earl Averill (.313/.414/.569 slash line) were left-handed sluggers who took advantage of the ridiculously short right-field fence at League Park. Odell Hale (101 RBI) and Joe Vosmik (.341 BA), who swung from the right side, were also big threats. But after 20-game winner Mel Harder and Monte Pearson's 18 wins, there was a big drop-off in pitching. In addition, there were rumblings that manager Walter Johnson was not popular with some of his players.

At the plate, the Red Sox had young third baseman Billy Werber, who hit .321 with 40 stolen bases in 1934, and left fielder Roy Johnson, who'd fashioned a lifetime .297 mark in six seasons with Detroit and Boston. First and second base had been major weaknesses in 1934, but the Sox were anticipating some punch from 24-year-old rookie first sacker Babe Dahlgren, a Pacific Coast League star from San Francisco. Boston had scored the third-most runs in the American League in 1934, but the pitching staff seemed like a house of cards ready to collapse. A return to form by Lefty Grove, coming off a terrible season in which he won only eight games with a 6.50 earned run average, would solve a lot of problems. It shaped up to be a four-team race, with the Tigers given a slight edge. Cochrane knew it would not come easy. His personality would not allow him to forget the sting of the Game Seven humiliation in the World Series. To have come so close, and to be devastated in the end, was a bitter pill to swallow. He would have to kick it into a higher gear as manager. He would have to out-work, out-prepare, and out-think the managers on the other side of the diamond. Anything else was unacceptable.

With John Dillinger out of the way, George "Baby Face" Nelson assumed the mantle of Public Enemy No. 1, albeit briefly. It did not take long for the 25-year-old gangster and bank robber to meet the same fate as Dillinger. A little over a month after Cochrane's G-Men had won the American League pennant, the nation's other G-Men, led by FBI Director J. Edgar Hoover, scored their biggest victory. In a wild shootout known as the "Battle of Barrington," the FBI killed the notorious Nelson. Hoover's G-Men suffered the loss of two fine agents, including Ed Hollis, the former Detroit bureau chief who had shot Dillinger.

In December, the first telephone line linking Japan and the United States was inaugurated. Secretary of State Cordell Hull exchanged pleasantries with Foreign Minister Koki Hirota over a crackly connection. Telephone calls notwithstanding, relations between the two nations were unsettled. By year's end, Japan announced that it would no longer be a party to the Washington Naval Treaty. Ratified at the end of World War I, the agreement set a limit on naval construction between the U.S., Britain, Japan, France, and Italy. Hull accepted Japan's abrogation of the treaty with what he called genuine regret.

Nineteen-thirty-four had been a good year for the Chevrolet Motor Car Company, with 876,000 automobiles rolling out of its U.S. and Canadian factories. That marked its sixth time in the last eight years as the world's biggest producer. New models would feature the powerful "Blue Flame" engine, providing improved performance at any speed. Henry Ford, meanwhile, was predicting a decided upturn in business. While he admitted that car dealers would not be jumping summersaults the way they had in 1929, there was reason for everyone to be hopeful. In 1935, he boasted, Ford vehicles would be longer, wider, roomier, and heavier. Engines would be more powerful. The company's lowest-price model was the five-window coupe, at $495. The station wagon, on the other hand, would set an American family back $670. It would be a tough sell for many households. The economy was showing signs of life, but unemployment remained high. In January 1935, Roosevelt sent an unbalanced budget to Congress that included nearly $5,000,000,000 for relief and recovery. One sign of a rebounding Motor City was the improved real estate market: Federal and city officials, as well as real estate and banking professionals, agreed that the area was on the cusp of a construction boom, which would alleviate Detroit's housing shortage. Even though Americans lacked the deep pockets to invest in real estate, they could always pretend that they did. A new board game called *Monopoly* debuted in February 1935. As players munched on their newfangled Ritz crackers, they could buy and sell imaginary prime properties like Boardwalk and Park Place, all with the goal of driving the competition into bankruptcy.

America thrilled to the daring exploits of a 37-year-old aviator from Kansas named Amelia Earhart. Braving clouds, fog, and capricious winds, Earhart became the first ever to fly solo from Hawaii to California. After covering 2,408 miles of Pacific Ocean, over a span of 18 hours and 16 minutes, her red plane touched down in Oakland at 4:31 pm on January 12, 1935, to the ovations of a welcoming crowd. Across the continent, the eyes of the world were riveted on a small courtroom in Flemington, New Jersey, where Bruno Richard Hauptmann stood trial for the suspected kidnapping and murder of the infant son of another famous flyer, Charles Lindbergh. "The Trial of the Century" lasted nearly six weeks and captivated the nation. On February 13, the jury finally reached a verdict on the fifth ballot: Guilty of murder in the first degree. Reports out of Berlin, meanwhile, threw all of Europe into a state of alarm. Scrapping the Treaty of Versailles, Nazi Germany decreed compulsory military service in the Reich, with an aim of quadrupling the size of its regular army to nearly 500,000. Great Britain and France issued a joint protest to Germany and the League of Nations, claiming that the new dictate threatened peace in the region.

Tigers fans were eager to welcome back the American League champions. The team's train arrived at Michigan Central Station at 7:30 on the morning of April 15, greeted by a throng of jubilant rooters. Cochrane ordered his men to report to Navin Field in four hours for a practice session. Baseball was back in Detroit, but the long, cold winter was not over yet. While snow swirled through the streets and arctic blasts blew between the downtown buildings, the first game at Navin Field had to be postponed one day. Wintry weather affected other openers as well, setting off a fresh round of the annual appeals to start the season a week later. Opined *The Sporting News*: "Loyal fans, it is true, continue to brave pneumonia in order to follow tradition and attend games on Opening Day, but their number is dwindling and will diminish to an even greater extent if common sense is not employed and the openings moved back to permit the early games to be staged under more favorable settings."[16] It is a refrain familiar to baseball fans of today.

A frigid Navin Field crowd of 24,000 was on hand to watch the Tigers begin the defense of their American League championship against the Chicago White Sox on Wednesday, April 17. Schoolboy Rowe was not sharp. Down 4–1 in the sixth, Goslin brought the fans to their feet with a three-run homer off 42-year-old starter Sad Sam Jones. But the Sox scored three runs in the eighth, highlighted by player-manager Jimmie Dykes's two-run triple. Former Bengal Whitlow Wyatt pitched two perfect innings of relief to close it out. The new electronic scoreboard in right field, 110 feet long and 30 feet high, showed a 7–6 Chicago victory on its red, green, and amber lights. Wrote H. G. Salsinger of the *Detroit News*, "No one has, as far as we know, ever compiled a list showing the total number of ways in which a ball game can be lost, but Detroit did fairly well yesterday in using a number of different methods and all of them with certain effectiveness."[17] Rowe confessed to having the Opening Day jitters; Goslin maintained that was perfectly natural. "Well, when the time comes when you don't feel that way," said Goose, "you're no longer a big leaguer."[18]

Any hopes of an undefeated season for the Sox were quickly dashed the next day, when the Tigers recaptured a little of that 1934 late-inning magic. The weather was slightly better, but Detroiters renewed that great baseball tradition of shunning the second home game of the year, as only about 5,000 attended. Tommy Bridges pitched tough despite not having good command; heading into the home half of the sixth, the score was tied at two. Detroit looked ready to blow the game open, however, when they loaded the bases with nobody out. That marked the end of the afternoon for Sox starter Les Tietje. In came Joe Vance, making his big league debut. The 29-year-old got Cochrane to pop to the catcher, and Gehringer bounced into a double play to end the inning.

In the seventh it was Gee Walker, recently emerged from Black Mike's doghouse, singling with two out to put Detroit on top. It was the team's first lead of the season, but it did not last long, as the Sox countered with a two-out RBI single of their own, this one by Jackie Hayes, to tie it in the eighth. The South Siders re-took the lead in the ninth thanks to Luke Appling's run-scoring single.

With his team down 4–3 in the bottom of the ninth, Goslin opened with a base knock and dashed home one out later on Walker's double off the left-field fence. The hustling Walker twisted his ankle sliding into second, and Pete Fox came in to run for him. At that point, the rookie Vance had trouble finding home plate. Two walks, sandwiched around a strikeout, loaded the bases, bringing up Cochrane with a chance to win it. Vance walked him as well, forcing in Fox to end the affair. It had not been pretty, but the Tigers' faithful whooped and hollered, knowing a victory was a victory. Still, the final score could not hide the fact that the home team left 16 men on base, while the Sox stranded 13.

After the game, Cochrane decided that Greenberg was not yet the answer at cleanup. The first basemen had only two singles in nine plate appearances, with no RBI. Goslin, on the other hand, had gone 6-for-9 with two doubles, a home run, and five RBI in the number five slot. Cochrane figured he would try Goslin at cleanup and move Greenberg down to sixth. With Walker out indefinitely from his ankle injury, Pete Fox became the new right fielder.

None of the changes helped. Detroit's bats were stymied in a 3–2 loss the following afternoon, ruining an excellent complete-game effort by Firpo Marberry. Goslin and Greenberg combined for one hit in seven at-bats. The White Sox, who had gone a woeful 5–17 against the Tigers in 1934, escaped the Motor City with an impressive series win. After the game, the Tigers optioned Dixie Howell to Birmingham of the Southern Association.

The hitting doldrums continued when the Indians rode into town. In a further attempt to shake things up, Cochrane shuffled Goslin from left field to right and put spring sensation Chet Morgan in left and batting eighth. Fox, meanwhile, was back on the bench. Elden Auker and newcomer Joe Sullivan pitched well in the first game on April 20, but Detroit could not deliver with men on base, falling in 14 innings, 2–1. There was no respite for the weary the following afternoon, a 13-inning affair that the Tigers won, 3–2, with Rowe throwing seven frames of relief for his first win. Willis Hudlin three-hit Detroit in the final game, a 5–0 loss; once again, the Tigers had struggled against a team they had dominated in 1934. Walter Johnson was not quick to draw any conclusions about Detroit, however. "You can't keep a gang like that down," he conceded.[19]

Arriving in the Windy City for a three-game set beginning April 23, Detroit looked to General Crowder to pull rank on the White Sox in the Comiskey Park opener. Instead, Chicago stripped the General of his medals, knocking him around for nine hits, three walks, and six runs in five innings. With Gehringer at cleanup the next day, the Tigers were limited to three hits. Trying to ignite the offense, Cochrane inserted himself fourth in the lineup for the finale. But Rowe, battling a cold, pitched poorly in a 9–8 loss as Chicago swept the series. Al Simmons, on the other hand, the man Tigers fans had salivated over in the off-season, went a combined 4-for-11 with a home run and five RBI. Expressing what was on everyone's mind, H. G. Salsinger wrote, "It is still very early in the season. If [the Tigers] suddenly started hitting everything would become different and the team is bound to begin hitting, sooner or later. The only danger is that it may start hitting too late."[20]

It was much of the same in Cleveland, where Detroit lost to the first-place Tribe, 11–3. Vociferous fans at League Park had not forgotten the spring-time spat between Cochrane and Walter Johnson. The Tigers' manager was the recipient of cacophonous queries of "Who are the Indians, Mickey?" Detroit suffered a 9–2 pasting on April 27, its sixth loss in a row. For the Indians, it was their fifth consecutive win. Detroit occupied the cellar in the American League, seven games behind the Tribe, with a record of two wins and nine losses. Cleveland was playing great baseball; five of their first eight wins were by one run or less.

The city of Detroit was in a near panic. In factories and cafés, streetcars and Cadillacs, the talk of the town was its ailing baseball team. The champs looked like chumps, unable to hit their way out of a paper bag. Cochrane was batting .200, Goslin .255, Rogell .225, and Greenberg .250 with no home runs. The pitching wasn't much better: Bridges boasted a 7.79 earned run average, with Rowe not far behind at 7.32. It was early, to be sure, but this was not how anybody had envisioned things. The entire organization, from Frank Navin down, had wanted to get off to a good start to show the world that 1934 was no fluke. The players, as a result, were straining under the weight of expectations. "Our hitters aren't hitting, and our fielders aren't fielding, and our pitchers aren't pitching," lamented Navin.[21] But he insisted that his team would come around.

Relief came from an unlikely source in Joe Sullivan. The rookie who had starred with the Hollywood Stars took the mound against the Indians on April 28. He wasn't flashy, but gutted it out the entire nine innings for his first big league victory. He pitched with the poise and confidence of a seasoned veteran. In another good sign, Greenberg banged out his first home run of the season, along with a double, as he was back in the cleanup position.

Sullivan's effort was something of a moral victory. Other pitchers threw faster and boasted better curves, but Sullivan had a knuckleball that he was able to harness extraordinarily well. He did not lack for confidence, as the *Detroit News* was quick to point out. "No pitcher ever got anywhere without it and regardless of what Sullivan lacks, here and there (and mechanically he lacks considerable) he does have the one big thing and that's what made Dizzy Dean a leading pitcher and that is what made Schoolboy Rowe the sensation of the American League last year. Joe's fine confidence carried him through yesterday's game."[22] The *Associated Press* proclaimed that Sullivan was "a mystery to the Tribesmen."[23] It was the Tigers' best-played game to date, with timely hitting and inspired fielding. Cochrane loved working behind the plate when Sullivan was on the mound because the kid could throw to a spot all day long. The catcher would hold up his glove, and Sullivan would throw it in there. Control, however, had not always been Sullivan's strong point.

He came from a family of itinerant farmers. His parents had tried scratching out a living first in Illinois, then in Twin Falls, Idaho, before finally gaining traction in Tracyton, Washington. His dad found work in the Bremerton Navy Shipyards. Sullivan began throwing the knuckleball in high school, where he first got the nickname "Tiger." His catcher, however, wasn't good at handling the unpredictable pitch and discouraged Sullivan from using it. After graduating, Sullivan played semipro ball in Bremerton, but it wasn't until he participated in a 16-team tournament that he caught the attention of Bill Essick, the Yankees' longtime scout covering the Pacific Coast League. Essick liked Sullivan's self-assurance on the mound and inked him to a contract posthaste.

He was assigned to the PCL's Hollywood Stars late in the 1930 season, but never got in a game. Finally his manager, Ossie Vitt, told him that he was being sent to the Tucson Cowboys of the Class D Arizona State League. But the team went bankrupt soon after his arrival, and he spent the winter wondering what a guy had to do to make a living at this game.

He stuck around Tucson and wound up signing with its new team, the Missions, which played in the recently rechristened Arizona-Texas League. With the Missions, Sullivan won 23 games as a raw-boned 20-year-old, drawing the attention of the Tigers, who swooped in and signed him before season's end. They sent him to Beaumont in 1932, which already had an abundance of starting pitchers, including Schoolboy Rowe and Luke Hamlin. Sullivan struggled with his control for the next two seasons, averaging over five walks per nine innings. Bob Coleman, his manager and a former big-league catcher, worked hard with Sullivan to overcome his wildness. His windup was altered, eliminating any superfluous movements in an attempt to simplify things. It was an ongoing process, however, and when Tigers management gave him a cursory look at spring training in 1934, they judged him still too wild. He was farmed out to the Hollywood Stars for more seasoning.

Sullivan blossomed, despite pitching in hitter-friendly Wrigley Field in Los Angeles. He won 25 games that summer, but, most importantly, he lowered his base on balls rate to just over four per nine innings. The Tigers took note. Now, less than three weeks into the 1935 season, the unflappable Sullivan's newfound control augured well.

Chapter Twelve

Hammerin' Hank
Sets the Pace

Early-season baseball, before the temperature rises, can be a low-scoring business. The reasons for this are varied, and new theories are constantly cropping up. Balls do not carry as much in the cooler, dry air. That home run in August might only be a long fly ball in April. Heat and humidity produce sweat on a pitcher's palms; with dryer hands in the spring, gripping the baseball is slightly easier, which could improve control (but it is a fine line; *too* cold and *too* dry, and the ball feels "hard" and more difficult to grip). Hitting in chilly weather poses its own set of challenges. Cold bats are less flexible, and this could deaden any ball they hit. There is also an element of pain: Get sawed off with an inside fastball in 40-degree cold and you won't forget the sting in your hands anytime soon. Many batters are still getting their timing down and do not fully find their groove until the warmer weather sets in. The Tigers' bats started slowly in 1935, but as the calendar turned to May, they began to heat up.

In St. Louis, Bridges and Crowder were back in fine form, as was the hitting, and Detroit took a pair from the Browns by a combined score of 29–3. Fewer than 900 hardy souls bothered to show up to Sportsman's Park for the two contests. Gee Walker was red hot: In four games since returning to action, he had gone 9-for-18 to raise his average to .519. He had also been blunder-free on the bases.

Showers wiped out the final two games of the series, and the deluge endured in Detroit, keeping the Tigers idle until May 4. That made for a well-rested staff, and Cochrane could have gone with any of his starters in a game against Boston. He bypassed Rowe and Bridges and gave the ball to the kid Sullivan, which raised some eyebrows. The lefty went the distance in a 5–2 victory, issuing only one base on balls. Walker got two more hits, as did Gehringer, who was now hitting .359. Sullivan was in trouble only once all afternoon. In the fifth inning, he hit Babe Dahlgren in the leg, loading the bases with one out and the Tigers nurturing a 2–0 lead. He then walked Wes Ferrell, forcing in a run. Many rookies could have cracked under the strain, but Sullivan kept his poise. He got Max Bishop to pop up to first and retired Billy Werber on a fly to Walker in left. "That boy knows how to pitch," Cochrane iterated after the game. "He has all the poise of a veteran and he seems to finally be the answer to our hope for a reliable starting southpaw."[1]

Tommy Bridges toyed with the lowly Athletics in a 5–3 win on May 7 at Navin Field, making it five in a row for Detroit. But the following afternoon saw one of those gut-wrenching games that give managers gray hairs. Schoolboy Rowe, wild all day long, was behind in the count with seemingly every batter. With Detroit nursing a 6–2 advantage with two on and two down in the top of the eighth, Bob Johnson tagged Rowe for a homer, his second of the game. Schoolboy struck out Jimmie Foxx to end the inning, but the implosion continued in the ninth. Leadoff man Pinky Higgins fanned, but two singles and a throwing error put runners on second and third. Cochrane headed out to the mound; Rowe's day was through. In came Auker, who struck out the first batter he faced, but then gave up a single that put the Athletics on top. Detroit gave it one last gasp, loading the bases in the ninth. But there was no joy in Tiger-town: Greenberg whiffed to end the affair, and the fans tore up their scorecards in disgust. Rowe's inexplicable funk was fodder for alarmists. Charged with all seven runs, his earned run average now stood at a putrid 7.39.

The Tigers closed out their home stand by winning three of five against Washington and New York. Sullivan once again stood sturdy against the Nats, walking only two in a complete-game, 8–4 victory on May 10. The most encouraging performance, however, was put in by Rowe three days later. Schoolboy threw a four-hitter, walking one and striking out five, besting the Yankees' Lefty Gomez in a 3–0 win. Rowe, wrote H. G. Salsinger, "for the first time this season, fully reached his 1934 form."[2] Walker hit his first home run of the season and was batting .451. Gehringer, at .349, was the only other regular hitting over .300. Sullivan suffered a tough loss on May 15, as Red Ruffing shut out the Tigers at Navin Field. It was the final game before Cochrane's men embarked on a 12-game, four-city eastern swing.

Despite some encouraging signs, the Tigers' offense lacked the punch of 1934. After 22 games, the team was hitting .261, with a woeful .371 slugging percentage. They were inspiring fear in nobody. Because of several postponements, the pitching staff had suffered from irregular work. With ten wins and 12 losses, it had become clear to the Tigers that repeating as American League champions was going to be a challenge. Before the Tigers and Yankees left town, Cochrane was a guest of honor at the Detroit Yacht Club. Lou Gehrig also got an invite, along with former Tigers outfielder Davy Jones. At the podium, Cochrane promised the 600-odd attendees that his club would be right up there come September.

Washington Senators owner Clark Griffith, in fact, had already written off Detroit. When the Tigers arrived in the nation's capital for a series beginning May 16, a reporter asked Griffith which teams he thought would be the contenders in the junior circuit moving forward. The Old Fox had won 237 games in his 20-year pitching career, and managed four different teams, before purchasing the Senators back in 1920. Griffith should have known to let sleeping Tigers lie. The teams to beat, he predicted, were the Indians, the Red Sox, and his own Senators squad (which was not exactly tearing up the league at 11–11). Detroit? They were done, he declared. Washington manager Bucky Harris concurred that his former charges lacked a certain zip. "The beating the Deans gave the Tigers last fall took something out of [them]," he appraised. No doubt notified of the disparagement, Detroit's batters swung inspired, putting up 37 runs as the Tigers took three of four in convincing fashion. Bridges, Crowder, and Sullivan all contributed solid starts, but Rowe took a step back, giving up seven earned runs in less than four innings of work to take the loss in game two. The Tigers were now 13–13, the first time they had reached the .500 mark in a month.

A turning point in the young season, however, came in the third game at Griffith Stadium, when center fielder and leadoff man Jo-Jo White was given the day off. White had excelled in the role in 1934, not just for his .316 batting average, but because he had walked 69 times, giving him an on-base percentage of .419. He was drawing more than a walk per game so far in 1935, with an on-base percentage of .366. Nevertheless, all Cochrane saw was White's anemic batting average of .196. He decided White needed some rest.

Taking White's place in center field was Pete Fox. Following his fine season the year before, Fox had played in only nine games so far in 1935, with two hits in 18 at-bats. He had not been in the starting lineup in three weeks. But batting leadoff against the Senators on May 18, he had a run-scoring single, and the next day he collected four hits, including a triple, with two RBI and two runs scored. Cochrane liked what he saw, and Fox remained in the lineup. In a further shake-up a few days later, he was shifted over to right field, which allowed Goslin to return to his favorite spot in left, while Walker continued to man center.

The Tigers departed Washington perhaps a notch or two higher in the estimation of Griffith and Harris. At Shibe Park, a three-run 11th inning powered Detroit to an 8–6 win over Connie Mack's Athletics on May 20. The City of Brotherly Love awoke the next day to a steady rain, and at nine o'clock Mack gave notice that he was cancelling that day's game, which was the home

Left to right: Goose Goslin, Jo-Jo White, and Pete Fox roamed the outfield for the Tigers (courtesy Ernie Harwell Sports Collection, Detroit Public Library).

team's prerogative. Three hours later the clouds broke and the sun burst forth, while the Tigers twiddled their thumbs back at the hotel. Cochrane complained to the league, contending that Mack called the contest in order to necessitate a doubleheader at some point in the future (apparently the Athletics could draw a bigger crowd for a twin bill than they could by playing two games in two days). Skies were clearer on getaway day; Fox led off the game by hammering a home run, and Auker went the distance for his first win of the year, 4–1.

The Tigers then took two out of three at Fenway Park, including a sparkling performance by Rowe. Following the awful 2–9 start, Detroit had won 15 of 20, leapfrogging to fourth place, three games behind Chicago. Pete Fox, meanwhile, continued his hot hitting. In seven games since being pressed into everyday duty, he had seven RBI, seven runs scored, seven extra-base hits, and an OPS of 1.348.

Fox, a 26-year-old native of Evansville, Indiana, had made a steady progression through the baseball ranks. Back in 1930, while toiling in a furniture factory by day and playing industrial-league ball on the weekends, Ervin Fox signed with the Tigers for $250 a month. That was a king's ransom compared to the $18 he brought home from the factory every week. He could pitch nearly as well as he could hit, but it was Bob Coleman, his first manager with the Class B Evansville Hubs in 1930, who made it clear that his ticket to the big leagues was written on his bat. Coleman, however, believed Fox was under too much pressure playing in his home town; after only seven games and a .222 average, Fox was sent to the Wheeling Stogies in the Middle Atlantic League. He could fly on the basepaths, stealing 27 bags that season while legging out 15 triples and batting .339.

After another .300 season at Evansville in 1931, he teamed with future Tigers Greenberg and Rowe to lead the Beaumont Exporters to a first-place finish. It was at Beaumont that Fox first picked up the nickname "Peter Rabbit" due to his speed, but soon his teammates just called him Pete. He led the Texas League with a .357 average, scored 103 runs, stole 30 bases, and hit 19 home runs, even though he missed most of August due to bone chips in his ankle. The Tigers needed outfield help heading into the 1933 season, so Fox was brought to spring training. Manager Harris, after watching the youngster gracefully glide after a fly ball, declared, "That Fox looks like an answer to my prayer."[3]

With his average hovering below .250 for much of the early summer of 1933, Fox appeared overmatched as a rookie. But he caught fire in July, hitting .409 for the month. His second half of the season included 98 base knocks, 53 runs scored, and a .315 average, to finish at .288. Two sets of statistics show how closely he was tied to the team's fortunes that year: In the 60 Tigers victories he played in, he hit .312; in 67 losses, he averaged only .262. Fox indeed was an answer to Harris's prayers, and now to Cochrane's as well.

Back on May 21, Henry Ford answered the prayers of many autoworkers when he restored the $6-a-day minimum wage. It was a return to the pay level of 1929, before the stock market crash, and benefitted 126,000 factory employees, including 81,000 in Detroit. That was not the only welcome news. In the last year, nearly 11,000 additional workers had found employment on the city's assembly lines. Before a week had passed, however, the Supreme Court ruled that the National Recovery Administration, a key component of Roosevelt's New Deal, was unconstitutional. Among the goals of the NRA was the establishment of minimum wages and maximum hours, but the high court unanimously held that the agency gave the President far too much power to dictate rules and codes, and that several provisions went too far in regulations affecting intrastate commerce. In response, industries across the nation announced that the ruling would in no way affect wage scales and working conditions. Labor, however, was uncertain how long things would remain status quo.

The Yankees, and nearly 30,000 Sunday worshippers, welcomed the Tigers to the Stadium in the Bronx on May 26. Joe Sullivan scattered five hits in a complete-game gem. His two big mistakes were a gopher ball to Bill Dickey in the second inning and a two-out wild pitch in the third that let in a run. The Yankees' rookie left-hander, Vito Tamulis, shut out the Tigers, improving his record to four wins and no losses.

Johnny Allen and Schoolboy Rowe locked horns the following afternoon in a classic pitchers' duel. Rowe, rounding into midseason form, fanned five and walked only two. But the Detroit bats were silent once again. Allen tossed a three-hitter, gave up only one unearned run, and registered his fifth win against no defeats. In the finale, Greenberg and Rogell each homered twice and drove in four runs, accounting for all the Detroit offense in an 8–3 victory. General Crowder held the Yankees at bay to gain win number four. It had been a successful eastern swing for the Tigers, winning eight of 12.

Less than successful had been the play of Marv Owen. His batting woes had begun in Lakeland and carried over to the regular season. As the Tigers left Gotham, Owen was mired in a 1-for-19 slump, while his average had plummeted to .184. Cochrane knew that he would have to make a change, and soon.

Tommy Bridges had emerged as Detroit's most dependable starter. In the first game of a May 30 doubleheader, the Browns lit up Elden Auker and three relievers to the tune of 16 hits in a 10–7 Tigers loss. But Bridges notched his second shutout of St. Louis in the second game. His parsimonious pitching limited the Browns to just three singles, and he struck out five in front of a celebratory Memorial Day crowd of 38,000. Bridges now had six wins in as many starts, with a 1.77 earned run average. The big blow the next day was delivered by Goslin, a bases-loaded, ninth-inning double that gave the Tigers a thrilling 6–5 victory. The *Detroit Times'* Bud Shaver noted with his usual hyperbole, "One sweet swish of Goose Goslin's mighty bat today must be recorded as one of the most far-reaching events in baseball history."[4]

Schoolboy Rowe's inconsistency, on the other hand, had the Tigers concerned. The pitcher labored through a complete-game loss to the White Sox on June 1, yielding five runs and walking five. Detroit had a chance to tie it in the bottom of the ninth. With Cochrane on first and two outs, Gehringer laced a single into right, with Cochrane sprinting to third. But Gehringer made the mistake of rounding too far off first base, where Zeke Bonura intercepted the throw from right. With Gehringer caught in a rundown, Cochrane made a mad dash for home; in the words of H. G. Salsinger, he "hurled himself at home plate in a desperate attempt to score the tying run. [Catcher Luke] Sewell went down under the impact but he kept hold of the ball and won the decision."[5] That was the ballgame, 5–4.

It was Rowe's fifth loss against only three victories. Had any pundits predicted before the season that Rowe would limp into June averaging 5.56 earned runs per game, they would have been told to re-check their math. Rowe's struggles were especially mystifying because the speed on his fastball was still there, along with his sharp curve and good control. But the Tigers never knew what they were going to get from Rowe on any given day. Unable to put together a string of good starts, Rowe had yet to resemble the pitcher who was one of the best in the American League in 1934.

The day after Rowe's loss to the White Sox, the man with 714 lifetime home runs finally had enough of Braves owner Judge Fuchs. In the middle of a game against the Giants, Babe Ruth told manager Bill McKechnie and the rest of the Braves that he was going to go on the voluntarily retired list for at least 60 days. It was a lost season for the flabby Bambino. His final burst of glory had come a week earlier, when he homered three times in a game at Forbes Field in Pittsburgh. But there was no hiding the fact that he was through. His .181 batting average read like a sinking stock price.

After the game, the 40-year-old Ruth huddled with the press. "I'm sorry to tell you this, boys, but I can't get along with Fuchs.... I like the Boston players and have the highest respect for McKechnie, but I'll never play another game as long as Fuchs is head of the club. He double-crossed me." A reporter asked how exactly the Babe had been double-crossed. Ruth related some cock-and-bull tale about wanting to go to New York the next day to represent baseball at a gala reception to welcome the French liner *Normandie*. Fuchs, said Ruth, had refused to give him time off to do so. That seemed unlikely, given that Ruth was not even playing due to a knee injury. In truth, Ruth's deep-seeded angst sprang from the realization that Fuchs never planned to make him manager in the first place.

Nobody seemed particularly surprised at the news. Most thought it a wonder that the charade between Fuchs and Ruth had lasted as long as it had. Braves pitchers, to a man, were relieved that the stationary Ruth would not be around anymore to turn routine fly balls into doubles. A few hours later, Fuchs read a prepared statement saying that Ruth was being unconditionally released. He added a final zing: "Nobody but an imbecile would act as Ruth did."[6] In the span of a year and a half, the Babe had gone from nearly managing the Tigers to *persona non grata* in Boston.

On June 5, Bridges won his seventh straight, a 5–4 decision against the Indians in the opener of a doubleheader at Navin Field. His own one-out, ninth-inning double scored Gee Walker to win it. It was the kind of late-inning magic that had so energized the Tigers the year before. The rousing victory put Detroit four games over .500 (22–18) for the first time in 1935. Because of a downpour, the game did not start until 3:10; by the time it was over, chances were slim of getting in the second contest. But the umpire called "play ball" at around 6:00, and dusk began falling by the time the Tigers came to bat in the sixth inning, trailing by a deuce. In the gathering gloom, a round-tripper by Cochrane, his first of the year, evened the score. "As he crossed the plate," wrote Sam Greene, "photographers took his picture with flashlights, the first time this has ever been done at Navin Field. The umpires decided that, night baseball not yet being approved by the American League, it was time to halt the proceedings."[7] William Kuenzel, a *Detroit News* photographer who had been snapping pictures for 31 years at Navin Field, pointed out after the game that never before had he needed to use a flash bulb to take a baseball shot. It was officially a tie, and the individual records stood.

Schoolboy Rowe's season reached its nadir the following afternoon at the corner of Michigan and Trumbull. For a while, he resembled the School-boy of old, holding the Indians hitless through the first six innings. The Tigers staked him to a seven-run lead. "Then came the most surprising reversal of the season," wrote H. G. Salsinger in the *Detroit News*.[8] Inexplicably, Rowe suddenly lost it in the seventh. Hal Trosky led off with a double to break up the no-no. The hits then came in rapid-fire succession: Another double, three straight singles, an RBI groundout, a single, and yet another double. Before Rowe knew what hit him, he was out of the game and was eventually charged with six runs in the inning. Detroit won it in the tenth on Goslin's RBI single, but all the fans could talk about as they exited the ballpark was how Rowe had imploded before their very eyes. Goslin, on the other hand, was hopeful that his game-winning hit would be the lift he was looking for. Coming into the contest with a .237 average, and hearing whispers that he was finished at age 34, he went 4-for-6 with five RBI. Gee Walker continued his hot hitting on June 7 against the second-place White Sox. His two-run homer in the ninth inning brought the Tigers to within a run in an eventual 9–8 loss. It was his second homer of the game.

Gee wasn't the only Walker in the Detroit lineup that day, however. His brother, Hub, recently called up from the Toledo Mud Hens, went hitless in a pinch-hitting appearance. It had been a long road back to the major leagues for Harvey Willos Walker.

He was never sure when, where, or how he had gotten his nickname. As a kid, everyone called him Hubby, which later was shortened to Hub. Of all the Walker Brothers (in addition to Gee and Hub, there was also Richard, Hilman, and Leonidas), it was generally acknowledged that Hub was the best athlete growing up. All four played football and baseball at the University of Mississippi, and Homer Hazel, the team's coach, called Hub "one of the greatest quarterbacks I have ever seen."[9] It was the hard-hitting Gee, however, with an inch or so and ten-odd pounds on his older brother Hub, who drew the most attention from baseball scouts. He signed with the Tigers in 1928; Hub hung around Oxford to get his degree before signing the following year. Reportedly, both had been wooed by scout Eddie Goosetree, who would also ink Schoolboy Rowe.

Hub was assigned to the Ft. Smith Twins of the Western Association his first year of pro ball. He hit .341 as a 22-year-old, earning a promotion to the Evansville Hubs the following year. Teaming up in the same outfield with Gee, the Hubs won the Three-I League championship. Hub batted .355, Gee .378. Their future in Detroit seemed bright. Both made the Tigers out of spring training in 1931 and had solid rookie seasons. Gee, despite spending nearly half the year at Double-A Toronto, batted .296. Hub suffered through various injuries, including a wrenched back, spiked hand, and broken collarbone, which negatively affected his swing. He still saw action in 90 games and hit .286.

Nevertheless, the Brothers Walker were headed in opposite directions. Manager Bucky Harris liked Hub's speed, but was intoxicated by Gee's potential as a hitter. Hub found himself back in the minor leagues, where, for the next three years, he struggled at the plate. His .261 batting average with the Toronto Maple Leafs and Montreal Royals in 1932 impressed no one. In 1933, he split time with the Royals and the Jersey City Skeeters, showing slight improvement at bat. At Montreal in 1934, he slumped to .256. The only part of his game keeping him in the lineup that year was his speed; he hit 11 triples and led the International League with 33 stolen bases. He spent hours before and after games in the batting cage, trying out different swings and hitting styles, but none of them seemed to work. While his kid brother was establishing himself in the majors, Hub appeared to be no better than a busher.

With the Mud Hens in 1935, however, Hub started to hit the way he always thought he could. Spraying the ball all over Toledo's Swayne Field, he maintained a plus-.300 average for much of the early season. That alone was not enough to punch his return ticket to Detroit, however. He needed a good break. He got one in Chet Morgan. The phenom who had looked like a future star in Lakeland had been a bust so far with the Tigers, appearing in only 14 games and hitting .174. Cochrane could no longer justify Morgan's continued presence on the roster. He was still high on Morgan's potential but wanted to give him more minor league seasoning. That meant the Tigers would need another spare outfielder. South to Toledo went Morgan, while north to Detroit went Walker.

The day after Hub made his first appearance in a big league game in over three years, the White Sox edged the Tigers, 3–2. All the scoring came via the long ball, with Rip Radcliff and Luke Sewell going yard for the Sox, and Greenberg and Owen doing the same for Detroit. Bridges tossed a five-hitter in the getaway game for his eighth win in a row. Greenberg homered again, his 13th, and Gee Walker added an RBI double in a 4–1 affair. Third baseman Marv Owen, however, went 0-for-3 and was batting .203. Such production out of the third base position was not going to win any pennants.

With the victory, the Tigers were 24–20, in fourth place, but only three games behind the Yankees. Cochrane's men headed back to Detroit, where they would enjoy some home cooking for the next 17 games. One player who did not make the trip, however, was Firpo Marberry. He had been a workhorse at the top of the rotation the past two years, with 31 victories. In 1935, however, he suffered from a sore arm. Winless in five appearances, he was finally given his outright release.

After an awful season in 1934, Boston's Lefty Grove was making a modest comeback. With eight starts under his belt in 1935, he had a 3–4 record and a very presentable 3.09 earned run average. In the opener of a doubleheader at Navin Field on June 11, he toyed with the Tigers, giving up only five hits and no walks in a 3–1 Sox win. Wasted was Joe Sullivan's solid six-hitter. Cochrane had decided to rest Owen, who not only had lost his stroke but was feeling physically weak. Taking his place at third base was the little-used Heinie Schuble. A 28-year-old Texan with five years of service in the majors, Schuble was a weak hitter with a solid glove. He didn't fare any better than the struggling Owen, going hitless in three at-bats. In the second game, Wes Ferrell bested General Crowder, who failed to pick up his sixth win.

Schoolboy Rowe had one of the best days of his life, both professionally and personally, on June 12. Celebrating the birth of his first child, he went the distance in a 4–1 victory, allowing a scant four baserunners while fanning five. He retired 20 in a row at one point. It was Schoolboy's first win in nearly three weeks, and it felt great. Cochrane, who was behind the plate, gushed that Rowe never had more stuff than he did that afternoon. Bridges was equally stellar the next day, racking up his ninth win in a row to improve his mark to 10–3. Among the offensive stars was Pete Fox, who had cooled down in recent weeks. Hitless in his last 14 at-bats, his average had dropped to .265, but he collected a single and a triple, good for two RBI and a run scored. He hoped it was the start of something good.

On June 14, before the fifth and final game with Boston, the Tigers raised their American League pennant to the top of the flagpole in center field. Will Harridge, president of the junior circuit, travelled from Chicago to be on hand for the ceremony. A military parade consisting of players from both teams, along with a marching band and "ten soldiers from Fort Wayne,"[10] made its way from home plate to deepest center. Fox picked up where he left off the day before, hitting a single, a home run, and driving in four runs. But the Tigers' bullpen spoiled the day, squandering a late-inning lead, as the Red Sox took three of five.

The June 15 trading deadline passed without the Tigers making any moves to shore up holes. Cochrane would have loved to add another experienced arm or two, but the market was bare. A spare outfielder and a third baseman would have given him flexibility as well, but once again, there just were not any available players. Third base had become a glaring weakness. Heinie Schuble was replaced by Flea Clifton, a good-field, no-hit rookie who clearly was not the long-term answer. Cochrane even pondered bringing up Dixie Howell from Birmingham, but scouting reports suggested the aspiring actor could not cut it at the hot corner.

Detroit took three from the Athletics at Navin Field, including a doubleheader on June 15. Greenberg hit his 15th home run in the opener, tying him with Philadelphia's Bob Johnson for the league lead. The power surge was a pleasant development; at the same point the year before, Greenberg had only seven homers. Both sluggers hit their 16th circuit clout the following day, and Rowe went the distance for win number five. The Tigers outscored Philly 34–7, setting up a four-game clash with the first-place Yankees, who rolled into town having won seven of ten. Detroit, at 29–23, was tied for second with the White Sox, four and a half games off the pace.

New York routed the Tigers in the first game of a doubleheader on June 19. General Crowder suffered the bulk of the beating in the 13–3 loss, while Gee Walker and Fox both homered. Bridges took the mound in the second game, gunning for his tenth win in a row. Tied at three in the top of the tenth, he gave up a solo shot to Ben Chapman, but Fox answered with his second homer of the day in the home half. In the 13th, with Bridges still in the game, New York's Red Rolfe led off with a chopper to first that deflected off Greenberg's glove. It was ruled a hit, and the next batter, Chapman, laid down a nifty bunt toward third base. The charging Clifton threw an off-balance peg in the general direction of third that wound up in the Yankees' dugout. With runners on second and third, Gehrig was passed intentionally to set up a force at any base.

Bridges then took Tony Lazzeri to a full count; on the next pitch, the Yankees' second baseman lined a single into center to score two. A third tally tripped across the plate on a force out to make it 7–4. The Tigers refused to go down quietly in their final at-bat. With two down and the fans headed for the exit ramps, Greenberg and Gehringer both homered to narrow the gap. To the plate strode Goose Goslin, who, at .268, was still trying to get untracked in 1935. The re-energized crowd shouted and stomped, but all Goslin could muster was a popup to end the nail-biter. "Tommy Bridges' winning streak," penned Bud Shaver in the *Detroit Times*, "expired with a soft little plop in Tony Lazzeri's gloved fist, like a punctured toy balloon."[11]

The third game started with a scare for the Yankees. In the first inning, a Joe Sullivan fastball struck Bill Dickey on the back of the skull. The catcher was carried off the field and later taken to a hospital, where an examination showed a slight concussion. Injuries had limited Dickey to only 104 games the previous season, and the Yankees could ill afford to lose him for any length of time in 1935. Despite his absence, New York scored three runs in the first and cruised to a 5–2 victory on the strong pitching of Johnny Allen. Joe Sullivan's control was not sharp, as he walked seven in seven innings. On the plus side, Fox banged out two hits for the sixth time in his last eight games.

His team desperate to avoid a three-game sweep, Schoolboy Rowe squared off against Red Ruffing on June 21. In one of the best-pitched games of his young career, Rowe gave up only four hits and three walks, fanning seven, in a 7–0 blanking. He even contributed a single and two RBI. Ruffing was cruising until Gehringer's leadoff home run opened the floodgates to a five-run sixth inning. "It really looks," wrote Sam Greene in the *Detroit News*, "as if the Schoolboy is ready to settle down to the serious business of the summer after a start that had everybody asking, 'What's wrong with Rowe?' and Mickey Cochrane groping in vain for an answer."[12] The Yankees, despite their loss, had taken three out of four; the Tigers slipped into fourth place, six and a half games off the pace.

Hank Greenberg had firmly established himself as the cleanup hitter. After the Yankees left town, the mediocre Senators shuffled in on June 22. Greenberg set the tone in the opener of a doubleheader with two RBI and two runs scored in a 7–0 pasting. Fox stroked a triple to run his hitting streak to ten games. In the nightcap, Greenberg's 18th home run lifted the struggling Elden Auker to only his third win. Goslin also banged out three hits; he now had a modest nine-game hitting streak of his own. A day later, Joe Sullivan pitched his worst game of the year, surrendering four earned runs and failing to last the second inning, while Greenberg hit a ninth-inning grand slam in a losing cause. The first baseman continued his hot hitting the following afternoon, doubling and driving in three runs. Goslin starred as well, driving in five runs in a game the Tigers won in the bottom of the 14th inning. The Senators finally bid adieu to Detroit with a 7–4 victory; Greenberg failed to homer, but he singled, tripled, and scored a run.

The Tigers finally left town following the long home stand. Hub Walker, however, was suddenly a man without a team. Having played in only nine games since his promotion from the minor leagues, Gee's brother had a mere four hits in 25 at-bats. The Tigers gave him the option of an outright release or a ticket to Beaumont. Hub chose the former. Within a few days, he signed a contract to rejoin the Mud Hens.

In a one-game stopover in the Windy City on June 27, Greenberg doubled and launched his 20th homer off former teammate Carl Fischer, whom the Sox had purchased back in May. Cochrane and Gehringer also hit round-trippers in the Tigers' 9–5 win, as did Fox, who ran his hitting streak to 15 games. Detroit then took four out of five from the Browns at Sportsman's Park, outscoring St. Louis, 49–19. Rowe and Auker both contributed brilliant starts. Goslin, who had hit in 16 straight, was finally held hitless on June 29, but he had raised his average to .293. Browns pitching, however, had no answers for Greenberg and Fox. The latter hit .520 with 12 runs scored and ten RBI in the series as his batting streak reached 20 games. Greenberg batted .400 with three home runs and ten RBI. With 23 four-baggers so far, there was talk that he could threaten Babe Ruth's single-season home run mark of 60, set back in 1927. He didn't seriously believe that he could break the record; besides, the mark he really wanted was Hack Wilson's RBI total of 190, which he established with the Cubs in 1930 (although historians later credited Wilson with 191). In Greenberg's view, RBI were more important than home runs, anyway. If he came to the plate with a runner on third and less than two out, he shortened his stroke, knowing that he was strong enough to drive the ball deep enough to score the run. Hammerin' Hank had no apparent weakness at the plate. He could hit any kind of pitch, in any location. His home runs had made him a national story as he assumed the mantle of superstar.

Returning to Navin Field on July 1 for the start of a five-game, home-away series with Cleveland, the Tigers won, 4–1, getting another fine outing from Auker for his sixth win. The sizzling Fox went 2-for-4 and scored a pair of runs. The Tigers and Indians were now in a virtual tie for second place, only three games behind New York. Bridges picked up win number 11 the next day, and Fox collected two more hits. Gehringer went 4-for-5 with a home run and three RBI, raising his average to .346. The next afternoon, Joe Sullivan, relegated to the bullpen to work on his control, threw 5⅓ innings of long relief in a win against the Tribe. That was followed by an Independence Day doubleheader sweep at League Park in Cleveland that gave the Tigers seven wins in a row. Leading off the second contest, Fox laced a single into center field, increasing his batting streak to 25 games.

In the last series before the All-Star break, Detroit made quick work of the Browns at Navin Field. In a 16–1 laugher in the opener, Greenberg hit his 24th and 25th homers, and Fox doubled twice and singled. Tommy Bridges started the second game, but after allowing six hits, three walks, and five runs, Cochrane had no choice but to remove him for a pinch-hitter in the second inning. Rowe came on in relief and, amazingly, pitched the rest of the game. The Tigers battled back to win, 7–6, capped by Gee Walker's RBI bunt single in the eighth. Fox, the hottest hitter in baseball, singled and scored three runs. He stroked a double the following afternoon, making it 28 games in a row, in a 12–5 triumph. He had this to say about his offensive emergence: "I believe I hit as many balls solidly last year, but more of them were caught. This year they have been falling safe. That's the difference."[13] The Tigers, meanwhile, were on a roll, having won ten consecutive games, the longest streak in the major leagues to that point in the season. They stood only one game behind the Yankees.

Not coincidentally, Detroit had put it into high gear once the bats had begun heating up. With the season's first half in the books, Gehringer was hitting .351, Fox .339, and Cochrane .326. Goslin and Gee Walker were at .299 and .298, respectively. Rogell was a solid .288. Greenberg had put up astonishing numbers, heading into the break with 25 home runs and 101 RBI. Even Marv Owen had picked up the pace. Back on June 27, with his average an unsightly .206, he was put back in the starting lineup for the first time in nearly three weeks. Playing regularly since then, he had batted an even .300, looking more and more like the Marv Owen of 1934. Jo-Jo White remained a huge disappointment, mired in a season-long slump and no longer an every-day player.

Little Tommy Bridges was the Tigers' most consistent starter. With 11 wins, he was turning into a bona fide ace. The up-and-down Schoolboy Rowe had eight wins and a 4.22 earned run average, and would have to straighten things out in the second half if the Tigers wanted to repeat as American League champions. Auker, with eight wins, and Crowder, with nine, had been solid if unspectacular.

The 1935 All-Star Game took place in Cleveland's cavernous Municipal Stadium. Opened in 1931, the horseshoe-shaped arena could seat nearly

80,000 patrons. The Indians tried playing in it a couple of seasons, with bad results, as the distant outfield walls robbed players of home runs. The stadium's sheer vastness made a crowd of 30,000 look more like a small get-together, while the game itself seemed a mere rumor to fans in the far reaches of the upper deck. The Tribe soon moved back to its old home, the cozy League Park. Municipal Stadium's huge seating capacity, however, made it a perfect choice for the All-Star Game.

The player selection process was a bit of a departure from the past. In 1933 and 1934, the fans voted for the starting players, while pitchers and reserves were selected by the previous season's pennant-winning managers. This was not a perfect system; many complained that fans mindlessly went with the established "name" players. The managers, however, could override the fans' choice if they felt another player was more deserving. For 1935, the fan vote was scrapped. Instead, the managers (in this case, Cochrane and Frisch) now had the honor of handpicking the rosters in their entirety. The only requirement was that each team had to have at least one player represented. From the Tigers, Cochrane nominated Charlie Gehringer as the American League starter at second, with Tommy Bridges and Schoolboy Rowe joining the pitching staff. Cochrane also selected himself, although not as a starter. In addition, Tigers coach Del Baker and trainer Dennis Carroll made the squad.

In what seems a curious decision over 80 years after the fact, Cochrane did not find a place on the roster for Greenberg, the American League's home run and RBI leader. In his autobiography, Greenberg had this to say about the omission: "That annoyed me because I had established myself with two good seasons in a row.... I thought to myself, What do you have to do to be selected to the American League All-Star team?"[14] In truth, Cochrane assembled a fine bunch even without him. Today's All-Star squads number 34 players. Cochrane, by contrast, had only 21 roster spots to work with, and a large pool of excellent players from which to choose. Permitted more space on the roster, he no doubt would have included Greenberg. Cochrane opted for Lou Gehrig as the starter at first base, a choice that is difficult to call into question. Cochrane did carry one other first baseman on the team, at least technically, in slugger Jimmie Foxx. But Cochrane wanted Foxx's bat for the entire game, not merely as a reserve threat. His clever strategy was to start Foxx at third base, a position he had played only twice to that point in 1935 (although he had some experience there in seasons past). A seemingly odd move, it only followed precedent, since American League manager Joe Cronin had done the exact same thing with Foxx in the 1934 game. Greenberg was a rising star having a great year, but the fact is that there is no shame in being passed over in favor of future Hall of Famers like Lou Gehrig and Jimmie Foxx.

Ultimately, Gehringer was the only Tiger who saw action in the game. He drew a base on balls in the first but was retired when Gehrig hit into a force play. He grounded out in the third, singled in the fifth off the Giants' Hal Schumacher, and doubled off Cincinnati's Paul Derringer two innings later. Foxx's two-run homer in the first inning was all the American League needed for a 4–1 win. Despite the fine weather, the turnout was somewhat of a disappointment at 69,812. That amounted to a net gate of $82,000, all of it earmarked for charity work among needy ballplayers. That is worth noting: Today, the All-Star Game is a pre-packaged brand drenched in hype and commercialization, a field day for the modern cynic. Yet, at its creation in the midst of the Depression, it had a simple, altruistic goal, which was to lend assistance to the destitute men who had given their youth and vigor to the game.

Chapter Thirteen

"Pulling game after game out of the fire"

Following the All-Star break, the Tigers began a 20-day, 18-game, five-city odyssey. Before boarding a train for the nation's capital, Cochrane was asked what he thought of the team's prospects moving forward. He admitted that he was pleased with how the pitchers had finally begun to hit their stride. The Yankees, he felt, were not as good as Detroit, and that would become clear in the weeks to come. "We can give our pitchers better batting and fielding support than the Yankees can." New York's pitching, by his estimation, was too thin. The Tigers, on the other hand, were beginning to click on all cylinders. "I believe we'll win the pennant by a wider margin than we did last year."[1]

Iffy the Dopester of the *Detroit Free Press* offered up this appraisal of the Tigers: "They are the only ball club in the league that is playing baseball as baseball should be played. They are lightning fast on the bases, they work the hit-and-run, the double steal, the squeeze; they bunt, they chop, they slug. They try anything and everything. Their heads are up and they are on their toes, pulling game after game out of the fire."[2]

On July 10 in Washington, the Tigers' ten-game winning streak appeared to be over before the fans had even settled into their seats. The Senators pummeled Tommy Bridges and a wild Joe Sullivan for seven first-inning runs and piled up a 12–4 lead by the end of five. Trailing 12–6 heading into the top of the ninth, Detroit scored five runs and had runners on first and second with only one out. But Gee Walker popped to first and Gehringer flied to left to put the game to bed. Fox collected another three hits, making it 29 games in a row for him. Even in defeat, however, the Tigers had shown their mettle, wrote H. G. Salsinger. "Detroit's ninth-inning rally demonstrated the team's spirit. Here they really looked like champions."[3]

The following afternoon, Schoolboy Rowe faltered again, giving up six earned runs in less than eight innings of work. The Tigers won the game, 7–6, in the tenth, but Fox went 0-for-4, snapping his brilliant batting streak. General Crowder's fine five-hitter helped Detroit take the finale, 2–1. It was Crowder's tenth win of the year.

Arriving in Philadelphia for a July 13 doubleheader, the Tigers were a mere game and a half behind the Yankees. Auker took a beating in the opener and was gone by the second inning, having given up seven runs, including a two-run shot by Bob Johnson. Clyde Hatter fared little better in the 18–5 drubbing. Fox drilled a two-run homer, his tenth. In the second game, Bridges rebounded from his bad afternoon in D.C., going the distance in a 6–3 victory, with Greenberg hitting home run number 26. The Jekyll-and-Hyde Rowe followed that up with a well-pitched game, but the Athletics won it in the tenth, 4–3, with Schoolboy taking the tough loss.

The Red Sox, despite their weak offense, had been able to hang near the fringes of contention on the strength of the arms of Lefty Grove and Wes Ferrell. Grove's renaissance had led to an 11–6 mark with an earned run average of 2.65. But Rowe was on his game at Fenway Park on July 18, blanking the Sox on five hits, while Ferrell was hit hard. Schoolboy also contributed at the plate with two singles, a triple, two runs scored and two RBI in the 8–0 win.

Detroit won again the next day, while the Yankees were losing to the Browns in the Bronx. The Tigers woke up on July 20 with an opportunity to do something that had eluded them all season: Move into first place. It was Goslin who played the hero that day; his ninth-inning single drove in Gehringer to break a five-all tie. In the bottom half of the frame, the Sox got the tying and winning runs at second and third with two down. But Auker, who had already pitched two fine innings of relief, retired Joe Cronin on a ground ball to third to slam the door. With the Yankees idle, the win put the Tigers in a virtual tie for the top spot in the American League. In the last game of the series, Detroit's bats pounced on Grove for six earned runs, the most he had given up all season. Pete Fox and backup catcher Ray Hayworth each collected three hits. Bridges, however, could not hold on to a 6–4 ninth-inning lead. None other than Wes Ferrell, one of the best-hitting pitchers in baseball history, blasted a three-run pinch homer to win it. The Yankees split with St. Louis and were back atop the leader board.

With a three-game face-off looming in the Bronx, Cochrane had a message for the Yankees:

> I'm going to throw Rowe against them twice, and when we leave New York next Thursday night we'll be out in front and there will be nothing left of the pennant race but the shouting. I'll start him against them Monday, even if they use [Lefty] Gomez, and close with him Thursday. There's half of the four game series. If we get the breaks and

take the other two games the Yanks will never catch us, and neither will anybody else in the league.[4]

Cochrane's assessment was supported by the numbers. Rowe was 5–0 versus New York in 1934, with an earned run average of 1.76 and a WHIP of 0.935, his best marks against any club. In July of that year, he started two games in a four-game series with New York and won both of them, the second on only three days of rest. He was 2–1 against the Yanks so far in 1935, having given up only three earned runs in 26 innings. Bridges, by contrast, had never pitched well against New York; his 5–16 career mark to that point did not inspire confidence.

The fickleness of Mother Nature threw a monkey wrench in Cochrane's best-laid plans. A downpour in New York on Monday, July 22, necessitated a doubleheader the following afternoon before 62,000 Yankees rooters. First-inning home runs by Cochrane and Greenberg gave the Tigers a quick 2–0 advantage. But Schoolboy Rowe once again was unable to find any kind of rhythm on the mound. Trailing 4–2 in the seventh, the Tigers tied it on RBIs by Rowe and Jo-Jo White. Finally withering in the broiling heat (90 degrees in the shade), Rowe walked leadoff man Red Rolfe in the home seventh. Cochrane pulled him and brought in Chief Hogsett. By the time the inning was over, the Yankees had scored three runs, and that was essentially the ballgame. Greenberg also homered, his 27th, as did Gehrig for the Yankees. By any measure, Rowe's afternoon had not been what the Tigers were expecting. He had given up only three earned runs, but walked five and rarely got ahead of hitters.

The second game of the twin bill was a pitchers' battle between little-used Vic Sorrell and Lefty Gomez, with Detroit prevailing, 3–1. It was only Sorrell's ninth appearance of the season, a complete game that gave the staff a big lift when it needed it most. The 34-year-old veteran and former anchor of the Tigers' rotation had kept quiet all summer, waiting patiently for Cochrane to hand him the ball. Given his opportunity, he made the most of it. "He pitched a great game," Cochrane remarked, "and was in great shape although he hasn't been in there for two weeks. That ought to be a lesson to some of these young pitchers who can't keep in shape even when they're working in regular turn."[5]

Crowder continued his solid mound work on July 24 in a 4–0 white-washing of New York. The win put the Tigers at 54–35, a half-game up on the Yankees, who had fashioned a 51–33 mark. More bad weather prevented the playing of the final game, but the Tigers had taken two of three. In little over a month, they had made up a deficit of seven and a half games on New York. Now, for the first time all season, they stood alone in first place, albeit by a razor-thin margin. H. G. Salsinger thought New York looked like a beaten team. "If Detroit had any fear for the Yankees it should have been dispelled by now. The Yankees of the last three games were a very weak ball club. Their hitting has been bad, their pitching not as good as Detroit's, their base-running stupid and their morale apparently shattered. They are in a very serious slump. Whether they will come out of this slump only the future can tell."[6] The Yankees hit only .231 in the series, and, in the words of Dan Daniel, "have themselves guessing."[7]

On the negative side, Detroit was now short-handed in the pitching department. With the demotion of Clyde Hatter, the spring phenom who had gotten into only eight games in 1935, the mound staff was down to seven men. Hatter's 7.56 earned run average would not be missed, but a team that expected to win a pennant would need a dependable arm or two to replace him. Both Cochrane and Navin hinted that, barring the sudden availability of a major league castoff, Detroit would have to plum the minor league ranks for reinforcements. But who would it be? One possibility was lefty Jake Wade, a Tigers farmhand who had recently tossed a no-hitter in the Pacific Coast League.

The rest of the staff was riddled with question marks. Crowder had been a pleasant surprise, but at 36 years old, he might not be able to hold up the entire season. Rowe and Auker had been wildly inconsistent. Since his ten-game winning streak, Bridges was 3–4 in nine starts with a 6.16 earned run average, and opponents had a .318 batting average in that stretch. Joe Sullivan, the rookie who had begun the season so well, had obviously lost the confidence of his manager. His old control problems, seemingly conquered, had mysteriously returned. He had pitched only twice in July. Chief Hogsett, on the other hand, remained reliable out of the bullpen, but was in danger of being overworked.

The Tigers descended on League Park in Cleveland, hoping to create some distance between themselves and the Yankees. Auker pitched well in running his record to 10–4 in a decisive 8–2 win on July 26. Bridges notched his 14th win, besting ace Mel Harder in a complete-game, 6–2 victory the next day. The enigmatic Rowe, however, followed that game up with a bad performance. Staked to a five-run lead in the opening frame, he lasted less than two innings, getting pummeled for seven hits and five runs. Chief Hogsett came on in relief and allowed only one run the rest of the way, while Detroit beat up on Tribe pitching in a 14–6 romp. Cleveland managed a win in the finale, but the Tigers returned home 2½ lengths in front of New York, who dropped three of four to the Senators at Yankee Stadium. Greenberg was on fire, going 11-for-19 with eight RBI in the four games in Cleveland, as was Goslin, who went 10-for-21.

Pennant fever was once again raging through the Motor City. To feed the hunger of fans for up-to-the-minute game accounts of their Tigers, radio station WMBC came up with a clever solution. Staff engineers installed a public address system on the third floor of the Stormfeltz-Lovely Building at the corner of Woodward and Grand, where the station had its offices. It also happened to be one of the busiest uptown corners during the day, with thousands of office workers scurrying from one place to another. Monitoring ballgame updates as they clicked across the telegraph wire was Bob Evans, WMBC's sports director and a huge Tigers fan. Evans' booming voice relayed every Greenberg homer or Gehringer double through the PA system to the expectant masses below. Gridlock naturally ensued, what with drivers pausing to stick their heads out car windows to catch the latest info. Detroit's finest were dispatched to keep traffic flowing, but the police force was understandably tolerant, and no orders were given to WMBC to remove the speakers.

For Cochrane, it only meant mounting pressure to win. Iffy the Dopester noticed the visible strain in Black Mike's face. "Cochrane is saturnine, dour, even sullen at times. His eyes are as black as his hair…. When he smiles it is like the sun popping out of the dark clouds and eager to escape. His grin is lightning on a dark night, a flash and it is gone."[8]

On July 30, Schoolboy Rowe squared off against the St. Louis Browns at Navin Field in his third bid for win number ten. It was the start of an extended home stand for the Tigers, who would not have to pack their bags again until August 28. Rowe was undone by two bad innings, a four-run fourth and a three-run seventh, and Detroit fell, 8–6. It was Rowe's ninth loss, dropping his record to .500. After the game, Cochrane reluctantly decided he had seen enough. He pulled last year's ace from the rotation. It was a bit of a psychological gambit on Cochrane's part. The threat of a train ticket to Beaumont had spurred Rowe to success in 1934; maybe watching the world from the bullpen would have a similar effect in 1935.

Following two wins against the Browns, rain delayed the start of a three-game series against Walter Johnson's Indians, necessitating a doubleheader on Saturday, August 3. Elden Auker, who had given up only two earned runs in his last 15⅓ innings, started the opener. Detroit got on the scoreboard first thanks to Greenberg's solo home run, his 29th. Auker was in fine form, with the Tribe constantly pounding his sinker into the ground. But with a 3–0 lead in the eighth, it quickly unraveled for the submariner. Joe Vosmik's one-out solo homer narrowed the gap; three batters later, Hal Trosky's two-run single evened the score. Bowed but unbeaten, Auker survived the inning. In the bottom of the eighth, the Tigers regained the lead on Greenberg's second solo round-tripper of the day. Cochrane let Auker start the ninth. He immediately rued the decision when the young pitcher coughed up a solo shot to light-hitting leadoff man Boze Berger, tying the game again.

The Indians had a chance to take their first lead in the tenth. Trosky was on second, Bill Knickerbocker on first after one-out singles off reliever Chief Hogsett. Catcher Ray Hayworth, having entered the game the previous inning as a pinch-hitter for Cochrane, noticed Knickerbocker dancing a little too far off first. Hogsett sneaked a fastball past hard-hitting Odell "Bad News" Hale, and Hayworth immediately whipped the ball down to Greenberg. Knickerbocker dove back to the bag too late to avoid the tag, and umpire Bill Dinneen called him out. The livid Knickerbocker, believing he was safe, put up a loud protest. Not caring for some of Knickerbocker's commentary, Dinneen wasted no time in tossing him from the game. When play resumed with two down, Hale hit a dribbler down to third; Owen charged the ball but could not make a play anywhere. With Trosky now 90 feet away, representing the go-ahead run, Berger bounced into a 6–4 force out, and the Navin Field faithful breathed a little easier.

In the 11th, the Tigers got runners on first and second with one out. Hogsett was due up. But Cochrane ordered Rowe to grab a bat. Schoolboy flied out, and though a wild pitch advanced the runners to second and third, Jo-Jo White grounded out to snuff the rally.

Rowe stayed in to pitch the 12th. Leadoff pinch-hitter Ab Wright hit a chopper to Rogell at short, an easy out for sure, but Rogell's throw to first was wild. Wright hotfooted it down to second base, but, not satisfied there, made a dash for third. Hayworth finally chased the errant ball down and made a strong peg across the diamond to Owen in time to nip Wright. For the strong-armed Hayworth, it was just like when he used to throw rocks at rabbits and squirrels as a kid back in North Carolina. Rowe, who no doubt owed Hayworth a drink later on, proceeded to walk Trosky. But Rowe settled down, got the next batter on a fly ball, and caught Hale looking for the third out. The fortuitous inning later proved to be a turning point in Rowe's season.

Hayworth, leading off the bottom of the 12th, got things going by beating out an infield hit. Gehringer laced a double to left, and Greenberg was walked intentionally to load the bases. That brought up Goslin, hitless in five at-bats, the crowd loudly beseeching for a merciful end to the nerve-wracking game. The Goose got a pitch to his liking and drilled it on a line to center field. Earl Averill caught it but had no chance to nip Hayworth, the Indians' nemesis for the day, who crossed the plate with the winning tally. Schoolboy Rowe finally had his tenth victory, and with it a shot of confidence.

His day had only begun. Much to everyone's surprise, Rowe started the second game, his bullpen exile apparently a *fait accompli*. He went the route, scattering eight hits, walking one, and fanning five. In the words of H. G. Salsinger, "He pitched very elegant ball."[9] Two wins in one afternoon was not a bad showing at all. "It was a thrill-packed afternoon for the fans," the *Detroit Times*' Bud Shaver wrote,

> a day which started under a cloudy and threatening sky and ended in the soft haze of ideal summer twilight. Straw hats sailed into the air as Hank Greenberg hit his twenty-ninth and thirtieth homers of the season in the first game. Rowe was the Schoolboy of old; fast, debonair and with iron control. He finished with a complete return of the poise and confidence which made him the pitching sensation of the league last year. In the ninth, he retired the last three men in order on exactly three pitches.[10]

Bridges had little trouble with the Tribe the next day, fashioning a four-hitter in a 7–0 blanking. His 16th victory, coupled with New York's tough 11–10 loss in the nation's capital, put the Tigers up 4½ games, a welcome bit of breathing room.

The first week of August brought relief from the humidity that had been baking the Detroit area, but there was no respite from the rising cost of putting food on the table. A dozen women, representing nearly a thousand homemakers, appeared before the Common Council to plead for the city's aid in lowering meat prices. Plans were under way to picket butcher shops throughout Detroit. One protest at a Mitchell Avenue meat packing plant resulted in the arrest of three women and one man. The following afternoon, a crowd of over 300 marched on the Davison Street Police Station, successfully demanding the quartet's release. The embattled women insisted that the fight had only begun, and soon the protests threatened to spread to Chicago as well.

One Detroit city official, meanwhile, described the local welfare problem as a "keg of dynamite."[11] Federal relief allotments were set to end within months, just as an additional 10,500 families would be joining the city's welfare rolls. There is an old saying that as General Motors goes, so goes the nation. With that in mind, prognosticators gained hope from Alfred Sloan, the president of GM. Citing improving business trends, he announced a $50,000,000 plant expansion program to increase auto production. The entire automobile industry anticipated an investment of nearly $100,000,000 for growth and development. Other economic indicators pointed positive. International shipping saw a spike, although there was a dark side: Much of the traffic had been in war materials such as scrap iron and steel, a sign that global tensions might soon be coming to a head. Indeed, with Mussolini's refusal to engage in peace talks over his planned Ethiopian conquest, another world war seemed inevitable. While heavy industry may have begun humming, there were still plenty of Americans struggling to find work. On August 15, Roosevelt signed the Social Security Act into law, with a goal of providing benefits for the unemployed and elderly. The president's detractors, however, saw it as further proof of his overreaching socialist agenda.

For much of the early summer of 1935, the Chicago White Sox were one of the most improved teams in the league. By the end of July, Jimmie Dykes's men had beaten the Tigers in eight out of 12 games. The Sox boasted a 51–37 mark, good for third place. Since then, they had apparently forgotten how to hit, losing six of eight games, including one tie. In Detroit on Thursday, August 8, General Crowder added to their misery, getting win number 13 with a 5–2 victory. He got off to a rocky start, giving up singles to the first three batters he faced. He eventually found his groove, however, and the Tigers pulled off four double plays in the game.

Cochrane handed the ball to Schoolboy Rowe the next day against Ted Lyons. In complete command of his pitches and throwing strikes, Rowe was dominant early on, retiring the first 13 batters. The big blow of the day for the Tigers was Greenberg's two-run shot over the scoreboard in left-center field, his 31st of the year. Rowe clung to a 4–3 lead heading into the ninth. He walked leadoff man Luke Appling on a full count, causing a collective groan from the Ladies Day crowd of nearly 27,000. Dykes, foreswearing the sacrifice, flied out. Jackie Hayes shot one through the box for a single, with Appling huffing it to third. Joe Sewell made a bid to tie the game with a hard liner toward center, but Gehringer made a spectacular backhanded stab for the out. Lyons, the pitcher, flied out to Goslin to put the game on ice, and Rowe had win number 12.

Bridges tossed a brilliant three-hitter the next afternoon, his second shutout in a row. Displaying, as the *Detroit News* put it, "almost faultless control and a world of stuff," he became the first American League pitcher that year to top 100 strikeouts.[12] Auker nearly matched him in the Sunday finale, allowing only four hits as Chicago's hitting doldrums continued. Gehringer collected three hits in the 4–1 win, played before more than 33,000 Tigers rooters. Pete Fox, whose latest hitting streak had reached 17 games, went 0-for-3. It was Detroit's ninth win in a row, leaving the Yankees in the rear-view mirror by six full games. The Sox, at 12 games back, had seen their slim pennant hopes exposed as a mere delusion.

After a tough extra-inning loss to the Senators on August 13, the Tigers looked to Rowe to get them back on the winning track. Detroit's offense erupted for 18 runs, and Rowe was the biggest star of the day, both on the mound and at bat. In an incredible display, he went 5-for-5 with a double and a triple, drove in four runs, and scored three. He went the distance, giving up only two runs, further evidence that the Tigers possessed perhaps the game's greatest two-way star. It was Rowe's fourth victory in a row since his brief bullpen sojourn.

The next day, the Senators stopped Tommy Bridges' streak of 23 consecutive scoreless innings, but Detroit still won, 6–3. In the eighth inning, Cecil Travis drove a shot through the box that caromed off Bridges, just above his knee. Staggering, Bridges threw out Travis to end the frame, but he was in too much pain to bat the next inning and exited for a pinch hitter. Still, he picked up win number 18. An examination afterward showed no serious damage, and it was expected that Bridges would not miss his next start. After a loss to Washington the next day, the Tigers welcomed the Yankees to Michigan and Trumbull for the final time in 1935.

New York's Lefty Gomez got the nod in the opening game on August 17. Gomez was in the midst of a down year by his standards. He had topped the American League with 26 wins in 1934, but had a pedestrian 10–12 record so far in 1935. He had pitched much better than his record indicated; in nine of his losses, New York had scored three runs or less, and two runs or less in six of them. Three times the Yanks were shut out while he was on the hill. With a respectable 3.22 earned run average, Gomez deserved a better fate.

Detroit's lead on the Yankees was six games. Opposing Gomez was General Crowder, seeking his 14th win. A packed house at Navin Field saw plenty of scoring opportunities on both sides, but Gomez and Crowder hung on to go the distance. The Tigers won it in the tenth, 3–2, thanks to a mental lapse by Yankees second baseman Jack Saltzgaver. With the bases loaded and one out, Cochrane worked Gomez to a full count before hitting a ground ball that Saltzgaver easily gobbled up. Saltzgaver started to throw to the plate, hesitated, and then inexplicably flung the ball to first as Rogell, the runner at third, streaked home with the game-winning tally. Crowder picked up the victory, while Gomez once again was the victim of poor support.

The game featured a kerfuffle that brought back memories of the Marv Owen-Ducky Medwick tussle in the World Series. In the sixth inning, Tony Lazzeri doubled to center field. As he tried to stretch it into a triple, Jo-Jo White made a strong throw to Gehringer, whose perfect peg to third baseman Owen nipped a sliding Lazzeri. In making the tag, Owen's left hand somehow got jammed between the bag and Lazzeri's foot. In the words of Owen, "I pulled up my hand, and pulled up Tony's foot with it. In doing so, I accidentally twisted his leg and that made him mad."[13] Lazzeri rushed at Owen, and the two would have come to blows were it not for the quick intervention of Yankees third-base coach Art Fletcher and umpire Brick Owens. Although both benches cleared, the disorder was speedily defused. Later in the game, to no one's surprise, Gomez plunked Owen on the shoulder with a fastball. Trotting to first, Owen glared at Gomez and shook his fist, but that was the extent of the hostilities.

Detroit increased its American League lead to eight games the following afternoon, buoyed by Rowe's three-hit shutout. He also blasted his first home run of the campaign and picked up his 14th win. After a tough loss on Monday, August 19, Cochrane gave the ball to Rowe for the final game of the series, despite the pitcher having only two full days of rest. There were a couple of reasons for the choice: Rowe, of course, always pitched well against the Yankees, and Tommy Bridges, Cochrane's other option, almost never did. Besides, Bridges was still nursing a bruised leg from the Cecil Travis line drive in his previous appearance. The strategy backfired, as a tired Rowe gave up six runs in only two innings of work. Greenberg hit his 32nd home run in a losing cause, but Detroit was happy to get a split of the series. According to Frank Navin, more than 120,000 paying customers made their way through the turnstiles for the four games.

Next, Detroit welcomed the third-place Red Sox. By now a distant 12 games back, Boston looked like a team that had decided to mail in the rest of the season. The Tigers won four of the five contests, including two masterful shutouts, one of them by Rowe in which he also homered and drove in three runs. Wrote Iffy the Dopester of the *Detroit Free Press,*

> Tell me, ladies and gentlemen, how Schoolboy Rowe is hitting and I'll tell you how he is pitching. He was hitting 'em again Friday and so he shut out those Boston Beanies. When Babe Ruth was fogging 'em over the plate for Boston it was the same way. Babe and the Schoolboy are natural sluggers. Most pitchers have an idea they should not even be asked to go to the plate—they are that temperamental. But the Schoolboy loves to hit, so when he has felt the thrill of hickory against horsehide, he's all tuned up to see that the opposition doesn't get its share of baseknocks.[14]

The other Tigers whitewash came courtesy of a 29-year-old, journeyman right-hander making his first appearance of the season. Roxie Lawson, whose three-year career with Cleveland and Detroit had consisted of 28 games, one victory, and a 7.09 earned run average, had nevertheless looked impressive down at Toledo, collecting 14 wins. In an effort to give his seven-man staff some much-needed rest, Cochrane called up Lawson to be another available arm in the bullpen. Sixteen-game-winner Lefty Grove was slated to pitch against the Tigers in the fifth game of the series, and Cochrane preferred not to waste one of his regular pitchers in a likely loss. With Detroit nursing a seven-game cushion at the top of the standings, Cochrane reasoned that he could afford to give Lawson the start.

It turned out to be one of the better-pitched games of the year on both sides. Lawson and Grove exchanged goose eggs until the bottom of the fifth inning. With the bases loaded and two down, Goslin rolled one down to first baseman Babe Dahlgren, who let the ball scoot under his legs for a two-run error. That was all that the side-arming Lawson needed in a five-hit shutout. Cochrane was thrilled with the pitching performance. "It looks like he will be able to go in there now and then and hold the opposition for a few innings and start a game once in a while if we need him."[15] Tigers coach Sam Perkins was even more effusive: "Relief pitcher, my eye! If that guy isn't a starting pitcher, I'm crazy, and I've never been in a lunatic asylum in my life."[16]

Lawson was not a complete unknown to Tigers fans. He was a September call-up back in 1933, but got into only four games. The seven-year veteran of the minor leagues did not have a whole lot of what scouts and coaches call "stuff." Instead, he survived on guile and deception with his side-winding delivery. The stringbean Iowa farm boy was once described as "tall, debonair, and casual."[17] He displayed a certain *sang-froid* whenever he took the mound.

Detroit wrapped up its lengthy home stand with six games in four days against the Philadelphia Athletics. The Bengals won five, benefitting again from back-to-back shutouts by Rowe and Lawson in the final two. The Tigers' lead in the American League was a comfortable nine games, but they were going to need every bit of cushion they could get: Of their final 24 games of the season, only five would be at Navin Field.

Hank Greenberg had continued his rampage, with a 1.127 OPS in the dog days of August. In a 13–3 Detroit win at St. Louis at the end of the month, he blasted home run number 35 and drove in five runs. Elden Auker notched his 14th victory. The Tigers took two of three from the Browns and then headed right back home for a Labor Day doubleheader against Chicago. It was a highly unusual morning-afternoon affair, something not seen at Navin Field since 1930. In the a.m. contest, the Sox plated a run off Schoolboy Rowe in the sixth inning, ending his scoreless-innings streak at 24. Not limiting his heroics to the mound, Rowe put a charge into the 31,000-strong breakfast crowd by launching a two-run homer "into the auto park across the fence from the left-field wall."[18] Goslin tallied his 100th RBI in the 6–1 Tigers win.

In the lunchtime game, Fox homered and drove in four runs, Auker tossed a seven-hitter, and Detroit prevailed, 5–0.

The Tigers then embarked on their final eastern swing of the summer, a 15-game, four-city trek that began with a doubleheader at Shibe Park on September 7. Despite not having his best stuff, Bridges won his 19th in the opener, while Auker was lights out in the second game. The submariner carried a no-hitter into the eighth inning, but a leadoff double by Jimmie Foxx broke the spell. Even Athletics fans had wanted to witness history. As Foxx stood on second after his hit, the Shibe Park crowd "booed, hissed and jeered him, and hundreds walked out of the park," reported the *Detroit News*.[19] It was a 15–1 drubbing that featured 20 hits by the Tigers. Baseball fans in the Motor City could not be faulted for wondering if perhaps the American League pennant was all but wrapped up. With the Yankees splitting their own twin bill against Cleveland, Detroit's lead stood at 10½ games.

Even Cochrane was not immune to speculation. "If we win in our league and the Cards win in theirs, then I believe we'll take 'em." Indeed, the first-place Cardinals looked to be in perfect position for their second consecutive National League pennant. "Our team will be less jittery than it was last year, and the pitching should be better. I think, on the whole, the Tigers are a better team than they were a year ago. I think they are good enough to beat the Cards." Black Mike quickly added, "But remember I said we've got to win in the American League first."[20] Frank Navin, meanwhile, wanted his ballpark to be ready in case the Tigers repeated as champions. As he had done in 1934, he arranged for the construction of temporary bleachers along the left-field wall, capable of squeezing in an additional 15,000 to 20,000 fans for the World Series.

As for the ballpark's infield, it was in terrible shape, and not just from the normal wear and tear of a 154-game baseball season. Since June, Navin Field had hosted nightly performances of "Opera Under the Stars," put on by a local theatrical company. The stage, assembled and torn down every evening, extended roughly from dugout to dugout, resulting in dead, patchy spots on the turf. Players had complained about its rough state, so finally Frank Navin ordered head groundskeeper Neal Conway to re-sod the entire infield. If another World Series was in store, Navin Field would have to look its best.

While the pennant was not yet secured, one scribe quipped that Tigers fans themselves were preparing projectiles should there be another cause for near rioting in the World Series. "There is a big run on apples, tomatoes, potatoes and turnips. There is no demand for spinach and such, because how can you throw spinach?"[21]

Chapter Fourteen

The Cubs Blow In

In the face of escalating American unease about the likelihood of war, at the end of August President Roosevelt signed a neutrality resolution to calm the fears of isolationists. "The policy of the Government," he declared, "is definitely committed to the maintenance of peace and the avoidance of any entanglements which would lead us into conflict. At the same time it is the policy of the Government by every peaceful means and without entanglement to cooperate with other similarly-minded governments to promote peace."[1] Violence hit close to home just over a week later: The country was stunned at the news that Huey Long, the controversial populist senator from Louisiana, was shot to death at the state capital building.

As pennant fever gripped Detroit, big changes were under way for the city's Brush Park neighborhood. The former enclave of Detroit's moneyed elite had fallen on hard times over the years. Once-grand brick mansions, long converted to rooming houses, sat decaying. With an eye to the future, the city earmarked a section of Brush Park for a massive slum clearance. Rising in its place would be the massive Brewster-Douglass project, the nation's first federally funded public housing development primarily for low-income African Americans. The first week of September, Eleanor Roosevelt arrived in town for a ceremony marking the demolition of the first dilapidated house. Hundreds more structures were on the docket for destruction. Taking one look at the run-down area, the First Lady deemed it a sore spot that must be eradicated. She predicted that Brewster-Douglass, ambitious in scope, would mean a great deal to the city and the country as a whole.

It was not the only sign of revival. Woodward Avenue, the main artery that split the city into east and west, had oozed class in its glory days. The past couple of decades, however, had seen it slowly overrun by "flea circuses and pitchmen."[2] The recent completion of a much-heralded widening of the thoroughfare promised to usher in a new business boom. Woodward had nearly approached functional obsolescence at only 66 feet across at its narrowest points. The addition of multiple lanes more than doubled the street's width. Almost ten years in planning and construction, the expansion had cost nearly $12,000,000. On September 20, the roadway's grand "re-opening" was marked by a spectacular parade called the "Pageant of Progress," a hopeful harbinger of prosperity. At 7 p.m., President Roosevelt flipped a ceremonial switch in his home in Hyde Park, New York, turning on the new lighting system that bathed Woodward in brilliance before 300,000 awed Detroiters. In a speech, Highway Commissioner Murray D. Van Wagoner touted the possibilities. "More than 100 years ago, your fore-fathers dared dream this dream. Much has happened since then. Detroit has grown to be one of the great cities of the Country.... It is estimated that $100,000,000 in new business places will fringe one of the finest pieces of pavement in Michigan."[3]

Further east in Pompton Lakes, New Jersey, heavyweight boxer Joe Louis took a break from a short workout at his training headquarters. He fielded questions from reporters about his upcoming fight with Max Baer. It was not always easy for Louis to find a few moments of downtime, what with the crowds of autograph seekers who descended daily on the camp. Today, how-ever, had a light schedule. Tomorrow he would get in the ring with his spar-ring partners, and again over the weekend. The main event with Baer would not be until September 24. Louis, however, felt like he was ready.

"I'll fight him like I've fought every one," he remarked with insouciance as he strolled around the grounds. "I'm not going to back away." Louis did not want to talk about the fight, however. Instead, his mind was on the Tigers. Born in Alabama in 1914, he was only 12 years old when his family joined the Great Migration of African Americans seeking better prospects in Detroit and other Northern cities. The man known as the "Brown Bomber" was a Tigers fan through and through. "They're just about in, I guess. I'm going to see them play the Yankees Thursday in New York. I think the Cubs will be the team they'll have to lick in the World Series."[4]

Just a couple of months ago, most observers would have called Louis cuckoo for his Cubs prophecy. On July 5, Chicago had been in fourth place, 10½ games behind the Giants. At that point, manager Gabby Hartnett's team went on an extraordinary 24–3 run to pull within a half-game of the top spot. As August turned to September, the Cubs were still 2½ back, but they once again refused to lose. By the time Louis made his prediction, Chicago was breathing down the necks of first-place St. Louis. A 13–3 drubbing of the Brooklyn Dodgers at Wrigley Field on September 12 gave the Cubs nine con-secutive victories. A mere game separated them from the Cardinals, them-selves winners of ten of 12. Chicago made it ten in a row the following afternoon, while at Sportsman's Park the Cards lost to the Giants in extra innings, 13–10, with Dizzy Dean taking the loss in relief. The Cubs' record stood at 89–52, only percentage points behind the Cardinals at 87–50.

Things were not as tight in the American League. After losing three of four in Washington, however, the Tigers' lead had shrunk to 7½ games. Looming next on the schedule were five games in the Bronx. The Yankees were sizzling, having won 12 of their last 15.

Elden Auker and Red Ruffing squared off in the first game on September 12. The Yankees' righty held the Tigers' bats in check for most of the afternoon, but Greenberg's RBI triple in the eighth, followed by a home run by Goslin, put the Tigers up, 5–4. Tony Lazzeri's pinch-hit RBI single scored Earle Combs to tie it in the bottom half of the inning. In the Detroit ninth, Owen led off with a triple against reliever Johnny Broaca. Auker was allowed to hit, but could only pop up to third for the first out. Jo-Jo White delivered the big blow, a home run that put the Tigers up by a deuce. It was only his second round-tripper of 1935. Detroit hung on to win it, with Auker getting credit for his 17th victory.

During batting practice the next day, Cochrane and a sharply dressed Joe Louis were all smiles as they posed for photographers, exchanging mock slugs. The Tigers played the role of heavyweights that afternoon, relentlessly attacking the Yanks' Lefty Gomez. Greenberg's three-run homer in the eighth inning was the blow that broke the game open, while Schoolboy Rowe survived a pair of blasts by Gehrig in the 13–5 win.

The two teams then split a doubleheader, including another outstanding effort by Roxie Lawson, who won his third game. After getting off to such a promising start when the season began, Lawson had become the odd man out on the staff, despite being virtually the only left-handed starter available to Cochrane. In the Sunday finale, Joe Sullivan took the mound for his first start in nearly three months. He failed to make the most of it. The Yanks lit him up for six runs in less than five innings of work in a Detroit loss. By taking three of the five games at Yankee Stadium, however, the Tigers had seemingly withstood New York's final challenge. When Tommy Bridges won his 20th game on September 16 in Boston, Detroit's lead stood at 9½ with 12 games left to play.

The following afternoon, the Red Sox held on to beat Detroit, 5–4, with Wes Ferrell going all the way for win number 24. Ferrell, a good hitting pitcher, stuck it to the Tigers again the following afternoon. Coming in to pinch-hit with the bases loaded in the ninth inning of a 3–3 tie, Ferrell singled off starter Schoolboy Rowe to win it. In the getaway game, Lefty Grove garnered his 19th win, outdueling General Crowder, 4–1. It was the end of a trying trip to Boston. Wrote Iffy the Dopester, "By the time [the Tigers] escape from Massachusetts and get back to the red flares and skyrockets of old Detroit's celebration, they will be so full of baked beans, tripe, scrapple, clams and lobsters the Tiger snarl will be a bi-carb wheeze."[5]

The Tigers briefly detoured to Detroit for their final three regular-season home games. Hundreds of fans greeted them as their train arrived at Michigan Central Depot. "At least half of the fans at the station were women," clucked the *Detroit News*.[6] The team swept a doubleheader against the Browns on September 21, including the pennant-clincher in the second game. Elden Auker, celebrating his 25th birthday, tossed a six-hit gem in the 1–0 victory that captured Detroit's second consecutive American League title.

Detroit News writer George W. Stark's account of the final moment evocatively portrays the outburst of delight.

> As the long shadows fell across the brilliant green outfield, the square-jawed, angular Auker hurled a third strike past Ed Coleman of the Browns and it was that very pitch that struck the proper statistical note. It signified the Tigers were in, definitely and mathematically. So, come on you Cubs! Or you Cardinals! Catcher Ray Hayworth, having received that third strike, politely passed the pellet back to pitcher Auker, who grinned happily and stuck the ball in his hip pocket to bear in triumph to Mrs. Auker, who will place it among her souvenirs. For with that ball all proceedings in the pursuit of the American League pennant of 1935 were, to all intents and purposes, over. Auker then loped into the dugout, pursued by his chattering teammates and some thousands of hysterical fans. Many thousands were at Navin Field and they proceeded, after properly serenading their heroes, to go their diverse ways, many of them doubtless to carry on their private celebrations into the night.[7]

Later, a festive banquet was held in honor of Frank Navin and Walter Briggs, lasting well into the early hours of the morning. Nearly 100,000 revelers jammed the downtown streets the day after the game as Hudson's department store, in a replay of 1934, unfurled a massive, six-story-high victory banner over its main entrance. "Champions, Detroit is Proud of You," it proclaimed, with a cartoon image of a smiling, crouching Tiger. On hand were Commissioner Kenesaw Mountain Landis, along with Cochrane and his five-year-old daughter, Joan. The manager elicited a delighted roar from the crowd when he shouted that the Tigers "would be the next world champions."[8]

An unknown St. Louis Brown by the name of Earl Caldwell held the Tigers to only three hits in the Navin Field season finale. It was a tough, 1–0 loss for Rowe, who turned in a pearl of his own, giving up four singles, no walks, and striking out ten. Another sellout crowd gave the Tigers a final 1935 attendance of 1,034,929, which led the American League for the second straight year. It was only the second time the franchise had topped a million customers, and the first since 1924. Before the Tigers left for Cleveland and Chicago to close out the campaign, the city honored them with a parade.

Forced to throw underhand because of a college football injury, Elden Auker won 77 games in six seasons with Detroit (courtesy Ernie Harwell Sports Collection, Detroit Public Library).

Riding at the head of a procession that began downtown before crawling along Michigan Avenue toward Navin Field, the players were feted with blaring bands and shrieking sirens. Once at the ballpark, they were presented with congratulatory gifts.

Iffy the Dopester praised the Tigers, indeed the national pastime itself, for injecting pride and joy into the hearts of Detroiters, two emotions that had been in short supply. "And in our darkest hours of despair when it seemed that our grandest dreams had been in vain, when our beloved Detroit was being advertised as a city of mushroom growth, a flash in the pan, a city that was—when our enemies, not only around the world, but within our gates, were denouncing us, vilifying our leaders, there came again the call of baseball."[9]

With the pennant wrapped up, the Tigers took their figurative foot off the gas pedal, losing six of their final seven games. The Yankees, meanwhile, closed their season with an 8–1 run, a case of too little too late. Detroit finished at 93–60, three games ahead of New York. While the Tigers were getting shelled, 14–7, before a handful of fans at League Park in Cleveland on September 24, Joe Louis was slugging his way to a knockout of Max Baer before a crowd of over 90,000 at Yankee Stadium in the Bronx. Back in Detroit, a giant neon sign atop the Garfield Building flashed round-by-round results of the fight to the masses huddled below on Woodward Avenue. For his 12 minutes of work that night, Louis earned just over $200,000. Only hours earlier, the Brown Bomber had exchanged nuptials with a Chicago stenographer named Marva Trotter. In the words of Paul Gallico, "[Louis] went from tenderness to terror, and there is no figuring, or knowing or even believing a man like that. He was supposed to fight Max Baer on his wedding night, but it was no fight, the four rounds that it went. It was a public pole axing. He smashed Baer bloody. He smashed Baer dizzy. He smashed him into the ground, and when he arose, he followed him coolly and smashed him down again."[10]

For the second straight year, the Tigers led the major leagues in batting average (.290), OPS (.801), and runs scored (918). Once again, their dynamic infield got most of the accolades. Greenberg continued his ascension, topping all of baseball in home runs (36), total bases (389), and runs batted in (168). He hit .382 with two outs and runners in scoring position. Gehringer was a model of consistency, leading the club in batting at .330 and in WAR with 7.8. Cochrane played in the fewest games of his career to that point (115), but he was the perfect number-two hitter all season long, drawing 96 walks to boost his on-base percentage to .452. Curiously, Black Mike hit only .271 at Navin Field, but stung the ball at a .365 clip on the road. Rogell scored 90 runs, and Owen overcame his dreadful start to hit .287 with 44 RBI in the second half. In the outfield, Goslin drove in 111, and Pete Fox's .513 slugging percentage was the second highest on the team behind Greenberg. Gee Walker batted .300 for the second time in his career, picking up the slack when Jo-Jo White struggled early.

The Big Three of Rowe, Bridges, and Auker combined for 58 wins, while Crowder stabilized the back end of the rotation with 16. The Tigers tossed more complete games (87) than any other team in the majors, while also topping both circuits in shutouts (16). Among American League clubs, only the Yankees gave up fewer hits or allowed fewer runs.

Meanwhile, the Chicago Cubs, Joe Louis's pick to go to the World Series against Detroit, had been unstoppable. Their winning streak reached 18 games thanks to Larry French's blanking of the Pirates on September 22. That was the final game of the year at Wrigley Field; the Cubs headed south to close out the schedule with five games in St. Louis. The Cardinals trailed Chicago by three games.

The Cubs drew first blood as Lon Warneke tossed a two-hit shutout, his 20th win of 1935. Big right-hander Bill Lee outpitched Dizzy Dean, 6–2, in the first game of a doubleheader two days later, the Cubs' 20th victory in a row. That clinched a National League pennant that had seemed a mere pipe dream back in midsummer. Chicago ran the streak to 21 in the second game, coming back from a 3–0 deficit in the seventh inning to tie it, scoring two in the ninth, and hanging on for a 5–3 win, their 100th of the year. The next day, facing another three-run hole in the ninth, they tied it up to send the game to extra innings. But St. Louis put a stop to the Cubs' improbable run when Ducky Medwick blasted a two-run, walk-off home run in the 11th frame. Chicago lost again on the final day of the regular season, but marched to the World Series with what looked to be unstoppable momentum.

Chicago's was a potent lineup, having scored the most runs in the National League (847), while posting the highest OPS (.761). Manager Charlie Grimm's squad proved the old maxim that baseball is a young man's game; no team in the National League possessed as much youth. Its brightest star was 25-year-old second baseman Billy Herman. A shrewd, hard-nosed player, he typified the aggressive style of the Cubs. "The only thing we had on our minds was to win," he said years later. "And if you didn't play hard, you wouldn't have a friend on the club and you wouldn't be there long."[11] Herman had the best year of his career, pacing the major leagues in hits (227) and doubles (57). His 6.9 WAR was the highest on the Cubs. He and his keystone partner, 27-year-old Billy Jurges, led the senior circuit in assists, putouts, double plays, and fielding percentage at their respective positions. Jurges had made headlines back in 1932 after an incident involving an admiring Cubs fan (and scorned lover) named Violet Valli (born Violet Popovich). Meeting him in his room at the Hotel Carlos in Chicago, Valli pulled a 25-caliber pistol on Jurges. A scuffle ensued. The gun fired three times, hitting Jurges in the finger and ribs, and Valli in the arm.[12] No one was seriously injured. Jurges admitted to reporters that he knew the 21-year-old Valli (described in the press as a "cabaret girl") only slightly and chose not to press charges.[13] With the incident behind him, he continued to develop into one of the finest fielding shortstops in baseball.

The Cubs' corner infield spots were manned by Stan Hack and Phil Cavarretta. The 25-year-old Hack, a California native, hit .311 with a .406 on-base percentage. Known as "Smilin' Stan," he was a Wrigley Field favorite. One player of the era observed that Hack had "more friends than Leo Durocher has enemies."[14] Hack had also supplanted Pittsburgh's Pie Traynor as the league's premier glove man at the hot corner. The scrappy Cavarretta, of Sicilian descent, had grown up less than three miles from Wrigley Field. At 18, he had taken over as the regular first sacker three days into the 1935 season and never stopped hustling, leading the team with 12 triples.

Twenty-three-year-old, switch-hitting left fielder Augie Galan led the league in runs scored (133) and stolen bases (22), while banging out 203 hits with 87 walks. He always maintained that were it not for baseball, he would have taken over his father's laundry business in his home town of Berkeley, California. An excellent fly chaser and a prototypical leadoff man, he formed an excellent hit-and-run combination with Herman, who batted second. In centerfield was Frank Demaree, another Californian, who hit .325 in only his second full season. Chuck Klein, the longtime Philadelphia Phillies slugger, had been acquired in a trade prior to the 1934 season. Hobbled by injuries, and without the benefit of Baker Bowl's cozy components, he had not been the same player the past two years. Nevertheless, he still managed 21 home runs and hit .293 while roaming right field.

The Cubs' most recognizable star was Gabby Hartnett, who, despite his 34 years and nearly 1,500 games caught, remained a force at bat. A Chicago institution, he drove in a team-high 91 runs with a .344/.404/.545 slash line in 1935, earning him Most Valuable Player honors in the National League. He also drew praise for his handling of a pitching staff that surrendered the fewest runs in the NL (596). The biggest studs were 20-game winners Lon Warneke and Bill Lee, who possessed one of the better late-breaking curve-balls in the league. Larry French, Tex Carleton, Roy Henshaw, and Charlie

Root all posted double-digit win totals. At 36, Root was the grizzled guru of the staff. A former flamethrowing ace for the Cubs, he had re-invented himself as a soft-tossing knuckleballer. After an arduous off-season of rowing, Root arrived in camp in 1935 noticeably more svelte. He enjoyed a renaissance on the mound, winning 15 games as a spot starter. Root, of course, is best remembered for having served up Babe Ruth's "called shot" in the 1932 World Series. Despite Chicago's youth, they were not lacking in experience. Many of the Cubs' kids had cut their teeth in that October classic in 1932, which the Yankees swept in four games. The bench had a couple of battle-tested veterans in infielder Woody English and fly chaser Freddie Lindstrom. Like the Tigers, the North Side franchise had a world championship drought of its own. Since defeating Detroit in consecutive World Series in 1907 and 1908, the Cubs had returned to the big dance in 1910, 1918, 1929, and 1932, losing every time.

Chapter Fifteen

"The most obscene language I ever had to take from anybody"

On September 29, President Roosevelt and 10,000 curious onlookers endured 100-degree temperatures to be on hand for the dedication ceremony of the Boulder Dam. Built at a cost of nearly $49 million (not to mention over 100 lives), the massive, concrete arch–gravity dam in the Black Canyon of the Colorado River was the latest testament to engineering's conquest of nature. In a speech broadcast over radio, Roosevelt opened by saying, "This morning I came, I saw, and I was conquered, as everyone would be who sees for the first time this great feat of mankind."[1] What Roosevelt did not do, however, was to mention the name of Herbert Hoover. In 1931, Secretary of the Interior Ray Lyman had tried to name the dam after Hoover, the Republican president at the time. With the economy in free-fall, however, it was a move greeted with scorn among Democrats. With Roosevelt's new Democratic administration now in power, the name became Boulder Dam, and Hoover was left off the dedication's guest list.[2]

Two days later, Charlie Grimm's men got their first look at Navin Field during the lone workout for both teams. The Tigers went through their usual practice drills, but as soon as they made their way off the diamond for the Cubs to take over, the skies opened up and a deluge commenced. Some took this as a bad omen, but Chicago, an unflappable squad, simply ducked back into the visitors' dugout and mugged for the shutterbugs, while the grounds crew frantically covered the field with canvas.

The squall soon let up, and the Cubs trotted onto the field. To a man, they were amazed at left field's new, pocket-sized dimensions. Frank Navin's massive temporary bleachers encroached nearly 15 yards into the greensward. The corner in left, at just over 300 feet from home plate, seemed close enough to spit at. It was an inviting target, even with the makeshift 20-foot screen, "the top half of which is only frail chicken coop wire," wrote the *Chicago Tribune*'s Irving Vaughan.[3] In batting practice, Jurges and Herman launched shots into the makeshift stands, while Hartnett slammed several that rattled against the screen.

The experts were predicting a competitive series. Most agreed it would last either five or six games. A poll of 57 *Associated Press* baseball scribes found 30 favored Chicago, while a majority of members of the Baseball Writers' Association of America leaned toward Detroit. Unlike in 1934, the Tigers were now deemed the more experienced team, if only slightly. The *Cleveland Plain-Dealer*'s Ed Bang put it thus: "There will be no tendency toward the jitters that handicapped Mickey Cochrane's crew last fall." *The Sporting News'* E. G. Brands crunched the numbers and calculated that "the Tigers should be a 25 percent better World's Series team than last year." Dan Daniel of the *New York World-Telegram* wrote, "Greenberg will give the Tigers a big edge in the Series." His associate Tom Meany added: "Rowe is mature and will not be rattled as he was last fall." E. Lansing Ray of the *St. Louis Globe-Democrat* echoed that sentiment: "Give me the cool and collected boys—the veterans— the Tigers." John Lardner of the *North American Newspaper Alliance* prophesied possible divine influence: "I doubt if anything but a miracle of inspiration … can win for the Cubs." Detroit was simply due, in the opinion of Joe Williams, sports editor of the *New York World-Telegram*: "The town has never won a World Series. This can't go on forever."[4]

Chicago, on the other hand, was "an up-and-coming team" in the eyes of the *Cincinnati Times-Star*'s Frank Grayson. "It took a lot of poise," pointed out Ed Zeltner of the *New York Daily Mirror*, "to win the league pennant and this bunch doesn't figure to blow up just because it's a World's Series and they are young." The Cubs, thought Damon Kerby of the *St. Louis Post-Dispatch*, "were hotter than the well-known firecracker." According to Maurice Shevlin, sports editor of the *St. Louis Post-Democrat*, the Cubs possessed a "brilliant array of hurlers." The *Philadelphia Record*'s Art West concurred: "The Cubs are geared to a high competitive pitch." The *International News Service*'s John C. Hoffman was at a loss when it came to the Chicago entry: "For the life of me I don't see how any team can beat the Cubs." From his desk at the *New York Herald-Tribune*, Arthur Patterson cut through the prattle and spoke straight: "Detroit is good but Chicago is better."[5]

The usual baseball swells rolled into Navin Field for Game One on October 2. Babe Ruth was perched in the press box, "dressed in a rhapsody of brown with a white carnation in his coat lapel, and a big, fat cigar in his face."[6] The Babe drew a crowd wherever he went. Getting out of the elevator at his hotel earlier that morning, so many autograph hounds waylaid him that he was forced to duck back behind the closing doors. Figuring the coast was clear a few minutes later, he sneaked out a back entrance, but not before stopping to grab a fistful of cigars from the smoke shop. Also spotted in the stands at Navin Field were Brooklyn Dodgers boss-man Casey Stengel and Cardinals skipper Frankie Frisch. The Fordham Flash took one look at the chummy left-field fence and quipped that Ducky Medwick would get sick if he could see it again. Cincinnati Reds manager Charlie Dressen boasted to anyone within earshot that the Tigers would finish no better than third in the senior circuit. Commissioner Landis, in his customary box seat, took a few moments before the game to announce that any fan interfering with a ball in play would be ejected posthaste. He made no mention, however, of littering left field.

All the eyes of the Motor City were focused on the game, and indeed all the ears as well: Frank Cody, superintendent of Detroit schools, instructed all principals to let their charges listen to the first two games on radio. The teams went with a pair of aces in the opener, Rowe for Detroit and Warneke for the Cubs, both of them sons of Arkansas. As expected, a taut pitchers' duel ensued.

Leadoff hitter Augie Galan took Rowe's first pitch of the game for a strike and fouled off the next offering. He then shot the ball a bit to the left of second base. Rogell tried to gobble it up, but it deflected off his glove and into center field. Galan rounded first and kept on going toward second. Neither Rogell nor Gehringer covered, and Galan made it to the bag standing up. It was ruled a double.

Rowe got two quick strikes on the next batter, Billy Herman, who hit a dribbler down the third base line. Rowe fielded it, but his throw to first hit Herman in the back, allowing Galan to score. It all brought back memories of the first inning of the 1934 Series, when the Tigers' infield had failed to make the

Chicago Cubs manager Charlie Grimm (left) and Mickey Cochrane before the start of the 1935 World Series (courtesy Ernie Harwell Sports Collection, Detroit Public Library).

routine plays. Herman advanced to second on a sacrifice, scored on Hartnett's line single, and, just like that, the Cubs had a 2–0 advantage before the Navin Field faithful had settled into their seats.

Rowe and Warneke then proceeded to exchange goose eggs. With two down in the second, Pete Fox banged a double off the left-field screen for the Tigers' first hit. Rogell hit a fly to Galan, who initially misjudged the ball before making a fine leaping stab to save a run and end the frame. Detroit looked like it might get to Warneke in the fourth. After one out, Greenberg and Goslin both walked, and the fans started to make some noise. Shortstop Jurges made a charging pickup on a slow roller off the bat of Fox, and while his throw was wide of first, Cavarretta made a nice reach for out number two. With runners on second and third, Rogell hit a grounder to Cavarretta to end the mild threat.

Rowe doubled with one out in the fifth but was stranded. Frank Demaree's ninth-inning home run over the makeshift screen in left gave the Cubs some unnecessary insurance. Warneke made amends for his disappointing performance in the 1932 Series, completely dominating the Tigers' bats in a four-hit blanking. Maybe it was the 14 hours of sleep he had gotten the night before. Either way, he was now 9–0 as a starter dating back to August 15. Cochrane, Gehringer, Greenberg, and Goslin, Detroit's 2-3-4-5 hitters, went a combined 0-for-13, and were the main culprits in a popgun attack. Navin Field, the scene of such brouhaha in Game Seven of the 1934 Series, was conspicuously quiet once the tenor of the afternoon had been set. Never before had 47,391 fans acted so politely.

Light snow fell in downtown Detroit in the early hours of October 3. Despite the sun that was out in full force for the start of Game Two, wintry winds swept through Navin Field. Game time temperatures were around 40 degrees in the shade. Wrote John C. Manning in the *Detroit Times*, "They came out today in fur coats and blankets and heavy ulsters and winter gloves and scarves and even a few bed quilts. They came in the face of weather conditions that would have daunted Admiral Byrd."[7]

The Tigers' greeting of Charlie Root was equally cold. The ageless right-hander was one of Chicago's best pitchers in the second half of the season, going 12–3 with a 2.54 earned run average, including a strong September in which he won four games, lost none, and posted a 1.054 WHIP. Root's sweeping delivery, however, was no mystery to Detroit.

Jo-Jo White led off the bottom of the first with a dying quail to left, good for a single. Cochrane drilled a double down the right-field line, scoring

White without a throw. Gehringer then swatted a long, high drive toward the corner in right as the crowd of 47,742 rose from their seats in hysteria. At the last second, a strong crosswind carried the ball foul before it was lost to view, landing somewhere on Trumbull Avenue. The throng begrudgingly sat back down. Given new life, Root tried to sneak a fast one past Gehringer, who punched it back through the box and into center field. Cochrane scored to put Detroit up by a deuce.

That brought Greenberg to the plate. He had ended the season on a down note: Homerless since September 17, he had failed to drive in a run in his last eight games, and yesterday's hitless affair made it nine. Before the Series, a reporter asked about his recent struggles. "That was just one of those things that occur in the life of every ballplayer," Greenberg pointed out. "A half a hundred guys have told me to do this or do that in order to get out of the slump. But I am not going to take their advice, even though I know it was well meant. If I go up there and try to remember what Joe Potatoes or Sam Zilch told me to do, I'll begin to press."[8]

Once in the batter's box, Greenberg took a few practice cuts against the soft-tossing Root. Although the Tigers' first baseman had driven in seven runs and hit .321 in the Series against St. Louis the year before, some critics complained that he had failed to deliver in the clutch. Well, here was a clutch moment, even if it was only the first inning. It was important to pad a lead early against Root, before he settled in. Offered a hanging knuckler, Greenberg drove a blast that Bud Shaver of the *Detroit Times* called "a whistling home run ... which rode the teeth of a northwest gale to land in the left field bleachers."[9] It gave the Tigers a four-run lead and marked the end of the afternoon for Root.

Reliever Roy Henshaw held Detroit at bay for the next couple of innings, but the wheels came off for Chicago in the bottom of the fourth following two quick outs. A hit batsman, a single, two walks, and a wild pitch plated the Tigers' fifth run, and brought up Gehringer with the bases loaded. His line-drive single to center drove in two, and Henshaw was promptly shown the shower.

Bridges, meanwhile, was cruising. Chicago could not manage a hit until Hartnett's base knock with two down in the fourth inning. In the fifth, a one-out single by Jurges scored Cavarretta, who had reached on the first of Greenberg's two errors that inning. With the score still 7–1 in the top of the seventh, Herman came to bat for Chicago with two out and runners on second and third. His single through the left side scored both, and he advanced to second on Goslin's throw home. But before any further damage, Bridges induced Freddie Lindstrom to pop out to Greenberg.

Cochrane led off the home half of the seventh by drawing a walk off right-hander Fabian Kowalik. Gehringer hit an easy grounder to second that looked like a sure double play. Herman scooped the ball up and tossed it to shortstop Jurges, who was upended on Cochrane's hard slide. The Tigers' skipper was ruled out, but his aggressive play prevented the twin killing. After Greenberg was hit by a pitch, Goslin lifted a lazy fly to Augie Galan in left for out number two (although it would have ended the frame had the double play been executed). The next batter was Fox, whose hard liner caromed off the pitcher's torso and into right field. Gehringer raced all the way home from second for the Tigers' eighth run, and when Greenberg noticed right fielder Frank Demaree's nonchalant toss back in to Herman at second, he made a dash for the plate. But Herman took the throw and made a strong peg to the catcher Hartnett. The ball and the sliding Greenberg arrived at the same time; umpire Ernie Quigley thrust his thumb into the air. Greenberg was out, and the inning was over. As the slugger rose slowly to his feet, he held his left wrist awkwardly. It hurt from the slide, but he remained in the game.

The 8–3 score held up, with Bridges pitching a complete-game six-hitter. He walked four and struck out two. "[He] pitched a swell ball game today," Cochrane beamed after the game, sitting in the wire cage that served as his clubhouse office. "He had plenty of stuff and good control and was never in danger. I was glad to see those base hits in the first inning. It's about time we started getting 'em. Isn't it? We've started hitting—now watch us go."[10]

Meanwhile the pain in Greenberg's left wrist got worse, and it started swelling badly. As soon as the game ended, he was taken to the hospital for x-rays. Dr. William E. Keane, the Tigers' team doctor, revealed that the tendons on the back of Greenberg's wrist had been injured in his hard slide into Hartnett. Despite the victory, a dark cloud hung over the Tigers' players. Would their big slugger be able to play in Game Three?

The answer to that question was not immediately apparent. X-rays revealed a left wrist sprain, and the initial diagnosis was that Greenberg would not have to miss any playing time. But the swelling continued, and the pain grew intolerable. Greenberg spent the entire train ride to Chicago that evening soaking his hand in hot water and alternately plunging it into a bucket of ice. By the morning of Game Three, the wrist "had swollen to twice its size," according to Greenberg.[11] Putting on a baseball glove was out of the question. He would not play that day. As to the rest of the Series ... well, he would rather not think about that yet.

Cochrane's options were limited. Before the game, Schoolboy Rowe begged his manager to put him in at first base. It was an enticing proposition. Rowe, an excellent athlete, could certainly hit, and, at 6'4" and 210 pounds, he made a sizable target as a first sacker. Nevertheless, he was totally unfamiliar with the position, and the risk of injury was too great. The last thing Cochrane needed was another star in the sick bay. "Stick around anyway," the manager told Rowe, "I may use you."[12] His words would prove prophetic.

A marginally better alternative would have been for Cochrane himself to play first base and put the reliable Hayworth behind the plate. But, like Rowe, Cochrane did not know a first baseman's glove from an oven mitt. With a surplus of outfielders, he could always go with White, Goslin, Fox, or Gee Walker at first, but they also were devoid of any experience there.

Finally, Frank Navin stepped in and gave the order for Cochrane to shift Marv Owen from third to first. Owen at least had the benefit of having played 27 games at the position back in his rookie season in 1931. Navin's subsequent directive was to put little-used Flea Clifton at third base. In 43 games in 1935, only his second full season in the majors, the 26-year-old Clifton had hit a decidedly weak .255. He possessed virtually no extra-base power. Despite his slight frame (or perhaps because of it), he possessed a certain tenacity and feistiness on the bases that made him a feared runner. He backed down to no one: If there was a brawl on the field, Flea Clifton could likely be found in the middle of the pile. This was no surprise, since he had long modeled his playing style after Ty Cobb, his boyhood hero.

The bleak childhood of Herman Earl Clifton was straight out of a Charles Dickens novel. Born in Cincinnati's hardscrabble West End, he remembered little of his father, killed in the Argonne Offensive in World War I while Herman was still a boy. At age 15, his mother was murdered by a drunken acquaintance of his stepfather's, strangled with Herman's own school necktie, no less. He never got along with his stepfather, who finally had enough of the lad and kicked him out of the house into the snow. Making his way to Kentucky, Clifton was left to fend for himself. Homeless and alone, living behind a garage, he huddled close to a potbellied stove and survived on the charity of locals. Often, the choice was to steal or starve.

Through all the hardship, he continued in school, where he was a strong student who loved to read. One book in particular caught his attention: A biography of Ty Cobb. Clifton himself loved to play baseball. To the impressionable youngster, "The Georgia Peach" became a hero to emulate, at least on the field, and Clifton dreamed of one day playing for the Tigers. Despite being a product of the streets, Clifton was determined to stay out of trouble and make something of his life. He starred on the Cincinnati sandlots and semipro leagues and was offered a contract by the St. Louis Cardinals. In the end, he signed with the Tigers for less money. He became a favorite of Greenberg's when the two first played in the minors together at Raleigh, North Carolina, in 1930. "He was a tough little guy," Greenberg recalled years later. Now, while the slugger licked his wounds, Flea Clifton found himself starting a World Series game.

Whatever had ailed the Cubs in Game Two, they hoped some home cooking would prove to be a cure in Game Three. Setting the tone for the day, owner Philip K. Wrigley had the 1935 National League championship banner hoisted up the flagpole in center field. This was a radical break with tradition: Pennant-winning teams had always reserved such ceremony for the following season. It was a frigid day, but Chicago Mayor Edward J. Kelly raised eyebrows by eschewing a topcoat as he sat in his box seat.

An energetic crowd of over 45,000 yelled and screamed itself hoarse from the very first pitch, a strike to Jo-Jo White from 25-year-old, sophomore right-hander Bill Lee. White swung and missed on a full count, but the ball got away from Hartnett, who had to retrieve it and throw to first to register the putout. Cubs fans roared their approval, an exclamation point to let everyone know they were at Wrigley Field now. The members of the press, over 400 strong, took note.

The Cubs put Elden Auker to the test almost immediately, with runners on first and second and one out in the bottom of the first inning. But a nifty 6–4–3 double play temporarily quieted the crowd. In the second, Billy Rogell banged the first hit for Detroit, a single with one out. He advanced to third on a groundout, but Clifton hit a high chopper that the 6'3" Lee leaped up to snare in his glove. The Cubs' pitcher tossed to Cavarretta at first to end the threat.

Leading off the Cubs' second was the right-handed-hitting Frank Demaree, who quickly got behind 0–2. Auker made a good pitch tailing away, but Demaree, who had hit only two home runs all season in 385 at-bats, reached out and caught the ball on the end of his bat, dunking his second round-tripper of the Series into the right-field bleachers. Before the frame was over, Chicago tacked on an unearned run set up by Clifton's fielding miscue.

The Tigers threatened again in the third. After two quick outs, Cochrane drew a walk and advanced to second on a Gehringer single. Goslin made a bid for an extra-base hit with a screaming drive to left, but Galan sprinted back at full speed, leaped, and made a fine snare at the base of the bleachers.

Auker's sinker had the Cubs constantly hitting the ball into the ground. In the fifth inning, he walked leadoff man Billy Jurges, who eventually scored on Augie Galan's seeing-eye single. Chicago had a chance for more with runners at the corners and only one out, but Auker got Lindstrom to ground into an easy 4–6–3 double play.

The Tigers finally got to Lee in the sixth on Pete Fox's RBI triple. With one out and Rogell at the plate, Fox began taking a sizeable lead off third base. On Lee's second pitch, catcher Hartnett rifled a throw down to Stan Hack. Fox dived back to the third-base bag, but Hack quickly put the tag down, and umpire Ernie Quigley yelled an emphatic "out!" Fox, for his part, accepted the verdict without any gripe, but third-base coach Del Baker got in Quigley's face to state his objections. Quigley didn't waste any time in giving Baker the boot. With the rally deflated, Rogell struck out as the folks at Wrigley Field thundered approval.

The Cubs had their own issues with the umpiring in the bottom half of the frame. Cavarretta, on first with two down, was thrown out attempting to steal. Manager Charlie Grimm, coaching at third, disagreed with the decision by second-base umpire George Moriarty. Grimm charged up to Moriarty, followed by five or six other bear cubs, to vent his dissatisfaction. Grimm may have figured that Moriarty harbored a bias for the Tigers. The ump, after all, had been a third baseman for Detroit from 1909 to 1915, and managed the club in 1927 and 1928. Either way, Moriarty took exception to something in Grimm's tone and ordered that he vacate the premises without further ado.

Lee had handcuffed the Tigers most of the day, but his armor began to crack in the eighth inning. Jo Jo White led off with a walk. One out later, Gehringer's sinking drive to right got past Demaree for a double, with White holding at third. Next, Goslin's hard-hit liner caromed off first base and over Cavarretta for a single. White and Gehringer both scampered home to tie the game, and Lee was done for the day.

The Tigers rudely greeted reliever Lon Warneke. Fox singled to left, with Goslin stopping at second. On a 2–2 count, Rogell shot one into center field; Goslin scored to break the tie, and the aggressive Fox streaked over to third. Rogell tried to steal second, but Hartnett's strong throw drove him back to first base. A rundown ensued, which the Cubs executed poorly; although Rogell eventually was tagged out, Fox saw an opportunity and bolted home with another run to make it 5–3, Detroit.

To start the eighth, Schoolboy Rowe replaced Chief Hogsett, who had relieved Auker an inning earlier. The Cubs' bench jockeys, meanwhile, kept up a steady stream of invective against umpire Moriarty. For his part, Moriarty did not hold back from cursing and ranting at Grimm's men. Having finally had his fill, the umpire strode over to the Chicago dugout and tossed Woody English and Tuck Stainback, a couple of reserves who apparently were making the most noise. English, the captain of the team, had played in only 34 games and hit .202 during the regular season. It was a long time since 1930, when he batted .335 with 100 walks, 214 hits, and 152 runs scored. Now, at age 29, his fine career was on a steady downward arc. He would have been better off keeping his mouth shut on this day; his unavailability later proved to be crucial.

Rowe set Chicago down in order. For the first out in the ninth, he got Cavarretta on a long fly that drove White to the wall. But three straight singles, two of them the pinch-hit variety by Chuck Klein and Ken O'Dea, cut the deficit to 5–4 and put runners at the corners. Rowe was fooling nobody, but Cochrane stayed with him. Jo-Jo White tracked down Galan's deep drive in center, but Klein jogged home with the tying run. Herman grounded out to Clifton to send the game into extras, but the damage had been done.

Goslin gave the Tigers a chance to take the lead with a two-out double in the tenth. Fox, however, managed only a weak pop fly to first. The Cubs threatened in the home half when Lindstrom drove Rowe's first pitch for a double. Grimm ordered Hartnett to bunt, a curious move on the surface given Hartnett's .344 average in 1935 with 91 RBI. But the man known as "Old Tomato Face" was also one of the best bunters in the National League. Hartnett did his job in this case, laying down a perfect sacrifice that advanced Lindstrom to third. Two easy groundouts by Demaree and Cavarretta, however, saved Rowe from the gallows and opened Grimm up to second-guessing for his small-ball strategy.

The Cubs finally coughed up the game in the 11th inning. Facing Larry French, Rogell started things off by hitting an easy grounder to shortstop, a ball that the sure-handed Jurges normally ate up. Jurges, however, was no longer in the game, having been pinch-hit for by Chuck Klein back in the ninth inning. With reserve shortstop Woody English ejected by Moriarty, manager Grimm had been forced to shuffle third baseman Hack over to short, a position he had never played in his life. Rogell's ground ball went right under the glove of Hack. It went as a hit, but the official scorer easily could have called it an error.

Chicago caught a break when Owen's bad bunt forced Rogell at second. That brought up Flea Clifton, who hit a garden-variety groundball to third. Had Hack still been playing there, the outcome may have been different. Center fielder Lindstrom, however, had replaced Hack at the hot corner. Lindstrom, a former third baseman back in his Giants days, had not played the position regularly in half a decade, and not at all since 1932. Understandably rusty, he fumbled Clifton's grounder and could not make a throw anywhere. That made it two key fielding blunders in the inning by two men playing unfamiliar positions. The Tigers had something going, with runners on first and second and only one out.

Rowe was due up, and Cochrane let him hit, figuring he was as good as anybody else on the Tigers' bench was. Schoolboy did not reward his manager's faith, however, as he whiffed on three pitches. Jo-Joe White bailed him out, slashing a single to center that drove in Owen and sent Clifton to third. White took second on the throw home. It was 6–5 Tigers, and Cochrane stood at the plate with the chance to drive in some insurance runs. All he mustered was a foul pop-up to the catcher.

It did not matter, as Rowe made short work of the Cubs in the bottom of the 11th, finishing things off with a strikeout of pinch-hitter Walt Stephenson. The Tigers, refusing to be intimidated by the electric atmosphere at Wrigley Field, had gutted out an impressive win in two hours and 27 minutes. "Eleven wild, thrilling, spectacular, even boisterous, umpire-baiting innings," wrote the *Chicago Tribune*'s Irving Vaughan.[13] Cochrane called it the toughest World Series game he had ever played in.

Charlie Grimm gave the Tigers credit, but also insisted that "in all my baseball I never have heard an umpire abuse members of a ball team with the language Moriarty used ... to Herman, to Jurges, to English, and to me, and then to the entire bench." Grimm claimed he was "showered with not only profane but the most obscene language I ever had to take from anybody." Even National League president Ford Frick, who had a ringside seat to the sparring, acknowledged that Moriarty had used "blasphemous language."[14] Commissioner Landis promised a thorough investigation. Second-guessing is as old as sports itself, but the Cubs walked off the field convinced that, were it not for the quick trigger of Moriarty in ejecting Woody English, the outcome of the game might have been very different indeed.

Chapter Sixteen

"This mad, delirious city"

The following morning, Landis summoned Grimm, English, Stainback, and the four men in blue who were working the Series. In the sober atmosphere of the commissioner's office at 333 North Michigan Avenue, each party stated its case. Later, Landis told reporters he would withhold any decision about the matter until after the Series.

As Game Four got under way, a chorus of boos rang down from the Wrigley Field stands as Moriarty was announced as the first-base umpire. Police officers stationed themselves on the rooftops along Waveland and Sheffield Avenues, in order to prevent freeloading fans from claiming those swell vantage points. Greenberg worked out with the Tigers beforehand, but it was obvious that he had trouble gripping a bat and could not play. Rowe was scheduled to start, but that was no longer an option, given his four innings of relief work the day before. The same was true of Larry French, who had pitched two frames. Cochrane, however, wasted no time deciding who his starter would be. He chose the experienced General Crowder; in fact, he notified him of his decision soon after the conclusion of Game Three. This allowed Crowder to retire early that night and get 11 hours of sleep.

Grimm went with Tex Carleton, the righty from Comanche who won 11 games in 1935, his first since coming to the Windy City via St. Louis. The previous year, he had pitched with little distinction in the World Series against the Tigers, adding an element of intrigue to the matchup. Of late, he had been the forgotten man of the Chicago staff, making only one appearance during the 21-game winning streak, and that only because no other hurler was available.

Detroit had him on the ropes in the second inning with the bases loaded and nobody out. But Owen popped up, and Flea Clifton, in the lineup again in Greenberg's absence, lined into a double play to foil the rally. Carleton settled down to turn in a fine performance, but Crowder was just a bit better. The old veteran, salvaged from the scrap heap the year before, gave up only a leadoff home run to Hartnett in the second. The next inning, Detroit put

194

runners at the corners with one out for Charlie Gehringer. The Mechanical Man drove a pitch toward right-center that a sprinting Freddie Lindstrom got a glove on, but the ball slipped out of his grip for an RBI two-bagger. Lindstrom badly jammed his thumb in the attempt but stayed in the game.

That is how things stood until the sixth inning, when Detroit took advantage of a pair of fielding flubs. With two outs, Flea Clifton poked a long, high fly to left. Galan, one of the league's premier fly chasers, dashed to the wall with his back to the plate. At the last moment, he turned, reached up to make the catch ... and the ball promptly popped out of his glove. Instead of being the third out, the speedy Clifton made it easily into second.

Great teams take advantage of the opposition's mistakes, especially when given additional outs in an inning. Crowder, the next batter, hit one softly to Jurges at short, who reached down nonchalantly for the ball ... and it wasn't there. It skittered under his glove for an error, and Clifton flew home with the second Tigers run.

In the bottom half of the frame, Billy Herman led off with a double, but the Cubs failed to bring him home. It was their last hit until the bottom of the ninth. With one out, Demaree and Cavarretta both singled, putting the tying run at second. Hack smacked a sharp grounder right at Rogell, who flipped it over to Gehringer to start a game-ending double play.

For Chicago, it was the first time they had lost three games in a row since the beginning of August. Detroit's offense was good enough, but just barely, having left 13 men on base in Game Four. After the game, Cochrane sat at his locker, puffing on a cigarette as he pulled off his leather shin guards. The strain of competition was beginning to show on Black Mike's visage; one had to wonder how much sleep he had gotten in the last week. Cochrane understood that a 3–1 Series lead could disappear quickly, and he was wary of overconfidence in his club. He praised Crowder's effort. "He pitched a smart, cunning game. It was marvelous. But those young Cubs certainly hit the ball hard. They're tough to beat."[1]

Gabby Hartnett was not as quick to give credit to the opposition. He insisted that Detroit's win was a product of luck. Galan made no alibis for dropping Clifton's long drive in the sixth, setting up the winning tally. "I just missed it—that's all. But I'm going to make a prediction that the Cubs are going to win the next three games. We're going to Detroit tomorrow night."[2]

If the Cubs were indeed going to return to the Motor City, they would have to go through Schoolboy Rowe first. A classic big-game pitcher, Rowe loved taking the ball when so much was riding on the outcome. It was a must-win for Chicago, and Rowe understood the basic tenet that it was imperative for a team to go for the jugular when the opposition was down. The Tigers, however, were banged up. Not only would Greenberg still not play, but Gehringer was also suffering from a slightly sprained left wrist. Owen, the man replacing Greenberg at first, had to scramble to find a first baseman's glove large enough to accommodate a swollen thumb sustained in Game Four.

The Cubs hitched their cart to Lon Warneke, the winner in the Series opener. They would be missing their regular center fielder, however: Like Owen, Freddie Lindstrom woke up that morning with a badly inflamed thumb, a result of his muff of Gehringer's fly ball the day before. Lindstrom could barely bend the digit, and the Cubs announced that he would be out for the rest of the Series.

When one door closes, another one opens. On October 6, 1935, one day short of his 31st birthday, the door opened for Chuck Klein. Benched for nearly the entire month of September, he was 1-for-4 in a primarily pinch-hitting role in the Series, and had scored the tying run in the ninth inning of Game Three. Klein was clearly on the downside of his great career. A prototypical left-handed slugger, he had averaged 36 home runs and 139 RBI for the woeful Philadelphia Phillies from 1929 to 1933. His detractors argued that Klein's numbers benefitted from the ridiculously short distance (280 feet down the line) to the 80-foot-high, right-field wall at Baker Bowl. In his five-plus years with the Phillies, he had hit an outrageous .420 at home and .296 on the road. He was the only marketable commodity for owner Gerald Nugent, whose franchise bled money. Klein won the National League's Triple Crown in 1933 with 28 homers, 120 RBI, and a .368 average. He also topped the circuit in hits (223), doubles (44), and OPS (1.025) for the second year in a row. The Phillies lost 92 games, drawing only 156,421 customers that year, and Nugent had little choice but to sell Klein to the Cubs in November. In return, he received $65,000 in cash and three aging players in Mark Koenig, Harvey Hendrick, and Ted Kleinhans, who contributed virtually nothing to their new team.

Klein arrived in Chicago in 1934 amid much ballyhoo. A serious leg injury in early May, however, hampered his production. By season's end, he had proven that Wrigley Field was no Baker Bowl, although most players would be satisfied with a .301 average and 20 home runs. In 1935, he failed to hit .300 for the first time in his career. Still a solid hitter, Klein was on the outside looking in as the Cubs roared to the pennant in September. Worse still, he had fallen out of favor with the Chicago fans and press.

Billy Herman led off the bottom of the third inning in a scoreless Game

Five by whacking a low liner toward the corner in left. It caromed off the wall and bounced past Jo-Jo White, allowing Herman to race into third. That brought up Klein. His moment of redemption came on a 1–1 count, when Schoolboy Rowe made a terrible pitch, down the middle, waist-high. Klein unleashed his powerful swing and launched a ball deep to right that sailed over the permanent bleachers and banged off a brick wall. The titanic blast put the Cubs up, 2–0, and the crowd of 49,237 shook Wrigley Field to the rafters. Cochrane, taking no chances, immediately ordered Elden Auker to start warming up in the bullpen.

Rowe quickly bounced back, however, retiring the next ten Cubs. Warneke was also in top form, allowing only three baserunners through the first six innings. But all was not well with the Cubs right-hander. In the third inning, he threw an overhand curve to Rowe and felt a sudden snap in his shoulder, followed by a twinge of pain. He kept quiet about it, but the arm bothered him the next frame, when the Tigers eked out two hits but could not score. Catcher Hartnett noticed a lack of zip on Warneke's first pitch in the sixth, and the pitcher's arm seemed to drop as if dead. Hartnett headed out to the mound to see what was up, but Warneke insisted he was okay. He gutted it out through a one-two-three inning, but then headed back to the dugout and gave Grimm the unhappy news: He could not go on. The pain was too much.

Jurges led off the seventh with a single and was bunted to second by Bill Lee, the new Cubs pitcher. Augie Galan cued one that hugged the grass on its way toward first base. Owen, who was playing first only because of Greenberg's injury, let the ball scoot under him and into right field. The speedy Jurges tore around third. Right-fielder Jo-Jo White's strong throw arrived at the plate the same time as the runner. Jurges barreled into Cochrane, who held onto the ball even as he tumbled backward. Umpire Moriarty called Jurges out. The Cubs put up an argument, and the fans booed their disapproval, but it made no difference. Galan took second on the play at the plate and scored an unearned run moments later when Herman doubled to right-center. Chuck Klein then worked Rowe to a full count before grounding out to Owen to keep the affair at 3–0.

No one could blame the Tigers for breathing a collective sigh of relief now that Warneke was back in the trainer's room. Lee, however, hung tough. Detroit threatened in the eighth inning with runners on first and second and two outs. Cochrane made a bid for a hit, but Cavarretta smothered his hot shot to first and tossed to Lee covering the bag for the third out.

Detroit refused to go down without a fight. Gehringer, Goslin, and Fox hit three straight singles to open the ninth, shaving the score to 3–1. With runners on first and second, Rogell hit a soft, shallow fly to Klein in center field for the first out. The runners stayed put. Pinch-hitter Gee Walker's excuse-me swing produced a slow roller to second; Billy Herman scooped it up and tossed to first. Now, with Goslin dancing off third and Fox off second, it was all up to Flea Clifton. Bill Lee fed him an inside fastball, and he skied a high pop fly on the first-base side. Phil Cavarretta drifted over next to the Tigers' dugout, reached his glove into the stands, and plucked the ball out of the October air to end the game.

For Schoolboy Rowe, it was a tough pill to swallow: Eight innings pitched, eight hits, two earned runs, one walk, three strikeouts, and one very bad pitch to Chuck Klein. As for Warneke, he had looked masterful before the injury. Back in the clubhouse, the Cubs' righty listened to the game's denouement on the radio. As he lay on the training table, an electric heat lamp burned the pain out of his shoulder, standard practice in the days before an ice pack was deemed the better solution. A reporter asked him why he had not come out of the game earlier. "I didn't tell Charlie I was through because I wanted to win," Warneke mumbled through his chaw of tobacco, a cigarette dangling from the corner of his mouth.[3] Grimm, for his part, insisted that the health of Warneke's arm was worth more than any championship.

For the second year in a row, the World Series headed back to Detroit with the Tigers one victory away from a championship. Probably nobody was more eager to get out of the Windy City than umpire George Moriarty, who had become public enemy number one. Cochrane's men had to hurry to catch their 5:00 train. Asked about his Game Six pitcher, he offered four parting words for the press: "Tommy Bridges will work."[4] Five hours later, a throng of thousands, eager to see their heroes, greeted them at Michigan Central Station. The crowd saved its biggest cheer for Hank Greenberg, whose status for the next day's contest was still very much up in the air. His manager swore that he would put his name in the lineup if it were at all humanly possible. The only certainty was that Detroit needed Greenberg's bat: Flea Clifton and Marv Owen, his replacements both offensively and defensively, were without a hit in the Series.

⚾ ⚾ ⚾

Baseball fans in Detroit were ready for this day. The 48,000-plus packing Navin Field were a boisterous bunch and did not have to wait long for the Tigers to give them something to cheer. Tommy Bridges, seeking his second win of the Series, set Chicago down in order in the first inning. His mound opponent, Larry French, was trying to avoid his second Series loss. Detroit got to him in the first inning. Singles by Cochrane and Gehringer put runners at first and second with two down. Next up, Pete Fox pulled one down the third base line; Hack dove to his right but was unable to get a glove on it, and the ball rolled into the corner. Cochrane raced home and Gehringer easily made it to third on the stand-up double. Not wanting to concede any more runs, Grimm ordered an intentional pass to Gee Walker, who was getting his first start of the Series in center field. The strategy worked. With the bases loaded, Billy Rogell bounced one right back to French, who tossed it to home to force Gehringer and squelch the rally.

Billy Jurges opened the Chicago third with a single up the middle. French muffed two attempts to lay down a bunt and eventually struck out. On a 3–2 count, Galan lined one just out of the reach of Gehringer, with Jurges taking third. Billy Herman roped a single into right that scored Jurges to tie the game. The speedy Galan, trying to make third, was gunned down by a strong throw from Pete Fox. Convinced that Clifton pushed him off the bag, Galan put up an argument with Moriarty, the third-base umpire. Moriarty, for his part, made a public display of jawing right back at Galan, which excited the crowd even further. Chuck Klein then made a bid for a home run with a deep drive to right, but Fox raced far to the scoreboard to make a spectacular catch.

The Tigers had French on the ropes in the fourth inning. Walker opened with a single and stopped at second on Rogell's base knock to left. With the infield drawn in, Stan Hack pounced on Owen's bunt down the third base line and threw a strong peg to Jurges to force Rogell. With runners at the corners, Bridges bounced into what looked to be an easy 5–4–3 double play, but the Tigers' pitcher, tearing down the first-base line, beat the relay throw from Herman by less than a step. Walker scored, and Detroit had a 2–1 lead.

Chicago took the advantage right back in the next inning, however. With one on and one out, Galan took a borderline pitch for strike three. He spun around and put up a squawk, but umpire Quigley let the critique pass. With a count of three balls and one strike on Herman, Bridges grooved a pitch that the Cubs' second baseman rocketed on a line over the fence in left. Chicago had its first lead of the afternoon, 3–2. The Navin Field crowd, in such a hopeful state just moments before, felt hints of panic set in.

A mild brouhaha occurred in the top of the sixth. With two outs, Hack doubled off the scoreboard in right. Jurges hit a chopper down to Clifton, who reached out to tag the charging Hack. The runner appeared to evade the swipe, but Moriarty thumbed him out, claiming he ran out of the baseline. Hack put up a howl, and Moriarty responded in kind with theatrical gestures, which only ignited the crowd further. Grimm, coaching at third base, stayed above the fray this time.

In the home half of the inning, French got two quick outs before Rogell drove one into the left-field corner that bounded into the stands for a ground-rule double. That brought up Owen, still hitless in the Series. In the biggest at-bat of his life, he came through, lining a single to left that plated Rogell to tie the affair at three. Bridges fanned, but then headed back out to the mound to try to keep Chicago in check.

After two scoreless frames, Stan Hack led off the top of the ninth inning for the Cubs. Twenty-five years old, Hack had hit .300 for the first time as a regular in 1935. He was 1-for-3 so far against Bridges, including a double in his last at-bat. This time, he got a pitch he liked and drilled it toward deep center field. It caromed off the flagpole at the base of the wall, and by the time Gee Walker could get it back to the infield, Hack was standing on third base with the potential go-ahead run.

All Billy Jurges needed was a long fly or deep infield grounder. The last thing he wanted to do was strike out. Like most of the Cubs, Jurges was a solid contact hitter, striking out only 39 times in 1935. Bridges, however, conceded nothing. With the infield pulled in for a possible play at the plate, he got Jurges to swing and miss on three straight pitches. That brought up French, and Charlie Grimm had a decision to make. Should he let his pitcher hit and thus keep him in the game, or should he pull him for a pinch-hitter with a chance to take the lead?

Grimm made his choice, and French stayed in to hit. He swung and missed on Bridges' first two offerings, then tapped a weak grounder back to the mound. Bridges fielded it, checked Hack back to the bag at third, and tossed to Owen at first for out number two.

From a twenty-first-century baseball perspective, the fact that Grimm allowed French to bat borders on the ludicrous. Today, all but the very best and most durable starting pitchers are usually long gone by the seventh inning. They certainly do not go to bat in the ninth inning of a must-win World Series game with the go-ahead run 90 feet away. In 1935, however, managers expected pitchers to finish what they started. French had pitched 16 complete games in 30 starts. Even more telling was that Cubs pitchers went the distance 81 times that season, the most in the National League. In all of baseball, only the Boston Red Sox (82) and the Tigers (87) pitched more complete games.

Even by the standards of the day, however, Grimm's declining to insert a pinch-hitter for French opened the manager up to criticism. After all, it was not as if French was tossing a perfect game; the Tigers had collected ten hits off him in eight innings. He was a lifetime .185 hitter, not bad for a pitcher. The Cubs' bench, however, had three other able bodies, any of whom would have been far likelier to deliver a key blow. There was backup catcher Ken O'Dea, who had delivered a clutch ninth-inning pinch hit in Game Three, as well as another receiver, Wally Stephenson. In addition, Woody English, the captain of the team and at one time the best player on the Cubs, had still not seen action in the Series. Couldn't Grimm take his chances with one of them

The unflappable Tommy Bridges was a three-time 20-game-winner with the Tigers. He etched his name in World Series lore with his gutsy performance in the ninth inning of Game Six in 1935 (courtesy Ernie Harwell Sports Collection, Detroit Public Library).

and then send in a relief pitcher capable of getting three outs in the ninth? Apparently not.

That left it up to Galan, who took a called strike, then flailed at strike two. Bridges' next pitch was an errant curve ball that bounced two feet in front of the plate. Cochrane, with the agility of a cat, got down to his knees and smothered it—keeping it from getting away and allowing the go-ahead run to score. Hack was forced to scamper back to third. Later, Frank Navin called Cochrane's block "the most important play of the Series."[5] Bridges came to the set and pitched again. Galan swung and lofted a high pop fly to shallow left field. Rogell, Clifton, and Goslin all converged on it as Hack headed for home. At the last moment, the charging Goslin made a fine catch, and the Chicago threat was over. Tigers fans exploded in cheers.

It was the most pivotal moment of the entire 1935 World Series. Had Hack been able to score the go-ahead run, Tigers history may have been very different indeed. Years later, Billy Herman could only shake his head and wonder what might have been. "When I think back to the 1935 World Series, all I can see is Hack standing on third base, waiting for somebody to drive him in. Seems he stood there for hours and hours."[6] Cochrane called it the finest exhibition of pitching he had ever seen in a World Series.

Clifton fanned on a three-two count to start the bottom of the ninth. Cochrane hit a smash up the middle; Herman ranged far to his right, knocking it down with his glove, but was unable to make a play. With the lefty French on the mound, Cochrane took a modest lead off first, as Cavarretta held him close. The next batter was the speedy Gehringer, a hard man to double up. As French wound and delivered, Cavarretta pulled slightly off the bag. The pitch was low and inside to Gehringer, who hit a scorching one-hopper right to the first baseman, a potential double-play ball. To Cavarretta, it seemed to explode right on top of him; decades later, he would remember it as the hardest-hit ball he faced in over 20 years of playing first base. He threw up his hands in self-defense; the ball tore right through the webbing of his mitt, but he was just able to stab it with his bare left hand. Normally, his instinct would have been to throw the ball down to second to get the lead runner, and, with any luck, a double play. But the ball had smacked so hard against his throwing hand, stinging it, that he did not want to hazard making a wild peg. "I was afraid it might wind up in left field," he would remark afterward.[7] Instead, he stumbled the few feet back to the bag for the sure out on Gehringer. He immediately risked a quick throw down to Jurges, but it was too late to get the sliding Cochrane, and the Tigers had a two-out threat.

To the plate strode Goose Goslin, exactly the man the Tigers wanted in a situation like this. Goslin was known as a clutch player, and he had hit .330

in 1935 with runners in scoring position. With first base open, the Cubs certainly did not need to pitch to him, and his run meant nothing. Grimm came out and huddled with French and his infielders to determine strategy. The reputation that had followed Goslin was that he was a sucker for left-handers. This was a bit unfair, as modern statistics point out: to that point in his career, Goslin had hit .290 against southpaws. Grimm wouldn't have known that, but either way he still preferred this lefty-on-lefty matchup. To walk Goslin meant facing Fox, a right-handed batter who had hit .321 versus portsiders that summer. Of course, Grimm could have ordered French to walk both Goslin *and* Fox, setting up a force at any base, while taking his chances with the right-handed Gee Walker, who hit lefties and righties equally well. Loading the bases in a situation like this, however, put an extraordinary amount of pressure on the pitcher: A wild pitch or a base on balls could end everything. It was settled: French would pitch to Goslin.

By now, the late-afternoon shadows had engulfed the entire infield, making it hard for hitters to pick up the ball out of the pitcher's hand. The Cubs, knowing that Goslin was primarily a pull hitter, shifted second baseman Herman slightly to his left and well beyond the infield dirt. "Herman was actually playing as a second right fielder," wrote Iffy the Dopester. "He was halfway out to the position of Klein."[8] On the first pitch, Goslin took a vicious cut, launching a drive high and far down the right-field line that brought the crowd to its feet—but it was clearly foul. At just before 3:30, French hurled his next offering toward the outside corner. Goslin shortened his swing this time, a one-handed poke that pulled the ball on an arc over Herman's outstretched glove into right-center field. Cochrane tore past third and scampered across home plate with the run that gave the Detroit Tigers their first World Series championship. Navin Field erupted in joy as Cochrane's men mobbed him. "A scene of indescribable confusion followed," wrote the *Detroit Times'* Bud Shaver.[9]

It was a wild, raucous picture moments later in the victorious clubhouse. The whooping and hollering Tigers tore into Goslin, pulling off his shirt and hauling him around the cramped quarters. "Hell—what a Series," shouted Cochrane. He threw himself into his office chair and shouted for a cigarette. "We beat a great ball club. I'm glad it's all over."[10]

Commissioner Landis and National League president Ford Frick squeezed their way through the mayhem to congratulate the new champions. "I never saw a greater World Series game," Landis boasted.[11] In the thrill of the moment, nobody was likely to disagree with him.

Even Frank Navin, who rarely stepped foot inside the Tigers' clubhouse, felt compelled to pop his head in and offer words of praise. One by one, he thanked every Tiger. He then buttonholed American League president William Harridge. "Will," he whispered, "I'm a sober man. But I have an almost irresistible inclination to get intoxicated tonight."[12] The two left the ballpark arm in arm, bound for the nearest Corktown watering hole.

"We did our best, so what the hell?" Charlie Grimm hollered to his men as they slouched in front of their lockers. "We still are National League champions and that's more than anybody expected. We are not world champions, but nobody can say we were badly beaten. It just wasn't in the books for us to win, so forget it and have a good time during the winter."[13] The Cubs' 21-game winning streak was their zenith; since then, they had lost six of eight.

Outside the ballpark, the party surged to the downtown area. Within two hours, an estimated 500,000 revelers were parading through the streets of Detroit, tossing streamers, blowing horns, banging trashcan lids, and hugging complete strangers. Office workers filled sacks with water and dropped them from upper-story windows onto the pavement below. Traffic came to a standstill along the main arteries, as countless vehicles clogged Woodward Avenue from Eliot to Jefferson. Scattered bonfires sprung up, prompting the city's fire fighters to rush to the scenes, their shrieking sirens adding to the general cacophony. Near Grand Circus Park, one group of rioters tried to tip over a streetcar. "After waiting 48 years," penned Grantland Rice, "the Detroit Tigers are at last baseball champions of the world. Nothing else matters in this mad, delirious city."[14]

It was a mob scene outside the entrance of the Book-Cadillac Hotel, the Series headquarters for the assorted league and team officials, as well as the press and visiting players. Mounted police tried desperately to restrain the crowds eager for a glimpse of any VIPs returning there for a party. A taxi carrying Goose Goslin, who stayed at the posh hotel, pulled up at the curb. The man of the hour, however, could not open his back-seat door for the press of people. He quickly directed his driver to whisk him away to an unknown location.

George W. Stark penned the postscript in the next day's *Detroit News*:

> It was the Goose who laid the Golden Egg. Goslin the Prophet, in the ninth inning of Monday's World Series base ball game between the Tigers and the Cubs, fired the shot heard round the world. Well, heard round that part of the world dedicated to the Game.
>
> He fired the shot that set a city on fire, that catapulted Detroit's first base ball title in almost half a century into its lap, that released a shower of gold into the pockets of his delirious teammates.
>
> And Detroit, most base ball-minded metropolis of the universe, staged a celebration the old town will never forget.
>
> Detroit the Dynamic was living up to its name and its reputation for ascending the grand scale.

In the years to come, when the myriad fans assembled there are in their easy chairs before the fire, they will tell this story to their children. They will tell the story not only of the galloping Goose, who fired the shot, but they will sing the saga of Tommy Bridges. Tommy who took a leaf out of good old General Crowder's manual of arms and pitched with a courage the amazed spectators never believed could reside in so small a frame.[15]

The citywide celebration continued long into the night. Never before had the Motor City seen such a torrent of joy among its citizenry. Not to be outdone by the rival *News* as a civic booster, the *Detroit Free Press* added its own paean praising Detroit and its Tigers:

It was an outburst of carnival spirit that gave the lie to the gloom-sayers of a few years ago who said that Detroit the Dynamic had become Detroit the Doomed.

Detroit, through the baseball team that is the symbol and the incarnation of its fighting spirit, had won the baseball championship of the world, and the world was to know it.

It was Detroit's salute to America.

Detroit had the dynamite. Mickey Cochrane and his Tigers provided the spark.

Detroit celebrated because it had won the world championship.

It celebrated because it was the city that had led the nation back to recovery.

It celebrated because it was the city that wouldn't stay licked; the city that couldn't stay licked.

It was Detroit the Unconquerable, ready to tell the world when the moment arrived. The moment had arrived, and the world was told.[16]

Epilogue

With a World Series victory came the inevitable financial windfall. Each member of the Tigers took home a winner's share of $6,554 (about $115,000 in 2016 dollars). It marked the highest figure in history up to that time, not surpassed until the 1948 Series. Salary records for the 1935 Tigers are incomplete, but we do know that Cochrane was the best paid at $20,000, which is understandable given his dual role as manager and player. Stars like Gehringer, Greenberg, Goslin, and Rogell all earned around $10,000. For nearly all the rest of the players, however, their World Series cut was more than their season's salary; indeed, it represented nearly five times what an average American worker made in a year.

Other Detroit teams quickly joined the Tigers in the championship ranks. On December 15, the National Football League's Lions beat the New York Giants for their first-ever title. The Red Wings of the National Hockey League captured their first Stanley Cup in April of 1936. The *Associated Press* honored undefeated heavyweight boxer Joe Louis with its "Athlete of the Year" Award in 1935. The sporting world hailed Detroit as the "City of Champions."

Tragedy quickly cast a pall over the Tigers' October euphoria, however. On November 13, Frank Navin died of a heart attack while riding his cherished horse, Masquerader, at the Detroit Riding and Hunt Club on Belle Isle. An experienced equestrian, he had taken the steed out nearly every morning for the previous 15 years. News of Navin's death at age 64 travelled swiftly, blindsiding the baseball world. His physicians had been warning him for years that the stress and excitement of owning a major league baseball team was taking a toll on his health. They had urged him to sell the franchise if he wanted to live a longer life. But the Tigers were Navin's pride and joy, never more so than at the very end.

Goose Goslin's winning hit in Game Six of the 1935 World Series, however, proved to be the final hurrah for the two-time American League champions. In December, Cochrane finally got his wish when the club purchased

The Tigers starting lineup poses in front of the Navin Field grandstand before a 1935 game (left to right: Jo-Jo White, Mickey Cochrane, Charlie Gehringer, Hank Greenberg, Goose Goslin, Billy Rogell, Gee Walker, Marv Owen, Schoolboy Rowe) (courtesy Ernie Harwell Sports Collection, Detroit Public Library).

slugging outfielder Al Simmons from the White Sox. It looked to be the move that would keep the Tigers on top in 1936. The New York Yankees, however, made an even bigger splash. They promoted a promising 21-year-old from Martinez, California, named Joseph Paul DiMaggio, effectively altering the American League's competitive landscape for the next 15 years. In his first regular-season game in the Bronx on May 3, he banged out three hits, including a triple, as the Yanks pounded the St. Louis Browns, 14–5. DiMaggio went on to hit .323 with 29 home runs and 125 RBI, as New York rolled to the American League pennant. The Tigers, with a record of 83–71, finished a distant second, 19½ lengths behind. Babe Ruth was long gone, but DiMaggio became the next Yankees immortal, leading the team to ten World Series titles in his 13 years as a player. Bridging the gap between two of the most dominant players in Yankees history, the Tigers' 1935 world championship was a kind of shooting star, a case of the right team taking advantage of the opportunity that history handed to them.

Mickey Cochrane took on the added duties of general manager in 1936. Ever since joining the Tigers, he had operated at a frenetic pace that would have worn lesser men ragged. He lived or died by every victory or loss, and his intensity slowly took a toll on his physical and psychological well-being.

The pressures and responsibilities only mounted once he also became the GM. The workload, coupled with his relentless drive, proved to be too much. On June 4, at Shibe Park in Philadelphia, Cochrane hit a bases-loaded, inside-the-park home run. After reaching home plate without a slide, he immediately ran toward the Tigers' dugout, where he collapsed. The Athletics' team physician, who treated him for over an hour, blamed it on strain, combined with the excitement of running out the home run. "I don't know what happened," Cochrane said after the game. "I started to go to bat but was suddenly seized by a dizzy feeling. Then my heart started beating at a rapid rate, and I thought I was going to die."[1] He revealed that he had had several fainting spells during the last month.

Doctors determined that Black Mike had suffered a nervous breakdown. He took time off from the team to convalesce at a ranch in Wyoming. He saw action in only five more games that season. He got off to a good start in 1937 before tragedy struck. On May 25 at Yankee Stadium, he blasted a third-inning home run off New York right-hander Bump Hadley. Two innings later, Hadley threw him a 3–1 fastball, up and in. Cochrane was unable to get out of the way, and the pitch fractured his skull. It was long before the days of batting helmets. While he never played again, he tried to return as manager in 1938, but the magic was gone. The team struggled, and he was finally fired in August, ending his days in the major leagues. Cochrane's legacy as a great catcher and field general endured, and in 1947, he became the first backstop elected by the Baseball Writers Association of America to the National Baseball Hall of Fame.[2]

After his wrist injury in Game Two, Hank Greenberg never played another inning of that 1935 World Series, making the Tigers' victory even more remarkable. Greenberg grew into one of the most prolific sluggers of his day, driving in 184 runs in 1937 and swatting 58 home runs the next year. He missed nearly 4½ years due to service in World War II during the prime of his youth. He returned in 1945, and his ninth-inning grand slam on the final day of that season gave Detroit the American League pennant. He gained election to the Hall of Fame in 1956.

The Mechanical Man, Charlie Gehringer, retired following the 1942 season, having amassed 2,839 lifetime hits with a .320 batting average. He finished with a career WAR of 80.6. Among Tigers, only Ty Cobb (144.7) and Al Kaline (92.5) have a higher figure. Voted into the Hall of Fame in 1949, he was Detroit's general manager for a little over two seasons beginning in August of 1951. He did not particularly care for the job, taking it on mostly as a favor to owner Walter Briggs. It was during that short tenure, however, that he signed Kaline, who at the time was an 18-year-old kid from Baltimore.

Goslin, the final part of the 1935 Tigers' Hall of Fame quartet, had one productive year left in 1936; the next October, Detroit released him. He played 38 games for the Senators in 1938, batting .158. After a multi-year stint as player-manager with the Trenton Senators of the Interstate League, he called it a career. The man they called Goose racked up 2,735 lifetime hits, with 500 doubles and 1,612 RBI. He retired to his farm, where he spent the remainder of his days on Delaware Bay hunting, fishing, and running his boat rental business.

Billy Rogell was a regular for only three more years in Detroit and wound up finishing his career as a backup with the Cubs in 1940. After retiring, he chose to remain in The Motor City, and began a nearly 40-year run on the Detroit city council. Just as tenacious in his second career as he had been as a ballplayer, Rogell took pride in developing a baseball school program for Detroit youth. It peaked in the mid–1950s with over 800 teams. On July 24, 2001, the wheelchair-bound Rogell threw out the first pitch before a Great Lakes Summer Collegiate League contest, the last baseball game ever played at the corner of Michigan and Trumbull. On Rogell's death at age 98 in 2003, longtime Tigers broadcaster Ernie Harwell said, "He was a feisty maverick. He was a good guy in baseball and politics."[3]

Marv Owen had a solid year in 1936, driving in 105 runs. In December 1937, the Tigers traded him along with Gee Walker to the Chicago White Sox. After his major league days were over, Owen was a player-manager for several seasons with the Portland Beavers of the PCL. He also skippered in the California League and the Georgia-Florida League. Later, as a scout, his most notable signing was future White Sox knuckleballer Wilbur Wood.

Jo-Jo White's playing time was reduced significantly in 1936 with the acquisition of Al Simmons. By 1939, he drifted back to the minors, but in the war years of 1943 and 1944 he returned to "The Show" with the roster-challenged Phillies and Reds. When hostilities ended, White's time in the big leagues was numbered. He went on to have some excellent years in the PCL, retiring from the Hollywood Stars at age 40 before embarking on a long coaching and managerial career. In 1967, he skippered the Dallas-Fort Worth Spurs, a team that featured a 28-year-old outfielder named Mike, who also happened to be Jo-Jo's son. Mike White had played in the major leagues with the Houston Colt .45s and Astros from 1963–1965.

Mickey Cochrane often called Pete Fox the club's most underrated player. One of the better outfielders of his era, he hit .302 in eight years as a Tiger before the Red Sox purchased him after the 1940 campaign. He retired in 1945 after a 13-year career in which he batted .298. He managed in the minors after hanging up his spikes, and scouted for the Tigers as well.

A lethal hitter, Gee Walker had a breakout campaign in 1936, hitting

.353 with a .924 OPS. He suited up for five teams in his 15 years in the majors, finishing with a .294 lifetime average and 1,991 hits. Walker was one of the most popular Tigers ever to wear the Old English D. Fans howled long and loud when the team traded him to the White Sox in December 1937; some vowed never to attend another Tigers game. Walker also played for the Reds, Senators, and Indians. He managed for five years in the minors before becoming a Detroit-based representative for a distillery.

Hub Walker, Gee's kid brother, played a couple of seasons for the Cincinnati Reds after 1935 and then disappeared into the minor leagues, seemingly never to be heard from again. In 1945, however, at age 38, he made an unlikely comeback with the Tigers, appearing in 28 games and going 3-for-23. He also banged out a pinch-hit double in that year's World Series, which Detroit won in seven games over the Cubs. Having reached the mountaintop, Walker promptly retired to a life of selling automobiles in suburban Detroit.

The consummate backup catcher, Ray Hayworth appeared in one game as a defensive replacement in the 1934 World Series and sat on the bench the entire 1935 fall classic. After his final season in Detroit in 1938, he shuffled around from Brooklyn to the New York Giants to the St. Louis Browns, and finally back to Brooklyn. He played in the majors until age 41 before briefly managing in the minors. He died at age 98 in 2002.

Forever remembered as the man who replaced Hank Greenberg in the 1935 Series, Flea Clifton played only two more years in the big leagues, averaging .200 for his career. He later suited up in the minors for Toledo, Oklahoma City, Fort Worth, and Minneapolis before leaving the game at age 34 to become a life insurance salesman.

Possessor of one of the best curveballs of his generation, Tommy Bridges topped the 20-win plateau three times with the Tigers. He also pitched in the 1940 and 1945 World Series for Detroit, and was finally released at age 39 after the 1946 campaign. He finished with 194 wins, every one of them in a Tigers uniform, and a career WAR of 52.5. In 1947, he caught on with the PCL's Portland Beavers, tossing a no-hitter in his first game. He pitched in the minors until 1950. The last two decades of his life were a difficult battle with alcohol, and Bridges died of liver cancer in April 1968.

Injuries limited General Crowder to only nine games and a 1.932 WHIP in 1936. A comeback the next season was not out of the question, but he decided to call it quits. He instead focused his energies on helping to establish an independent team for his home town of Winston-Salem. Known as the Twins, they began play in the Piedmont League in 1937. Crowder even took to the mound, but after only two rocky appearances, he exchanged his uniform for a front office position with the team.

Elden Auker won 130 games in his ten-year career with Detroit, the Red Sox, and the Browns. After baseball, he found great success in the abrasives business and died a wealthy man in 2006 at age 95. He and his wife Mildred had been married 73 years. Auker was the last surviving member of the 1935 world champion Tigers.

After only three relief appearances with the Tigers in 1936, Chief Hogsett was traded to the St. Louis Browns, where he struggled as a full-time starter. He also pitched briefly for the Washington Senators; later, the American Association's Minneapolis Millers purchased his contract. After six seasons in the minors, Hogsett had a cup of coffee with the Tigers in 1944, another example of a player benefitting from the shortage of able bodies during World War II. A born storyteller, he dabbled in the sporting goods business before finding his niche as a liquor salesman.

Joe Sullivan never pitched in the World Series and lasted only one more season in Detroit, posting a 1.895 WHIP in 1936. After stints with the Braves and Pirates, he hung around for nearly a decade in the minors. Sullivan loved the Pacific Northwest and settled there after baseball, attaining the rank of fire chief in Bremerton, Washington.

After ten years as a steady, if unspectacular, pitcher with the Tigers, Vic Sorrell toiled in the minors for a few years before retiring. He served in the navy at the Wilmington, North Carolina, shipyards during World War II. After scouting for the Tigers, he became the baseball coach at North Carolina State University, a post he held for 20 years.

One of the most successful relief pitchers of his time, Firpo Marberry threw briefly for the Giants and Senators in 1936. He played in the minors until age 42. A car accident in 1949 cost him his left (non-throwing) arm, but he recovered well enough to play in old-timers' games.

Roxie Lawson won as many as 18 games for the Tigers in 1937, but for most of his nine-year career, he was a nondescript spot starter. He later played, managed, and umpired in the minors. After baseball, he became a navy gunner at a base in Michigan. He was also a car salesman and the owner of a restaurant.

Clyde Hatter's big-league career consisted of eight games with Detroit. Once a promising prospect, and he won 16 games at Double-A in 1936. At the end of that season, however, he suffered a nervous breakdown. His 1937 campaign was a disaster from the start. His drinking led to disciplinary problems, and the Toledo Mud Hens suspended him for 30 days. An overdose of sleeping pills led to a trip to the emergency room that summer. Following his sudden death in October of 1937, the coroner listed heart disease as the cause.

Dixie Howell never made it to the majors, although he played eight years in the Pacific Coast League and the American Association.[4] During World War II, he saw service in the United States Navy. He had a stint with the Washington Redskins of the National Football League for one season and went on to coach college football for many years. He was inducted into the College Football Hall of Fame in 1970 (as a player). Howell's Hollywood career never quite panned out, although he had an uncredited role in a 1936 film, *The Adventures of Frank Merriwell*. His name lives on in American Literature: Dixie Howell is referenced by Scout, the narrator in Harper Lee's 1960 classic, *To Kill a Mockingbird*.

Perhaps no member of the 1934–1935 Tigers experienced as many highs and lows in baseball as Schoolboy Rowe. Plagued by arm problems throughout his career, he never lived up to the greatness predicted of him. After winning 19 games again in 1936, injuries limited him to only two starts the next season. He spent most of 1938 back in the minor leagues with Beaumont, trying to find his way and his health. He had a comeback in 1940, a year the Tigers went to the World Series. Rowe notched 16 wins in 23 starts with a 1.260 WHIP that season, although he lost two games in the Series against the Reds.

More arm woes ensued. After another stretch in the minor leagues and an unsuccessful comeback with the Brooklyn Dodgers, Rowe had seemingly reached the end at age 32. There was still some life left in his old arm, however. He caught on with the Philadelphia Phillies, who played at Shibe Park, on the same field where his bid for a 17th consecutive victory had failed miserably so long, long ago. In five seasons as the Phils' grizzled veteran (interrupted by two years in the Navy), he twice won 14 games and made the All-Star team in 1947.

Schoolboy Rowe's baseball odyssey continued past age 40. His fastball long gone but his wits still about him, he toiled in minor league outposts like Shreveport, Louisiana, and San Diego, California. He rejoined the Tigers' organization as a pitcher-manager for Williamsport, Pennsylvania, in the low bushes in 1951. At the time, he was the last member of the 1935 champions still playing professional baseball. He skippered the Triple-A Buffalo Bisons the following year and finally made it all the way back to Detroit, this time as a first-base coach beginning in 1954. After a heart attack in spring training three years later, he returned to baseball in 1958 to manage the Montgomery Rebels, the Tigers' Class D team.

His health, however, was failing. He left the everyday grind of the game to take up scouting for Detroit, covering the Louisiana-Mississippi-East Texas area. A second heart attack on January 8, 1961, proved fatal. Schoolboy Rowe would have turned 51 three days later (although some reports erroneously claimed his age was 48). He was survived by his beloved wife Edna, as well as a son and a daughter. His major league *oeuvre* read 158 wins and 101 losses. "When he died," said the *Detroit Free Press*, "a bit of those golden, unforgettable Tiger pennant summers of 1934 and 1935 went with him."[5]

As they sipped their morning coffee while perusing the sports page, Tigers fans in 1930s Detroit had plenty of fine baseball writers to enjoy. The *Detroit Free Press* boasted Charles P. Ward's droll metaphors and M. F. Drukenbrod's straightforward analysis. The paper also featured the astute reportage of Jack Carveth, W. W. Edgar, and Tod Rockwell, the former University of Michigan quarterback turned journalist. Redoubtable scribes Sam Greene and H. G. Salsinger headed a lineup at the *Detroit News* that also included Jack Weeks, Alan Gould and George W. Stark. The lyrical beat writer Bud Shaver of the *Detroit Times* may have been the best of the bunch, despite his propensity for hyperbole.

No local baseball writer had as wide or devoted an audience, however, as Iffy the Dopester of the *Detroit Free Press*. His periodic musings, alternately quirky and irreverent, erudite and playful, were always entertaining. A well-read man, Iffy the Dopester was as likely to quote Thucydides as Connie Mack. His exact identity was supposedly shrouded in mystery, and readers willingly played along with the charade. Iffy might promise in print to make a public appearance at such-and-such time, and such-and-such place, only to not show up under a flimsy pretense. It was all a running gag; the whole town knew Iffy to be none other than Malcolm W. Bingay, the managing editor of the *Free Press*.

Though born in Ontario, Canada, Bingay was raised in Detroit and became one of the city's most ardent civic boosters. As a young teen, he landed his first job with the *Detroit News* as a printers' devil; by age 21, he was named sports editor. He eventually moved on to the *Free Press*, where he also wrote a daily discourse called "Good Morning." Needing an outlet with which to expound on his beloved Detroit Tigers, he created Iffy, whose idiosyncratic style soon found a following among readers. The cartoon mug shot atop Iffy's column portrayed him as a bald, bespectacled, white-bearded geriatric, a kind of crazy old uncle. In Bingay's view, the crusty character was a response to other newspaper writers, who were forever lamenting about "*If* the Tigers had only done this," or, "*If* the Tigers had only done that." Thus, Iffy was born, and he quickly became a *Free Press* staple.

The Dopester always supported the home team. It was not a blind, naive support, however, nor did he expect such from his readers. Bingay credited Detroit sports fans with having minds of their own. His job was to give the facts and let the public form its own opinions. He applied the term "dopester" to any writer, whether of sports or politics, who insulted his readers' intelligence.

> These dopesters are well-known journalists and professional politicians. They speak a common language and know the technique of the game as played in the "smoke-filled back room." They become so indurated to the finesses of the game that they forget the people are not chips of the sport but are sovereign. The people in a democracy have a way of making up their own minds without paying much attention to the dopesters. They follow their instincts, not any set of rules.[6]

Iffy the Dopester became Bingay's doppelganger, a voice of humor and honesty in an increasingly cynical press.

As Detroit's World Series celebration raged around him on that late afternoon in October 1935, Iffy the Dopester closed the curtain on a wondrous summer. "When the years have rolled on and this baseball generation is no more, high tales still will be told of that ninth inning finish. And as the tale is told by the troubadours of another time, the baseballic Homers will give their recital a name. They will title it 'Courage.'"

Iffy grasped the import of the moment, both for the Tigers' organization and for the city that it called home. When Stan Hack tripled in the ninth inning, he wrote, it looked like fate had decreed that Detroit was never to have a world championship ballclub. Tommy Bridges, however, displayed more courage than Iffy had seen in all his decades of baseball watching. Mickey and the G-Men, Schoolboy and the gang, had captured the sport's ultimate prize. "And now, my hearties, the play is over. With heavy heart Old Iffy says farewell to his comrades of the happy summer days."[7]

Chapter Notes

Preface

1. A. Bartlett Giamatti, "The Green Fields of the Mind," *Yale Alumni Magazine and Journal*, November 1977.

Chapter One

1. Sam Greene, "Hint Harris Will Go to Red Sox; Could Have Stayed with Detroit," *Sporting News*, September 28, 1933, 1.

2. *Ibid.*

3. Ken Belson, "Apples for a Nickel, and Plenty of Empty Seats," *New York Times*, January 26, 2009, B11.

4. *Associated Press*, "Babe Ruth Mentioned as Harris's Successor," *Reading Eagle*, September 25, 1933, 11.

5. "10,000 Fans Greet Ruth in Honolulu," *New York Times*, October 20, 1933, 23.

6. Harry Grayson, "Why Can't Baseball Find Place for Ruth, Its Foremost Figure?" *Evening Independent*, February 7, 1945, 14.

7. Dink Carroll, "Playing the Field," *Montreal Gazette*, May 17, 1947, 15.

8. Wins Above Replacement (WAR) is a statistic that, according to the website *Fangraphs*, "is an attempt by the sabermetric baseball community to summarize a player's total contributions to their team in one statistic." Essentially, a WAR of 5.0 means that a player provided five more wins in a season than a typical Triple-A replacement player. Any number of 5.0 or above is considered all-star quality.

9. "Cochrane on All-Time Eleven Picked at Boston University," *New York Times*, November 29, 1931, 113.

10. John Kieran, "Sports of the Times," *New York Times*, April 22, 1931, 34.

11. James C. Isaminger, "Philadelphia Gains Both Batting Kings," *Sporting News*, October 5, 1933, 3.

12. Malcolm W. Bingay, "Mickey So Real His Life Scheme Defies Analysis," *Detroit Free Press*, August 12, 1934.

13. One account has the Athletics' owner offering both Cochrane and ace hurler Lefty Grove for $200,000.

14. "Rumor of the Sale of Grove Persists," *New York Times*, November 1, 1933.

15. C. William Duncan, "Mickey Cochrane, Always a Fighter, Should Bring Back to Detroit Tigers Scrappy Ways of Ty Cobb," *Sporting News*, December 21, 1933, 3.

16. James C. Isaminger, "Philadelphia Fans Ready for Bad News," *Sporting News*, December 7, 1933, 5.

17. "Cochrane Deal Is Sure Thing," *Detroit News*, December 10, 1933.

18. H. G. Salsinger, "Bank Demands Compel Mack to Wreck Club," *Detroit News*, December 11, 1933.

19. Mack himself had no plans to step down as the Athletics' skipper. In fact, he would hang on to the job until the conclusion of the 1950 season, giving him a whopping 50 years at the helm of the Athletics. Of course, Mack was also the owner that entire period, and even though Philadelphia was mostly terrible in the 1930s and 1940s, he was never willing, whether due to financial reasons or pride, to fire himself.

20. "Cochrane 'Poison' as Foe, Welcomed to Tigers' Lair," *Detroit News*, December 19, 1933.

21. *Associated Press*, "Mack Sells Grove and 4 Other Stars," *New York Times*, December 13, 1933.

22. *Associated Press*, "Mack Lays Deals to Wage Demands," *New York Times*, December 19, 1933.

23. George Kirksey, "Mack Wrecks A's in Baseball's Biggest Deal," *Pittsburgh Press*, December 13, 1933, 28. With Cochrane gone, the only star remaining from the Athletics' glory days was Jimmie Foxx, and he would be traded to the Boston Red Sox after the 1935 season. As for Johnny

Pasek, the catcher Mack acquired for Cochrane, he never played a game for the Athletics. He was immediately traded, along with former World Series star George Earnshaw, to the Chicago White Sox for catcher Charlie Berry and $20,000. Berry hit .253 in his four years with Philadelphia until his eventual release. Pasek appeared in all of four games for the White Sox in 1934 before vanishing forever into the minor leagues.

24. Al Demarr, "Caught Between Imperial and Victorian Rooms at the Palmer House," *Sporting News*, December 21, 1933, 5.

25. "Echoes from the Lobbies at the Majors' Meetings in Windy City," *Sporting News*, December 21, 1933, 6.

26. "Cochrane Is Insured by Tigers for $100,000," *New York Times*, December 16, 1933.

27. That Senators team featured 36-year-old Walter Johnson, who won 23 games. It was managed by Bucky Harris, Cochrane's predecessor as Tigers manager. Harris also played second base and batted .268.

28. Frank Young, "Poor Fielding Nullifies Good Battery," *Washington Post*, December 2, 1923.

29. Lawrence S. Ritter, *The Glory of Their Times* (New York: Harper Perennial, 2010), 279.

30. H. G. Salsinger, "Why Cochrane Gave Stone for Goslin," *Detroit News*, December 14, 1933.

31. "Goose to Add More Power to Outer Posts," *Detroit Free Press*, December 14, 1933.

32. Sam Greene, "Cochrane Reaches Terms with Navin," *Sporting News*, December 21, 1933, 7.

Chapter Two

1. "New York to Detroit: My First Trip to the West—Railroad Reflections—Buffalo—The Great Lakes and the New Steamboats—Safe in Detroit," *New York Daily Times*, July 13, 1854, 3. This correspondence was sent from the Biddle House in Detroit. Built in 1851 at the corner of Randolph and Jefferson, it hosted General Ulysses S. Grant in 1865. Once the finest hotel in the city, its best days were numbered when the luxurious Russell House opened in 1857. Today, the land where the Biddle House once stood is occupied by the Renaissance Center Complex, which currently houses the headquarters of General Motors.

2. It had taken months for Ford to build the prototype quadricycle in his Bagley Avenue shed. When the morning of the trial run arrived, he realized with horror that the contraption would not fit through the door. Wielding an axe, he doubled the size of the opening by banging out a few bricks, and the rest is automotive history.

3. "Ford's $28,000 'Shoestring' Now $409,000,000," *Michigan Manufacturer & Financial Record*, September 9, 1922, 14.

4. J. G. Taylor Spink, "Three and One," *Sporting News*, February 1, 1934, 4.

5. "Four Killed in Riot at Main Ford Plant as 3,000 Fight," *New York Times*, March 8, 1932, 1.

6. "Cochrane Reaches Terms with Navin," *Sporting News*, December 21, 1933, 7.

7. *Ibid.*

8. Richard Bak, *Cobb Would've Caught It: The Golden Age of Baseball in Detroit* (Detroit: Wayne State University Press, 1992).

9. *Detroit Free Press*, February 29, 1896.

10. Sam Greene, "Cochrane Is Big Hit as Resident Leader," *Sporting News*, January 18, 1934, 2.

11. Sam Greene, "Intra-League Games on Tiger Spring List," *Sporting News*, January 25, 1934, 3.

12. Sam Greene, "Rogell to Practice Bunting Technique," *Sporting News*, February 1, 1934, 5.

13. Sam Greene, "Goslin Puts Tigers Among First Three," *Sporting News*, February 8, 1934, 6.

14. Steve Steinberg and Lyle Spatz, *The Colonel and Hug: The Partnership That Transformed the New York Yankees* (Lincoln: University of Nebraska Press, 2015), 222.

15. Dan Parker, "Al Lang Grows Healthy, Wealthy, Wise in Florida," *Sporting News*, February 8, 1934, 5.

16. Ernie Pyle, "Attending to Baseball Business Keeps Al Lang Busy; Makes Him a Happy Man," *St. Petersburg Times*, April 25, 1940, 3.

17. Cinnamon Bair, "Landing Tigers a 1934 Home Run," *Lakeland Ledger*, March 26, 2001, 17.

18. Rick Rousos, "The Tigers' Live in Lakeland: A Sweet 60th Anniversary," *Lakeland Ledger*, March 1, 1996, 1.

19. "Taxi Strikers Seize Cabs, Rip Off Doors and Force Theatre Crowds to Walk," *New York Times*, February 4, 1934.

20. "Pay Increases Given 20,000 Ford Workers," *Detroit Free Press*, February 7, 1934.

21. Sam Greene, "Cochrane Will Sift Tigers from 32 Men," *Sporting News*, February 15, 1934, 7.

Chapter Three

1. *Associated Press*, "News from Other Major League Baseball Training Camps," *New York Times*, March 8, 1934.

2. John Kieran, "Sports of the Times: The Tigers of the Baseball Jungle," *New York Times*, March 19, 1934, 24.

3. "Tigers Down Reds in Ninth," *Detroit Free Press*, April 3, 1934.

4. *New York Times*, March 27, 1934, 27.

5. Charles P. Ward, "Rowe Returns to Mound and Tigers Blank Montreal, 10–0," *Detroit Free Press*, April 7, 1934.

6. Associated Press, *New York Times*, April 9, 1934.

7. H.G. Salsinger, "Cochrane Is Likely to Fan Out Rowe," *Detroit News*, May 1, 1934.

8. Associated Press, "Tigers Down Reds, 7–4," *New York Times*, April 16, 1934.

9. Sam Greene, "Greenberg Slated for Clean-Up Post," *Sporting News*, April 5, 1934, 7.

10. John Kieran, "Sports of the Times: Clinical Notes on the Grand Opening," *New York Times*, April 17, 1934.

11. Associated Press, "Teams Ready for Opening of Season," *Boston Globe*, April 17, 1934.

12. H. G. Salsinger, "Salsinger Picks Tigers to Finish Third in Race," *Detroit News*, April 17, 1934.

13. Associated Press, "First Wide Open Pennant Race in Many Years Predicted for American League," *Detroit Free Press*, April 1, 1934.

14. John Drebinger, "Hubbell to Pitch Opener for Giants," *New York Times*, April 17, 1934.

15. Grantland Rice, "The Spotlight: Play Ball! Batter Up!" *Boston Globe*, April 17, 1934.

16. Paul Gallico, "One Touch of Nature Makes Baseball Fans Cheerful Kin," *Detroit Free Press*, April 18, 1934.

17. "Still Leading," *Detroit Free Press*, March 15, 1934.

18. "Auto Strike Settled: Text of President Roosevelt's Peace Plan," *Detroit Free Press*, March 26, 1934.

19. "Detroit Hits Stride in Recovery's Van with Strike Settlement," *Detroit Free Press*, March 27, 1934.

20. Edward Burns, "Cochrane to Make His Debut as Detroit Pilot," *Chicago Tribune*, April 17, 1934.

21. M. F. Drukenbrod, "Mickey Almost Guessed It," *Detroit Free Press*, April 7, 1934.

22. "Mark Up One for the Sick List," *Detroit Free Press*, April 18, 1934.

23. H. G. Salsinger, "The Umpire," *Detroit News*, April 18, 1934.

24. Bud Shaver, "Mickey Brings Colorful Nine For 1st Game," *Detroit Times*, April 22, 1934.

25. *Baseball Magazine*, April 1912.

26. Ralph J. Yonker, *Detroit Times*, April 20, 1912.

27. Paul Hale Bruske, "Detroit's Day," *Sporting Life*, April 27, 1912.

28. H. G. Salsinger, "Typical Tiger Attack Keeps Detroit in Lead," *Detroit News*, April 25, 1934.

29. Edward Burns, "Tigers Amuse 24,000 in Snow, Whip Sox, 7–3," *Chicago Tribune*, April 25, 1934.

30. *Ibid.*

31. Sam Greene, "Tigers 'Sold' to Fans in First Home Game," *Detroit News*, April 25, 1934.

32. Malcolm W. Bingay, "Good Morning," *Detroit Free Press*, April 25, 1934.

33. Charles P. Ward, "Rowe Chased Early and Browns Defeat Tigers, 7–2," *Detroit Free Press*, May 1, 1934.

34. Sam Greene, "Rowe Tightens Grip on Berth," *Detroit News*, May 3, 1934.

35. Charles P. Ward, "Tigers Stage Rally in Eighth to Defeat Browns, 5 to 4," *Detroit Free Press*, May 2, 1934.

36. Sam Greene, "Tigers Pick Up Power As Goose's Bat Honks," *Sporting News*, June 7, 1934, 3.

37. M. F. Drukenbrod, "Druke Says: West Goes East, Test for Tigers, They Need Pitching," *Detroit Free Press*, May 4, 1934.

38. Charles P. Ward, "Yankee Sluggers Hammer Out 10–6 Victory Over Tigers," *Detroit Free Press*, May 6, 1934.

39. H. G. Salsinger, "Ruth Hits Two Homers, Fischer Beaten Pitcher," *Detroit News*, May 6, 1934.

40. James C. O'Leary, "Rowe's Mighty Hit Wins For Tigers," *Boston Globe*, May 7, 1934.

41. Charles P. Ward, "Rowe's Homer in Eleventh Beats Boston Red Sox, 8 to 6," *Detroit Free Press*, May 8, 1934.

42. Wilson, *Boston Sights and Insights*, 152.

43. James C. O'Leary, "Rowe's Mighty Hit Wins for Tigers," *Boston Globe*, May 7, 1934.

Chapter Four

1. Jim Hawkins and Dan Ewald, *The Detroit Tigers Encyclopedia* (Champaign, IL: Sports Publishing, 2003), 58.

2. Bak, *Cobb Would Have Caught It*, 191.

3. John Kieran, "Sports of the Times: Conversation Around Second Base," *New York Times*, June 20, 1934.

4. Bak, *Cobb Would Have Caught It*, 192.

5. John Kieran, "Sports of the Times: Conversation Around Second Base," *New York Times*, June 20, 1934.

6. Charles P. Ward, "Tigers Take Third

Place Alone By Beating Yankees in Opener, 5–4," *Detroit Free Press*, May 18, 1934.

7. Charles P. Ward, "Tigers Down Yanks, 10–8, and Advance to Second Place," *Detroit Free Press*, May 19, 1934.

8. Bud Shaver, "Shavings," *Detroit Times*, May 4, 1934.

9. Edward Burns, "Sox Stopped By Rowe; Tigers Triumph, 3–1," *Chicago Tribune*, June 2, 1934.

10. Charles P. Ward, "Rowe Beat Sox, 3–1, and Tigers Crowd Close to Second," *Detroit Free Press*, June 2, 1934.

11. Edward Burns, "Marberry Holds Sox to Four Hits; Tigers Triumph, 12–0." *Chicago Tribune*, June 3, 1934.

12. Edward Burns, "Sox Drop 7th Sunday Game in Row," *Chicago Tribune*, June 4, 1934.

13. Charles P. Ward, "Tigers Return Home Determined to Seize League Lead," *Detroit Free Press*, June 5, 1934.

14. Sam Greene, "Top Is Neared by Gehringer," *Detroit News*, June 6, 1934.

15. Sam Greene, "Showing of Tigers Best in Ten Years," *Sporting News*, June 14, 1934, 1.

16. H. G. Salsinger, "Tigers Lifted Closer to Top By Goslin's Bat," *Detroit News*, June 4, 1934.

Chapter Five

1. H. G. Salsinger, "The Umpire," *Detroit News*, April 21, 1934.

2. Irving Vaughan, "Bridges' Curve Is Respected as American League's Best," *Chicago Tribune*, September 28, 1934.

3. James C. O'Leary, "Tigers Grab Game in One Round, 4–2," *Boston Globe*, June 13, 1934.

4. James C. O'Leary, "Red Sox Top Tigers in Slugfest, 15–13," *Boston Globe*, June 14, 1934.

5. James C. O'Leary, "Durocher's Homer with Bases Full Kills Braves' Chances at St. Louis—Yankees Pass Idle Tigers," *Boston Globe*, June 15, 1934.

6. Charles P. Ward, "Yankees Increase Lead By Beating Tigers in Series Opener, 8 to 4," *Detroit Free Press*, June 17, 1934.

7. James P. Dawson, "55,000 See Yanks Split with Tigers," *New York Times*, June 18, 1934.

8. James P. Dawson, "Rally By Tigers Turns Back Yanks," *New York Times*, June 19, 1934.

9. H. G. Salsinger, "Fearless Leadership Keeps Tigers in Fight," *Detroit News*, June 19, 1934.

10. John Lardner, "Yanks or Washington? Just Wait, Says Mickey," *Detroit News*, June 19, 1934.

11. Dan Daniel, "Collapse of Yankees Recalls Plight of Huggins' 1925 Team," *Sporting News*, May 31, 1934, 1.

12. H. G. Salsinger, "Tigers Getting Breaks Pennant Winners Need," *Detroit News*, June 21, 1934.

13. Denman Thompson, "Cronin Still Preaching Flag, But His Men Won't Believe Him," *Sporting News*, July 19, 1934.

14. Jeff Lenburg, Joan Howard Maurer, and Greg Lenburg, *The Three Stooges Scrapbook* (Chicago: Chicago Review Press, 1982), 77.

15. "After Much Tall Talk, Mussolini Takes a Bad Licking in North Africa," *Life*, February 10, 1941.

16. "20,000 Nazi Friends at a Rally Here Denounce Boycott," *New York Times*, May 18, 1934.

17. "Toledo Mobs Gather Anew," *Milwaukee Journal*, May 29, 1934.

18. Cynthia Clark Northrup, *The American Economy: A Historical Encyclopedia* (Santa Barbara, CA: ABC-CLIO, 2003), 254.

19. RMY Auctions (Middleton, ID), Auction: August 5, 2016, "Crime and Punishment." Lot 1272: *1934 John Dillinger, "Handwritten Letter to Henry Ford Praising His Getaway Car."* Original photo.

20. "Police Protect Goebbels Party," *Jewish Telegraphic Agency*, June 14, 1934.

21. Robert S. Wistrich, *Who's Who in Nazi Germany* (London: Routledge, 2013), 186.

22. William Shirer, *The Rise and Fall of the Third Reich* (New York: Simon & Schuster, 2011), 218.

23. Richard J. Evans, *The Third Reich in Power* (New York: Penguin, 2006), 40.

24. Grantland Rice, "The Spotlight: Play Ball! Batter Up!" *Boston Globe*, April 17, 1934.

25. Sam Greene, "Cochrane Thinking, If Not Talking Flag," *Sporting News*, July 5, 1934.

26. Sam Greene, "Cochrane Is Big Hit as Resident Leader," *Sporting News*, January 18, 1934.

27. Charles P. Ward, "Mickey Shifts Tiger Lineup," *Detroit Free Press*, March 29, 1934.

28. Scott Ferkovich, ed. *Detroit the Unconquerable: The 1935 World Champion Tigers* (Phoenix, AZ: Society for American Baseball Research, 2014), 141.

29. John Kieran, "Sports of the Times: Running a Few Bases," *New York Times*, July 2, 1934.

30. Charles P. Ward, "Boston Red Sox Beat Tigers, 5 to 4, and Square Series," *Detroit Free Press*, May 10, 1934.

31. Charles P. Ward, "Tigers Drop First of Series to Browns in the Tenth, 4 to 3," *Detroit Free Press*, July 1, 1934.

32. Sam Greene, "Mickey Cochrane's Novel

Idea Makes Tigers Judge Each Other," *Sporting News*, July 12, 1934.

33. Charles P. Ward, "Walker Suspended By Cochrane for Poor Base Running," *Detroit Free Press*, July 2, 1934.

34. Charles P. Ward, "Walker Banned Ten Days as Team Votes Him New Chance," *Detroit Free Press*, July 6, 1934.

35. Greene, "Mickey Cochrane's Novel Idea."

36. Tod Rockwell, "Walker Says He's Sorry and He'll Be Good," *Detroit Free Press*, July 3, 1934.

Chapter Six

1. Jack Carveth, "Hustling Tigers and Double Bill Bring Out Fans—38,000 of 'Em," *Detroit Free Press*, July 5, 1934.

2. Harvey Woodruff, "Stars Play Baseball's Biggest Game Today," *Chicago Tribune*, July 6, 1933.

3. "15 Hits By Tigers Top Senators," *New York Times*, July 12, 1934.

4. "Babe's Old Wrist Snap Lacking; So Are Those Oldtime Base Hits," *Detroit Free Press*, July 13, 1934.

5. James P. Dawson, "Yankees Bow, 4–2, Drop League Lead," *New York Times*, July 13, 1934.

6. Bud Shaver, "Babe Smashes 700th Blow of Career," *Detroit Times*, July 14, 1934.

7. Charles P. Ward, "Ruth Hits 700th Home Run and Yanks Beat Tigers 4–2," *Detroit Free Press*, July 14, 1934.

8. James P. Dawson, "Ruth Hits 700th as Yanks Score, 4–2," *New York Times*, July 14, 1934.

9. James P. Dawson, "Tigers Halt Yanks to Regain the Lead," *New York Times*, July 15, 1934.

10. Sam Greene, "Tiger Bats Develop Powerful Attack," *Sporting News*, July 19, 1934.

11. Dawson, "Tigers Halt Yanks."

12. Daniel M. Daniel, "Inspired Tigers Fill Yanks with Alarm," *Sporting News*, July 19, 1934.

13. Dawson, "Tigers Halt Yanks."

14. *Ibid.*

15. Charles P. Ward, "Tigers Score Four in Ninth, Win 12–11, and Regain Lead," *Detroit Free Press*, July 15, 1934.

16. Leo A. Donovan, "Joyous Detroit Fans Look to the World Series," *Detroit Free Press*, July 16, 1934.

17. Daniel, "Inspired Tigers."

Chapter Seven

1. Sam Greene, "No Hurdle Too High for Inspired Tigers," *Sporting News*, July 26, 1934.

2. Bak, *Cobb Would've Caught It*, 225.

3. H. G. Salsinger, *Detroit News*, September 12, 1935.

4. "Adds Ferocity to Tigers," *Sporting News*, August 2, 1934.

5. Jack Carveth, "Jimmy Foxx's Homer Gives Macks Victory Over Tigers, 5–4," *Detroit Free Press*, July 21, 1934.

6. "Red Sox Lose First Game of Detroit Series By 7–2," *Boston Globe*, July 24, 1934.

7. "Tiger Cub Proves Too Clever for the Red Sox," *Boston Globe*, July 25, 1934.

8. *Ibid.*

9. Irving Vaughan, "Sox Get Only 3 Hits; Tigers Triumph, 11–1," *Chicago Tribune*, July 29, 1934.

10. Charles P. Ward, "Tigers Regain First Place by Beating White Sox, 11 to 1," *Detroit Free Press*, July 29, 1934.

11. Irving Vaughan, "Rowe's Homer Beats Sox, 16–15," *Chicago Tribune*, July 30, 1934.

12. "Rowe Is Man of Hour When Veteran Moundsmen Bog Down," *Detroit Free Press*, July 30, 1934.

13. Jack Carveth, "Right-Hander Is Purchased in Aid to Drive for Pennant," *Detroit Free Press*, August 5, 1934.

14. Tod Rockwell, "'Glad to See You,' Says Tigers to Crowder," *Detroit Free Press*, August 8, 1934.

15. "Tiger Rally Tops the Browns, 12–8," *New York Times*, August 8, 1934.

16. Charles P. Ward, "Tigers Boost Lead Over Yanks by Beating Browns, 12–8," *Detroit Free Press*, August 8, 1934.

17. G. W. Daley, "Yankees to Start 1st-Place Battle," *New York Times*, August 14, 1934.

18. Charles P. Ward, "Tigers Invade N.Y. for Crucial Series of Pennant Race," *Detroit Free Press*, August 14, 1934.

19. John Drebinger, "79,000 See Tigers Top Yanks Twice," *New York Times*, August 15, 1934.

20. Paul Gallico, "Fans Hang on Rafters as Crowd Riots Outside," *Detroit Free Press*, August 15, 1934.

21. Bud Shaver, "Broaca Stops 15th Tiger Victory; Bridges Loser," *Detroit Times*, August 15, 1934.

22. "Yankees, Tigers to Play Two Games Today; New Yorkers Confident They Will Win Both," *New York Times*, August 17, 1934.

23. Sam Greene, "Rowe Shows Fiber of Tigers' Courage," *Sporting News*, August 23, 1934.

24. *Ibid.*

25. Charles P. Ward, "Rowe a Wonder Even to His Teammates," *Detroit Free Press*, August 18, 1934.

26. *Ibid.*
27. "Says Ruth Will Stay," *New York Times*, August 18, 1934.
28. Greene, "Rowe Shows Fiber of Tigers' Courage."

Chapter Eight

1. "Il Duce Warns Fascists to Get Ready for War," *Detroit Free Press*, August 25, 1934.
2. "Louisiana House Makes Huey Dictator with Power 'Greater Than Mussolini's'; Threats of an Armed Revolution Uttered," *Detroit Free Press*, August 17, 1934.
3. David J. Wilkie, "Tigers' Pennant Race Steals Thunder of the Politicians," *Detroit Free Press*, August 24, 1934.
4. "'Long Way to Go,' Says Cochrane," *Boston Globe*, August 19, 1934.
5. Gerry Moore, "Tigers Prove Magnet to Draw 46,995," *Boston Globe*, August 20, 1934.
6. James C. O'Leary, "'Schoolboy' Rowe Wins 15th in a Row," *Boston Globe*, August 22, 1934.
7. The major league record for most consecutive wins, over the course of *more than one season*, belongs to the Giants' Carl Hubbell. He won 24 consecutive games from July 17, 1936, to May 27, 1937.
8. Tim Murnane, "No Record for Wood," *Boston Globe*, September 21, 1912.
9. Henry W. Thomas, *Walter Johnson: Baseball's Big Train* (Lincoln: University of Nebraska Press, 1998), 101.
10. Larry D. Mansch, *Rube Marquard: The Life and Times of a Baseball Hall of Famer* (Jefferson, NC: McFarland, 1998), 111.
11. "Rowe's Goal Is 20 in Row," *Detroit Free Press*, August 26, 1934.
12. "It's a Big Day for Edna and All El Dorado," *Detroit Free Press*, August 26, 1934.
13. Frederick G. Lieb, "Schoolboy Rowe, Ace Tiger Twirler in '30s, Dies at 51," *Sporting News*, January 18, 1961.
14. Frank Reil, "Rowe, New Pitching Sensation of Tigers Too Good for Baseball," *Brooklyn Eagle*, May 2, 1933.
15. Another version of the story recounts that it was Schoolboy's mother who answered Goosetree's knock at the door.
16. "Meet Schoolboy Rowe, the Spinach Eatin' Fireballer," *Chicago Tribune*, August 26, 1934.
17. J. Alva Waddell, "Pugilism Almost Knocked Out Rowe's Diamond Ambition," *Sporting News*, November 22, 1934.

18. Lieb, "Schoolboy Rowe, Ace Tiger Twirler."
19. Sam Greene, "Rowe Shows Color Along With Ability," *Sporting News*, April 20, 1933.
20. Sam Greene, "Injuries Give Tiger Staff a Severe Test," *Sporting News*, August 24, 1933.
21. *Ibid.*
22. Donald Honig, *Baseball When the Grass Was Real* (Lincoln, NE: Bison Books, 1993), 47.
23. Irving Vaughan, "Fans Keep Rowe's Pen Busy, But His Hat's Same Old Size," *Chicago Tribune*, September 26, 1934.
24. James C. Isaminger, "Rowe, Killed By Kindness and Hindered By Handshakers, Missed AL Hill Record," *Philadelphia Enquirer*, September 2, 1934.
25. Sam Greene, "The Schoolboy! He's in a Class By Himself," *Sporting News*, August 30, 1934.
26. "Meet Schoolboy Rowe, the Spinach Eatin' Fireballer."
27. Bud Shaver, "Shavings," *Detroit Times*, August 29, 1934.
28. "Mickey Tells How It's Done," *Detroit Free Press*, September 6, 1934.

Chapter Nine

1. Hank Greenberg and Ira Berkow, *The Story of My Life* (Chicago: Ivan R. Dee, 2001), 16.
2. John Rosengren, *Hank Greenberg: Hero of Heroes* (New York: New American Library, 2013), 37.
3. John Lardner, "Yanks or Washington? Just Wait, Says Mickey," *Detroit News*, June 19, 1934.
4. "Hank's Rosh Hashonah," *Detroit Jewish Chronicle*, September 14, 1934.
5. Dick Farrington, "Greenberg, Young Tiger Star, 'Just Tumbled into Game,'" *Sporting News*, October 4, 1934.
6. *Ibid.*
7. "Greenberg's Homers Defeat Red Sox 2–1," *Boston Globe*, September 11, 1934.
8. Charles P. Ward, "Greenberg's Two Home Runs Give Tigers 2 to 1 Victory," *Detroit Free Press*, September 11, 1934.
9. Jack Carveth, "Henry Prayed and Swung His Way to Baseball Glory," *Detroit Free Press*, September 11, 1934.
10. "Hank's Rosh Hashonah."
11. Iffy the Dopester, "Hanks Homers Strictly Kosher," *Detroit Free Press*, September 11, 1934.
12. "Ruth Admits Lead of Tigers Seems Safe," *New York Times*, September 18, 1934.
13. "Crowder, Tigers, Blank Yanks, 3–0," *New York Times*, September 18, 1934.

14. Jack Carveth, "Yankees' Pilot Won't Give Up," *Detroit Free Press*, September 18, 1934.
15. Bud Shaver, "Shavings," *Detroit Times*, September 18, 1934.
16. Iffy the Dopester, "The Flag Is in the Bag," *Detroit Free Press*, September 18, 1934.
17. Tod Rockwell, "Billy Rogell Ready to Count His World Series Cash Now," *Detroit Free Press*, September 19, 1934.
18. Iffy the Dopester, "Promising Young Man" *Detroit Free Press*, September 19, 1934.
19. "Cochrane Names Rowe for Opener," *New York Times*, September 23, 1934.
20. Tod Rockwell, "Rotarians See Navin Break Down and Make Confession," *Detroit Free Press*, September 20, 1934.
21. "Cochrane's Feat Rare in Baseball," *New York Times*, September 25, 1934.
22. Of the 12, the first was Al Spalding, who won it with Chicago in 1876. Since that was the National League's inaugural year, some "first-year" manager was going to win it by default. The same can be said of Clark Griffith, who won the pennant with Chicago in 1901, the American League's first season.
23. "Cochrane's Feat Rare in Baseball."
24. "Tiger Banner to Be Unfurled," *Detroit Free Press*, September 29, 1934.
25. Bud Shaver, "We'll Win World Series, Mickey Pledges," *Detroit Times*, September 25, 1934.
26. Iffy the Dopester, "When Flag Was Won," *Detroit Free Press*, September 24, 1934.
27. John Stone, the man whom the Tigers dealt for Goslin, hit .317 in his five years with Washington, so it was a trade that benefitted both clubs.
28. Goslin hit only .286 lifetime at Navin Field, the lowest average of any park he played in (minimum of 50 games).
29. "Grateful Detroit Showers Detroit with Presents," *Chicago Tribune*, September 26, 1934.
30. "Scribbled by the Scribes," *Sporting News*, October 4, 1934.
31. J. G. Taylor Spink, "Brief Tales About Those Tigers," *Sporting News*, October 4, 1934.
32. Iffy the Dopester, "The Nation Will Live," *Detroit Free Press*, September 29, 1934.

Chapter Ten

1. William McNeil, *Dodgers Encyclopedia* (New York: Sports Publishing, 2000), 346.

2. Vince Staten, *Ol' Diz: A Biography of Dizzy Dean* (New York: HarperCollins, 1992), 147.
3. Iffy the Dopester, "The Pitiless Light," *Detroit Free Press*, September 26, 1934.
4. Dick Farrington, "Spotlight Swings on Deans and Rowe," *Sporting News*, October 4, 1934.
5. William C. Richards, "This Is Detroit, the Series City," *Detroit Free Press*, October 3, 1934.
6. Iffy the Dopester, "A Cavalry Charge," *Detroit Free Press*, September 27, 1934.
7. "Tigers and Giants Certify 23 for Series," *Sporting News*, September 20, 1934.
8. Charlie Bevis, *Mickey Cochrane: The Life of a Baseball Hall of Fame Catcher* (Jefferson, NC: McFarland, 1998).
9. Arch Ward, "Talking It Over," *Chicago Tribune*, October 4, 1934.
10. Sam Greene, "Cochrane to Play Aces Against Aces," *Sporting News*, September 27, 1934.
11. Bud Shaver, "Dizzy Tames Tigers as Infield Errors Yield Four Runs," *Detroit Times*, October 3, 1934.
12. "Dizzy Admits He Wasn't So Hot in Opener," *Chicago Tribune*, October 4, 1934.
13. "Dizzy Dean Has a Busy Day, and More Are Coming," *Chicago Tribune*, October 4, 1934.
14. "Wray's Column," *St. Louis Post-Dispatch*, October 4, 1934.
15. Westbrook Pegler, "Dizzy Makes Good on Brag," *Detroit News*, October 4, 1934.
16. Iffy the Dopester, "Just a Lucky Stiff," *Detroit Free Press*, October 4, 1934.
17. Irving Vaughan, "St. Louis Wins, 8–3, in World Series," *Chicago Tribune*, October 4, 1934.
18. Jack Weeks, "Corktown Gets Every Thrill as Tigers Fight for Crown," *Detroit News*, October 4, 1934.
19. "Dizzy Dean Tells Byrd All About It," *St. Louis Post-Dispatch*, October 4, 1934.
20. "Gossip of First Game," *Sporting News*, October 11, 1934.
21. "Dean (Himself) Takes the Air," *Detroit Free Press*, October 4, 1934.
22. Arch Ward, "Talking It Over," *Chicago Tribune*, October 5, 1934.
23. "Dan Howley Substantiates Collins' Charge That Fan Flashed Mirror in His Eyes," *St. Louis Post-Dispatch,* October 6, 1934.
24. Bud Shaver, "Goslin Wins Game After Walker Hit Ties Score in 9th," *Detroit Times*, October 4, 1934.
25. W. J. McGoogan, "Defeat Angered Cards But They Regained Spirits Quickly," *St. Louis Post-Dispatch*, October 5, 1934.

26. *Ibid.*
27. "Cardinals Rage Into Clubhouse; Blame Breaks," *Chicago Tribune*, October 5, 1934.
28. Herman Wecke, "Tigers Not Hitting Up to Season's Averages," *St. Louis Post-Dispatch*, October 5, 1934.
29. Alan Gould, "Rowe Stands Today Among the Greats," *Detroit News*, October 5, 1934.
30. Paul Gallico, "Young Ajax…The Schoolboy Comes to Manhood," *Detroit Free Press*, October 5, 1934.
31. "'They Can't Beat Us Sign Hangs Over Cards' Door," *Chicago Tribune*, October 6, 1934.
32. Sam Greene, "Cochrane Shifts Batters; Auker in Box," *Detroit News*, October 6, 1934.
33. Bob Murphy, "Cochrane Rallies Team to Fighting Pitch," *Detroit Times*, October 6, 1934.
34. Lynwood Thomas "Schoolboy" Rowe, "'I'm Glad the Deans Aren't Triplets,' Says Schoolboy Rowe After Seeing Paul Win," *St. Louis Post-Dispatch*, October 6, 1934.
35. John Heidenry, *The Gashouse Gang* (New York: PublicAffairs, 2008), 247.
36. J. Roy Stockton, "Greenberg Leads 13-Hit Attack with Four Blows," *St. Louis Post-Dispatch*, October 7, 1934.
37. Damon Runyon, "Greenberg's Lusty Smash in Seventh Defeats Cardinals," *Detroit Times*, October 7, 1934.
38. "Dean Says He's Ready to Pitch in Today's Game," *Chicago Tribune*, October 7, 1934.
39. *Ibid.*
40. Iffy the Dopester, "Found: A Detonator," *Detroit Free Press*, October 7, 1934.
41. "Dean Says He's Ready to Pitch."
42. W. J. McGoogan, "Bridges to Pitch for Tigers Today and Rowe in Next Game," *St. Louis Post-Dispatch*, October 7, 1934.
43. Richard Goldstein, "Billy Rogell, 98, Star Shortstop in the 1930's, Dies," *New York Times*, August 13, 2003.
44. J. Roy Stockton, "Detroit Can Win Its First World Title Today," *St. Louis Post-Dispatch*, October 8, 1934.
45. Tod Rockwell, "Mickey's Star Pitcher Vows He'll Finish Job," *Detroit Free Press*, October 8, 1934.
46. Grantland Rice, "Dizzy's Waterloo," *Detroit Free Press*, October 8, 1934.
47. "Jubilant Tigers Sure Rowe Will Win Title Today," *Chicago Tribune*, October 8, 1934.
48. W. J. McGoogan, "Breadon Denies Reported Plan to Sell Cards to Ford," *St. Louis Post-Dispatch*, October 9, 1934.
49. Rosengren, *Hank Greenberg*, 101.
50. Leo Durocher "'That Boy Paul Has Ice Water in His Veins,'" *St. Louis Post-Dispatch*, October 9, 1934.
51. Rosengren, *Hank Greenberg*, 100.
52. Tod Rockwell, "Mickey Cochrane is Kept in the Hospital Overnight as Physicians Debate Whether to Let Him Play in Deciding Game Today," *Detroit Free Press*, October 9, 1934.
53. Bud Shaver, *Detroit Times*, October 10, 1934.
54. Westbrook Pegler, "'Disgraceful, Delightful,' Says Pegler of Final Game," *Detroit News*, October 10, 1934.
55. J. Roy Stockton, "Dizzy's Pitching and Batting Potent Factors in Winning Title Game," *St. Louis Post-Dispatch*, October 10, 1934.
56. San Greene, "Detroit Gives Cards Credit," *Detroit News*, October 10, 1934.
57. "Cards Hilarious Over Capture of World Title," *Chicago Tribune*, October 10, 1934.
58. Paul Gallico, "Echoes of the Series," *Detroit Free Press*, October 11, 1934.
59. Sam Greene, "Tigers Find Solace in Series Dividends," *Sporting News*, October 18, 1934.
60. M. F. Drukenbrod, "Joe to Blame, Landis Insists," *Detroit Free Press*, October 10, 1934.
61. "A Psychological Uplift," *Sporting News*, October 18, 1934.
62. Iffy, the Dopester, "No Regrets, Mickey," *Detroit Free Press*, October 10, 1934.

Chapter Eleven

1. Charles P. Ward, "Mickey to Plan Tiger Trades on Way to Hawaii with Al Simmons," *Detroit Free Press*, October 11, 1934.
2. Sam Greene, "Cochrane Jabs New Puncture into Gehringer Trade Bubble," *Sporting News*, December 6, 1934.
3. Sam Greene, "Yankees Interested in Deal For Walker," *Sporting News*, February 21, 1935.
4. Charles P. Ward, "National League Owners Vote to Permit Night Baseball," *Detroit Free Press*, December 13, 1934.
5. "License 102 Gives Mickey a Goal," *Detroit Free Press*, December 30, 1934.
6. "Tigers' Camp Again to be in Lakeland, Fla.," *Detroit Free Press*, October 21, 1934.
7. Sam Greene, "Mickey Cuts Down Bengal Camp Grind," *Sporting News*, January 10, 1935.
8. Charles P. Ward, "Cochrane Copies Mack's Trait in Experiment with Grid Star," *Detroit Free Press*, March 12, 1935.
9. Sam Greene, "Dixie Howell Shines at Third Base Test," *Sporting News*, February 21, 1935.

10. Charles P. Ward, "Schoolboy Rowe Sets Goal at 25 Victories During 1935," *Detroit Free Press*, March 6, 1935.

11. W. W. Edgar, "The Second Guess," *Detroit Free Press*, March 7, 1935.

12. Sid C. Keener, "Cards in Condition, Look Good to Frisch," *Sporting News*, April 4, 1935.

13. Bud Shaver, "Walker Steps Into Cochrane's Favor," *Sporting News*, April 18, 1935.

14. Ed Bang, "Flag Hopes Flare in Cleveland as Indians Seize Close Contests," *Sporting News*, May 2, 1935.

15. Charles P. Ward, "Hank Decides Clouting Is His Hope for Fame," *Detroit Free Press*, March 5, 1935.

16. "Game Postponed—Snow," *Sporting News*, April 25, 1935.

17. H. G. Salsinger, "The Umpire," *Detroit News*, April 18, 1935.

18. Tod Rockwell, "'Nuts!' Is Mickey's Verdict and Dressing Room's Silent," *Detroit Free Press*, April 18, 1935.

19. W. W. Edgar, "The Second Guess: Johnson Peers at Pennant Race from Indians' Dugout," *Detroit Free Press*, 23, 1935.

20. H. G. Salsinger, "Early Hitting Slump May Ruin Tiger Morale," *Detroit News*, April 26, 1935.

21. W. W. Edgar, "The Second Guess: Tigers' Slump Doesn't Worry Mr. Navin," *Detroit Free Press*, April 27, 1935.

22. H. G. Salsinger, "Sullivan Wins Berth as Starting Southpaw," *Detroit News*, April 29, 1935.

23. Associated Press, "Joe Sullivan Is a Mystery to the Tribesmen," *Frederick* (MD) *News Post*, April 18, 1935.

Chapter Twelve

1. "Makes Nickname Fit," *Sporting News*, May 16, 1935.

2. H. G. Salsinger, "Rowe Needs Four Weeks to Win First Start," *Detroit News*, May 14, 1935.

3. H. G. Salsinger, "Fox Answers Harris' Prayer," *Detroit News*, May 11, 1933.

4. Bud Shaver, "Swat in Ninth Sends Team to Victory," *Detroit Times*, June 1, 1935.

5. H. G. Salsinger, "Ninth-Inning Rally Fails and White Sox Conquer Tigers," *Detroit News*, June 2, 1935.

6. Paul Shannon, "Fuchs Ready to Follow Bambino Out of Boston Braves' Picture," *Sporting News*, June 6, 1935.

7. Sam Greene, "Tigers' Hopes Ride on Rowe Comeback," *Sporting News*, June 13, 1935.

Just over a month prior, the first night game in major league history had been played at Crosley Field in Cincinnati.

8. H. G. Salsinger, "Poor Pitching Spoils Detroit Outlook," *Detroit News*, June 7, 1935.

9. *Hattiesburg American*, November 12, 1926, 13.

10. Sam Greene, "Tigers Functioning with Big Four Staff," *Sporting News*, June 20, 1935.

11. Bud Shaver, "Tigers Beaten Twice, Drop to Fourth," *Detroit Times*, June 20, 1935.

12. Sam Greene, "Rowe Keeps Yankees from Reaching Third Base," *Detroit News*, June 22, 1935.

13. Sam Greene, "Tigers Make Bold Prophet of Mickey," *Sporting News*, July 11, 1935.

14. Greenberg, *The Story of My Life*, 92.

Chapter Thirteen

1. Sam Greene, "Tigers Make Bold Prophet of Mickey," *Sporting News*, July 11, 1935.

2. Iffy the Dopester, "Lancers Against Rifles," *Detroit Free Press*, July 14, 1935.

3. H. G. Salsinger, "Tigers Lose But Show 1934 Fight," *Detroit News*, July 11, 1935.

4. "Cochrane Picks Rowe to Beat Yankees Twice," *Chicago Tribune*, July 21, 1935.

5. Bud Shaver, "Rowe Offers No Excuses for Loss," *Detroit Times*, July 24, 1935.

6. H. G. Salsinger, "The Sidelines," *Detroit News*, July 25, 1935.

7. Dan Daniel, "Yankees and Giants Teeter Around Top," *Sporting News*, August 1, 1935.

8. Iffy the Dopester, "Hugh and Mickey," *Detroit Free Press*, August 4, 1935.

9. H. G. Salsinger, "Detroit Beats Cleveland Twice—Both Victories Credited to Rowe," *Detroit News*, August 4, 1935.

10. Bud Shaver, "Greenberg Collects 29th, 30th Homers in Opening Contest," *Detroit Times*, August 4, 1935.

11. "Mayor to Face a Relief Crises on His Return," *Detroit Free Press*, August 3, 1935.

12. H. G. Salsinger, "Bridges Allows Three Hits, Winning his Seventeenth Game, 4 to 0," *Detroit News*, August 11, 1935.

13. Sam Greene, "Effective Pitching Guards Tiger Lair," *Sporting News*, August 22, 1935.

14. "Iffy the Dopester Rises to Remark," *Detroit Free Press*, August 24, 1935.

15. Sam Greene, "Lawson Gives Bengals Another Winning Stripe," *Sporting News*, August 29, 1935.

16. Burlington (IA) *Hawk Eye*, October 2, 1968, 21.

17. "Completes Apprenticeship: Roxie Lawson," *Sporting News*, September 5, 1935.

18. Edward Burns, "White Sox Lose Two to Tigers, 6 to 1 and 5 to 0," *Chicago Tribune*, September 3, 1935.

19. H. G. Salsinger, "Tigers Beat A's in Two Games, Jumping Lead to 10 Games," *Detroit News*, September 8, 1935.

20. Sam Greene, "Navin Jumps Over Mickey's 'If,' Goes Ahead with Extra Seats," *Sporting News*, September 12, 1935.

21. Daniel M. Daniel, "Rambling Round the Circuit with Pitcher Snorty Casey," *Sporting News*, September 12, 1935.

Chapter Fourteen

1. Marc Cogen, *Democracies and the Shock of War: The Law as a Battlefield* (New York: Routledge, 2016), 198.

2. "300,000 Line Up 10 Deep to Hail Wider Woodward as a Signal of Detroit's Record Stride to Front," *Detroit Free Press*, September 21, 1935.

3. *Ibid.*

4. "Louis Picks Cubs to Meet Tigers in World Series," *Chicago Tribune*, September 11, 1935.

5. "Iffy the Dopester Rises to Remark," *Detroit Free Press*, September 18, 1935.

6. "Tigers Home Amid Cheers," *Detroit News*, September 20, 1935.

7. George W. Stark, "Third Strike Whizzes By; Tiger Pennant Flies Again," *Detroit News*, September 22, 1935.

8. "Cochrane Predicts Victory for Tigers in World Series," *St. Louis Post-Dispatch*, September 22, 1935.

9. "Iffy the Dopester Rises to Remark," *Detroit Free Press*, September 23, 1935.

10. Paul Gallico, "The Executioner," *Detroit Free Press*, September 24, 1935.

11. Joseph Wancho, "Billy Herman," The Baseball Biography Project, http://sabr.org/bioproj/person/d6297ffd#sdendnote11anc, accessed May 25, 2016.

12. That episode, along with a parallel one involving the Phillies' Eddie Waitkus in 1947, was the likely inspiration for the shooting scene in Bernard Malamud's classic 1952 baseball novel, *The Natural*.

13. "Letter Solves the Shooting of Bill Jurges," *Chicago Tribune*, July 7, 1932.

14. Bill Nowlin, ed., *Van Lingle Mungo: The Man, the Song, the Players* (Phoenix, AZ: Society for American Baseball Research, 2014), 130.

Chapter Fifteen

1. Michael Hiltzik, *Colossus: Hoover Dam and the Making of the American Century* (New York: Simon & Schuster, 2010). *xii.*

2. Twelve years later, Hoover received vindication when the dam was officially renamed after him.

3. Irving Vaughan, "Cubs Aim Home Runs at Short Tiger Fence," *Chicago Tribune*, October 2, 1935.

4. "Majority of Experts Support Detroit," *Sporting News*, October 3, 1935.

5. *Ibid.*

6. "Detroit Crowd Has to Like It, Only Boos Once," *Chicago Tribune*, October 3, 1935.

7. John C. Manning, "47,742 See Tigers Win 2D Game," *Detroit Times*, October 3, 1935.

8. Charles P. Ward, "Tigers Back in Winning Ways for Series, Mickey Says After Impressive Workout; Grimm Is Just as Confident for His Cubs," *Detroit Free Press*, October 2, 1935.

9. Bud Shaver, "Four Runs in Opener All Bridges Needed to Beat Cubs," *Detroit Times*, October 4, 1935.

10. "'We're Hitting; Watch Us Go,' Cochrane Says," *Chicago Tribune*, October 4, 1935.

11. Greenberg, *The Story of My Life*, 81.

12. "Cochrane Says 'No!' to Rowe as Greenberg's Sub," *Chicago Tribune*, October 5, 1935.

13. Irving Vaughan, "Cubs Lose, 6–5; Use Carleton Today," *Chicago Tribune*, October 5, 1935.

14. Edward Burns, "Landis Investigates Cub Feud with Umpire," *Chicago Tribune*, October 5, 1935.

Chapter Sixteen

1. "Tigers Praise Clever Pitching of Al Crowder," *Chicago Tribune*, October 6, 1935.

2. *Ibid.*

3. "Warneke Mum; Hartnett First to Sense Injury," *Chicago Tribune*, October 7, 1935.

4. *Ibid.*

5. Rosengren, *Hank Greenberg: The Hero of Heroes.*

6. Bevis, *Mickey Cochrane: The Life of a Baseball Hall of Fame Catcher*, 6.

7. Honig, *The October Heroes*, 222.

8. "Iffy the Dopester Rises to Remark," *Detroit Free Press*, October 8, 1935.

9. Bud Shaver, "Bridges Holds Cubs in 9th After 1st Batter Triples," *Detroit Times*, October 7, 1935.

10. "Riotous Tigers Gang on Goslin After Victory," *Chicago Tribune*, October 8, 1935.

11. *Ibid.*

12. Tod Rockwell, "Impulse Grips Frank J. Navin," *Detroit Free Press*, October 8, 1935.

13. Irving Vaughan, "Young Chicago Team Puts Up Gallant Fight," *Chicago Tribune*, October 8, 1935.

14. Grantland Rice, "'Here It Is!' Magic Words for All Detroit," *Detroit Free Press*, October 8, 1935.

15. George W. Stark, "Goose's Fame Hangs High as City Wildly Celebrates," *Detroit News*, October 8, 1935.

16. "Detroit Hails Its Champion Tigers as a Symbol of the City Dynamic," *Detroit Free Press*, October 8, 1935.

Epilogue

1. Charles P. Ward, "Victory Over A's Costs Bengals," *Detroit Free Press*, June 4, 1936.

2. Catchers Buck Ewing, Roger Bresnahan, and Wilbert Robinson had previously been voted in by the Hall's Committee on Old-timers.

3. George Hunter, "Ex-Tiger Rogell Was Scrappy," *Detroit News*, August 10, 2003.

4. He is not to be confused with Millard "Dixie" Howell, who pitched for the Cleveland Indians, Cincinnati Reds, and Chicago White Sox from 1940–1958, compiling a 19–15 record. There was also a Homer Elliott "Dixie" Howell, who caught for the Reds, Dodgers, and Pirates from 1947–1956.

5. Bob Pille, "Rowe's Big Line: 'How'm Ah Doin', Edna?'" *Detroit Free Press*, January 9, 1961.

6. Malcolm W. Bingay, "Good Morning," *Detroit Free Press*, April 11, 1940.

7. "Iffy the Dopester Rises to Remark," *Detroit Free Press*, October 8, 1935.

Bibliography

Anderson, William M. *The Detroit Tigers: A Pictorial Celebration of the Greatest Players and Moments in Tigers History*. Detroit: Wayne State University Press, 2008.

_____. *The Glory Years of the Detroit Tigers 1920–1950*. Detroit: Wayne State University Press, 2012.

Angelo, Frank. *Yesterday's Detroit*. Grand Rapids, MI: Four Corners Press, 1977.

Auker, Elden. *Sleeper Cars and Flannel Uniforms: A Lifetime of Memories from Striking Out the Babe to Teeing It Up with the President*. New York: Triumph, 2001.

Badger, Anthony J. *The New Deal: The Depression Years, 1933–40*. New York: Hill and Wang, 1989.

Bak, Richard. *A Place for Summer*. Detroit: Wayne State University Press, 1998.

_____. *Cobb Would've Caught It: The Golden Age of Baseball in Detroit*. Detroit: Wayne State University Press, 1992.

Benson, Michael. *Ballparks of North America*. Jefferson, NC: McFarland, 1989.

Betzold, Michael. *Queen of Diamonds: The Tiger Stadium Story*. Farmington Hill, MI: Northmont, 1997.

Bevis, Charlie. *Mickey Cochrane: The Life of a Baseball Hall of Fame Catcher*. Jefferson, NC: McFarland, 1998.

Brinkley, Alan. *Voices of Protest*. New York: Alfred A. Knopf, 1982.

Brokaw, Tom. Foreword. *The Hall: A Celebration of Baseball's Greats: In Stories and Images, the Complete Roster of Inductees*. New York: Little, Brown, 2014.

Brown, Henry D. *Cadillac and the Founding of Detroit*. Detroit: Wayne State University Press, 1976.

Cogen, Marc. *Democracies and the Shock of War: The Law as a Battlefield*. New York: Routledge, 2016.

Cohen, Irwin J. *Tiger Stadium—Comerica Park: History and Memories*. Boreal Press, 2011.

Cohen, Robert W. *The 50 Greatest Players in Detroit Tigers History*. Lanham, MD: Taylor Trade, 2016.

Dixon, David. *Never Come to Peace Again: Pontiac's Uprising and the Fate of the British Empire in North America*. Norman: University of Oklahoma Press, 2014.

Dunbar, Willis F., and George S. May. *Michigan: A History of the Wolverine State*. Grand Rapids, MI: Wm. B. Eerdmans, 1995.

Eliot, Thomas Hopkinson. *Recollections of the New Deal: When the People Mattered*. Boston: Northeastern University, 1992.

Evans, Richard J. *The Third Reich in Power*. New York: Penguin, 2006.

Falls, Joe. *The Detroit Tigers*. New York: Macmillan, 1975.

Ferkovich, Scott, ed. *Detroit the Unconquerable: The 1935 World Champion Detroit Tigers*. Phoenix, AZ: Society for American Baseball Research, 2014.

Fitts, Robert K. *Banzai Babe Ruth: Baseball, Espionage & Assassination During the 1934 Tour of Japan*. Lincoln: University of Nebraska Press, 2012.

Golway, Terry. *Together We Cannot Fail: FDR and the American Presidency in Years of Crisis*. Naperville, IL: Sourcebooks MediaFusion, 2009.

Greenberg, Hank, and Ira Berkow. *The Story of My Life*. Chicago: Ivan R. Dee, 2001.

Hawkins, Jim, and Dan Ewald. *The Detroit Tigers Encyclopedia*. Champaign, IL: Sports Publishing, 2003.

Heidenry, John. *The Gashouse Gang*. New York: PublicAffairs, 2008.

Hiltzik, Michael. *Colossus: Hoover Dam and the Making of the American Century*. New York: Simon & Schuster, 2010.

Honig, Donald. *Baseball When the Grass Was Real*. Lincoln, NE: Bison Books, 1993.

_____. *The October Heroes*. Lincoln, NE: Bison Books, 1996.

Lenburg, Jeff, Joan Howard Maurer, and Greg Lenburg. *The Three Stooges Scrapbook*. Chicago: Chicago Review Press, 1982.

Lieb, Frederick G. *The Detroit Tigers*. New York: G. P. Putnam's Sons, 1946.

Lochbiler, Don. *Detroit's Coming of Age*. Toronto: Copp Clark, 1973.

Mansch, Larry D. *Rube Marquard: The Life and Times of a Baseball Hall of Famer*. Jefferson, NC: McFarland, 1998.

Martelle, Scott. *Detroit: A Biography*. Chicago: Chicago Review Press, 2012.

Mason, Philip P., and Charles K. Hyde. *Detroit in Its World Setting: A Three-Hundred Year Chronology*. Detroit: Wayne State University Press, 2001.

McCollister, John. *The Tigers and Their Den*. Lenexa, KS: Addax, 1999.

McNeil, William. *The Dodgers Encyclopedia*. New York: Sports Publishing, 2000.

Neyer, Rob. *Rob Neyer's Big Book of Baseball Lineups: A Complete Guide to the Best, Worst, and Most Memorable Players Ever to Grace the Major Leagues*. New York: Fireside, 2003.

Northrup, Cynthia Clark. *The American Economy: A Historical Encyclopedia*. Santa Barbara, CA: ABC-CLIO, 2003.

Nowlin, Bill, ed. *Van Lingle Mungo: The Man, the Song, the Players*. Phoenix, AZ: Society for American Baseball Research, 2014.

Pietrusza, David. *Judge and Jury: The Life and Times of Judge Kenesaw Mountain Landis*. South Bend, IN: Diamond Communications, 1998.

Poremba, David Lee. *Detroit: A Motor City History*. Charleston, SC: Arcadia, 2001.

Rader, Benjamin G. *Baseball: A History of America's Game*. Urbana: University of Illinois Press, 2008.

Rajtar, Steve. *A Guide to Historic Lakeland, Florida*. Charleston, SC: History Press, 2007.

Ritter, Lawrence S. *The Glory of Their Times: The Story of the Early Days of Baseball Told by the Men Who Played It*. New York: Harper Perennial, 2010.

Rosengren, John. *Hank Greenberg: The Hero of Heroes*. New York: New American Library, 2013.

Schlesinger, Arthur M. Jr. *The Age of Roosevelt: The Coming of the New Deal*. Boston: Houghton Mifflin, 1958.

Shaw, Peterson Joyce. *American Automobile Workers, 1900–1933*. Albany, NY: SUNY Press, 1987.

Shirer, William. *The Rise and Fall of the Third Reich*. New York: Simon & Schuster, 2011.

Smith, Jean Edward. *FDR*. New York: Random House, 2007.

Snyder-Grenier. *Brooklyn!: An Illustrated History*. Philadelphia: Temple University Press, 2004.

Staten, Vince. *Ol' Diz: A Biography of Dizzy Dean*. New York: HarperCollins, 1992.

Steinberg, Steve, and Lyle Spatz. *The Colonel and Hug: The Partnership That Transformed the New York Yankees*. Lincoln: University of Nebraska Press, 2015.

Sullivan, George. *The Detroit Tigers*. New York: Macmillan, 1985.

Thomas, Henry W. *Walter Johnson: Baseball's Big Train*. Lincoln: University of Nebraska Press, 1998.

Watkins, Tom H. *The Great Depression: American in the 1930's*. New York: Little, Brown, 1993.

Watts, Steven. *The People's Tycoon: Henry Ford and the American Century*. New York: Knopf Doubleday, 2009.

Wilson, Susan. *Boston Sights and Insights*. Boston: Beacon Press, 2004.

Wistrich, Robert S. *Who's Who in Nazi Germany*. London: Routledge, 2013.

Woodford, Arthur M. *This Is Detroit*. Detroit: Wayne State University Press, 2001.

Woodford, Frank B., and Arthur M. Woodford. *All Our Yesterdays: A Brief History of Detroit*. Detroit: Wayne State University Press, 1969.

Index

Numbers in **_bold italics_** indicate pages with illustrations